Blueprint for a
Sustainable Economy

David Pearce
Edward Barbier

EARTHSCAN

Earthscan, London

First published in the UK in 2000 by Earthscan
Reprinted 2001, 2006

A catalogue record for this book is available from the British Library

ISBN-10: 1-85383-515-3
ISBN-13: 978-1-85383-515-5

Typesetting by MapSet Ltd, Gateshead, UK
Printed and bound in the UK by Cromwell Press, Trowbridge
Cover design by Andrew Corbett

For a full list of publications please contact:
Earthscan
8–12 Camden High Street
London, NW1 0JH, UK
Tel: +44 (0)20 7387 8558
Fax: +44 (0)20 7387 8998
Email: earthinfo@earthscan.co.uk
Web: **www.earthscan.co.uk**

Earthscan is an imprint of James and James (Science Publishers) Ltd and
publishes in association with the International Institute for Environment and
Development

This book is printed on totally chlorine-free paper

Contents

Tables, Figures and Boxes

Tables

Figures

Boxes

Acronyms and Abbreviations

CA	conjoint analysis
CAC	command and control
CBA (COBA)	cost-benefit analysis
CCA	compliance cost assessment
CFC	chlorofluorocarbons
CITES	Convention on International Trade in Endangered Species
CSERGE	Centre for Social and Economic Research on the Global Environment
CVM	contingent valuation method
DETR	Department of the Environment, Transport and the Regions
EC	European Commission
EFTEC	Economics for the Environment Consultancy
EIA	environmental impact assessment
EKC	environmental Kuznets curve
EU	European Union
FAO	Food and Agricultural Organization (United Nations)
FCCC	Framework Convention on Climate Change
FSC	Forest Stewardship Council
GDP	gross domestic product
GEF	Global Environment Facility
HPM	hedonic price method
IFPRI	International Food Policy Research Institute
IIED	International Institute for Environment and Development
ISEE	International Society for Ecological Economics
ITTO	International Tropical Timber Organization
Kh	human capital
Kn	natural capital
Kp	physical capital
LEEC	London Environmental Economics Centre
MBI	market-based instrument

NAFTA	North American Free Trade Agreement
NGO	non-governmental organization
NNP	net national product
NOAA	National Oceanic and Atmospheric Administration (US)
NPV	net present value
NUV	non-use value
OECD	Organisation for Economic Co-operation and Development (OECD)
PSE	producer subsidy equivalent
RUM	random utility model
SACTRA	Standing Advisory Committee on Trunk Road Assessment
SPM	solid particulate matter
SSSI	Site of Special Scientific Interest
TCM	travel cost method
UCL	University College London
UNCED	United Nations Conference on Environment and Development
UNEP	United Nations Environment Programme
WCED	World Commission on Environment and Development (Brundtland Commission)
WCMC	Wildlife Conservation Monitoring Centre
WTA	willingness to accept
WTP	willingness to pay
WWF	World Wide Fund For Nature

Preface

Blueprint for a Green Economy (Pearce et al, 1989) set out an agenda for containing environmental degradation based on the now widely-accepted observation that most environmental problems have their origins in the misworkings of the economic system, and that their solutions therefore lie in the correction of those misworkings. The book tried to set out the implications of that basic idea in a fairly simple way and we were heartened by its reception worldwide. We made no claims that it was new in concept since what we wrote then encapsulated and distilled much of what had been learned from the discipline of environmental economics over the previous 30 years or so. We did try to piece together a coherent story about how to assess priorities, how to identify the fundamental causal factors at work, and how to design environmental policy based on economic incentives. While some objected, and continue to object, to component parts of the overall story, we have heard little that would lead us to change these central messages, and a great deal that reinforces what we had to say. As the 20th century closes, for example, we detect little intellectual opposition to the idea of making users of the environment pay for its services, and our view of the meaning and interpretation of sustainable development has gained increasing acceptance. Probably the most resisted issue remains the idea of placing money values on environmental assets, the so-called monetization of the environment. Most of the critics do not focus on the practice but on the very idea of monetization, arguing that this somehow debases the case for environmental conservation, or, at least, places the environment at risk should the economic benefits of conservation be shown to be small. We address these concerns in Chapters 1 and 3 and consider most of the criticisms to be false. Some, it has to be said, emanate from plain ignorance of what monetization is all about. However, some criticisms reflect genuine worries and it is right that we try to address those as constructively as possible.

Since *Blueprint for a Green Economy* there have been four other volumes in the series. *Blueprint 2* (Pearce, ed, 1991) applied the ideas of *Blueprint 1* (as *Blueprint for a Green Economy* became known) to world environmental problems. *Blueprint 3* (Pearce, ed, 1993) returned to the context of *Blueprint 1* and showed how sustainable development was threatened in the UK and how progress towards sustainability could be measured using monetary values of environmental damage. *Blueprint 3* thus demonstrated a clear use for monetary valuation in terms of national economic accounting procedures. *Blueprint 4* (Pearce, 1995) set out an agenda for solving world environmental issues based on the concept of a global bargain, a mutually beneficial agreement based on the interests of the various parties. *Blueprint 5* (Maddison et al, 1996) was the first volume to address a sectoral issue, the all-important transport sector. It showed that road users pay only a fraction of the true costs of road transport, contrary to the claims of most motoring organizations. It also showed another use of monetary valuation, for the conclusion that motorists pay too little for their use of the roads could not have been demonstrated without monetizing the environmental damages they impose.

The current volume revisits *Blueprint 1*, bringing the ideas and empirical illustrations up to date, but also extending the remit to cover global and international issues. A reassessment is justified because of the rapid growth in the environmental economics literature in the last decade, including its application to developing world problems where it has proven particularly fruitful. Environmental economics has become a truly exciting subject. We have done our best to convey a little of that excitement in what follows. Ultimately, however, the real measure of success will be the added armoury in defence of the environment and human well-being. While some critics suggest that environmental economics is a source of the problem, not its cure, we can only say that our experience in the practical world of policy making is precisely the opposite. It is true that, for many environmental assets, it is too late. The world in general has taken too long to realize what is happening and has acted too slowly when the realization has come. But the practical arena for the application of economic solutions to environmental problems is vast and we continue to feel that there is real hope in this context. In the end, it is only by adopting all sound arguments and all sound appeals to conscience and morality that any progress will be made. The message of this *Blueprint* is that we know how to address environmental problems. The challenge is to get on with the job and apply those policies in practice.

Acknowledgements

Blueprints 1 and 2 were produced when we were both at the London Environmental Economics Centre (LEEC) which was a joint venture between the Department of Economics at University College London (UCL) and the International Institute for Environment and Development (IIED). Blueprint 1 grew out of a report for the then UK Department of the Environment (now the Department of the Environment, Transport and the Regions) – the so-called Pearce Report – and we continue to be grateful to our friends at DETR for having the vision to sponsor the report. LEEC closed down in 1993. We had gone our separate ways, David Pearce to form the Centre for Social and Economic Research on the Global Environment (CSERGE) at UCL and the University of East Anglia in 1991, and Ed Barbier to help found the Department of Environmental Economics and Environmental Management (now the Environment Department) at the University of York in 1993.

Blueprints 3, 4 and 5 were CSERGE products. This sixth volume, Blueprint for a Sustainable Economy, is a joint product of UCL's Economics Department and York's Environment Department. We thank our colleagues in UCL and York for the continuing years of stimulating ideas and research; we have borrowed freely from their work, notably on the measurement of sustainability and on monetary valuation.

Earthscan, our publishers, have been stalwart supporters of the teams that have produced not just the Blueprints but other volumes as well and we are especially grateful to Jonathan Sinclair Wilson and his colleagues. A continuing supporter and inspirationist was Richard Sandbrook, who retired from IIED in 1999. The Earth has had few friends as dedicated as Richard and we salute him here.

David Pearce's thanks go, as always, to Sue for tolerating repeated absences to write these and other books. The original Blueprint, the blue Burmese cat, still thrives, now with six feline mates and Rocket and Rosy, German Munsterländer, who are decidely not his friends.

Ed Barbier wishes to thank Jo and Lara, plus Smokey the cat, all of whom have made life in Hovingham wonderful, except for the headless rabbits in the bathroom.

Duddenhoe End, London, Hovingham and York

DWP
EB

1

Introduction

The Blueprint Theme

Blueprint for a Green Economy (*Blueprint* 1) argued that the source of most environmental problems lies in the failure of the economic system to take account of the valuable services which natural environments provide for us (see Box 1.1). It also argued that environmental functions are important not just for everyday human well-being, but for the grander objective of sustainable development. This is because environmental assets are akin to other capital assets like machinery and roads and the stock of knowledge and skills. Increasing one form of asset while running another one down is likely to be a short-sighted prescription to increasing human well-being. Yet in many ways this has been the history of past economic development.

Environmental or ecological services and functions include:

- the provision of non-renewable natural resources such as coal and oil, bauxite and iron;
- the provision of renewable natural resources such as timber, fish and water;
- the provision of waste sinks to receive and assimilate solid, liquid and gaseous wastes from economic systems;
- the provision of amenity;
- the provision of biogeochemical cycles which help stabilize climates, provide nutrients to living things, and purify water and air; and
- the provision of information in the form of genetic blueprints and behavioural observation.

Box 1.1 *The Original Themes of* Blueprint for a
Green Economy

Environmental assets are important not just in themselves (so-called intrinsic value) but in economic terms, that is in terms of the economic services they provide.

Economic importance relates to the contribution that those assets make to human well-being.

Human well-being embraces everything that gives humans happiness and satisfaction. It is not confined to the satisfaction derived from material goods and services nor is the motive for being happy or satisfied confined to self-interest.

Economic value is most commonly revealed and observed in the market place.

But the contributions that environmental goods and services make to human well-being may or may not be channelled via functioning markets. In a great many cases, they are not. We say there are missing markets.

Economic importance can be demonstrated by placing monetary values on environmental assets and services, values which reflect human preferences, just as if there was a market. This is the process of non-market valuation.

Non-market valuation matters for several reasons, but they are summarized in the paradigm of demonstration and capture:

- Non-market valuation helps to demonstrate the economic importance of environmental assets, placing them in the same political dialogue as economic assets;
- It reminds us that economic activity may increase or decrease those assets. If it decreases them, then it reduces the asset base that supports the whole process of creating human well-being. This is the essence of unsustainable development, running down the asset bases on which future well-being depends;
- It helps to avoid the most common reason for environmental degradation, namely the failure of environmental services and assets to compete in the market place with competing economic activity. If land has an economic value for housing, but no apparent economic value in conservation, it is hardly surprising that we develop the land for housing and ignore its impact on the environment;
- It points us towards solutions. If we know what the economic value of an environmental asset is, we can work towards the capture of that value by creating a market for the asset. If we know how people value an asset we can, for example, find the price that could be charged to those people for using the asset. That price translates to a revenue which, in turn, can be used, at least in part, to finance conservation.

Once we know an asset has economic importance, we can focus on the policies to conserve it. But policies are not effective unless they address the root cause of the problem, and those root causes often lie in the structure of the economic system. Hence economic solutions are required for environmental problems.

Policies need to be biased towards economic incentives, measures that make it in the financial interest of the various stakeholders to conserve rather than destroy. In particular, the focus needs to be on market-based instruments such as taxes and tradable quotas.

Box 1.2 *Are We Running Out of Resources?*

One popular way of measuring the physical scarcity of natural resources is to compute the period of time before available resources are exhausted. Where available reserves in the current year are Q, the level of extraction (consumption) is q, and the annual rate of growth of consumption is g per cent, the exponential scarcity index is given by:

$$T = ln([Qg/q]+1)/g$$

T is the number of years before the resource is exhausted. Clearly, if a resource is getting scarcer we would expect the value of T to decline over time. The world estimates below show that, for the materials selected, T has in fact increased, not decreased, with lead as the only exception. The analysis is based on what T would have looked like if estimated in 1970 and in 1994.

	T (1970)	T (1994)
Aluminium	31	104
Copper	21	25
Iron	93	115
Lead	21	11
Mercury	13	20
Coal	111	139
Gas	22	42
Oil	20	35

One reason for the result is that new discoveries are regularly made so that the reserves figure is not a fair representation of the availability of the resource. Other factors are at work too. Reserves that were previously uneconomic to exploit become economic as the technology of extraction and processing changes. More subtly, a given quantity of resources is used more efficiently over time – the productivity of the resource increases. Finally, some materials are recycled to a greater and greater extent, lowering the rate of growth of consumption of the 'virgin' material.

Economic systems are generally good at providing only the first of these. While some commentators still express concern about the exhaustion of fossil fuel energy and mineral resources, the functioning of market systems can, to a considerable extent, be relied upon to signal when these resources are approaching exhaustion. These signals will include rising prices, which constitute an early warning that we should be moving out of those resources and into others, such as into renewable energy sources. Moreover, the rising prices themselves stimulate new discoveries, substitution of now relatively cheaper resources, and encourage technological change. We can argue about the precise pace at which this transition should happen, but the evidence is that what we might call old-fashioned resource exhaustion is not a major environmental problem (see Boxes 1.2 and 1.3).

Box 1.3 *The Growth in Efficiency of World Energy Use*

A simple measure of the efficiency with which a resource such as energy is used is the ratio of economic output to resource input. The figures below show how much of the gross world product (GWP) is produced per kilogramme of energy, measured as total primary energy (TPE) in tonnes of oil equivalent (TOE). Over the past 30 years or so, the efficiency with which energy has been used has improved from about US$2.73 to 3.56 per kilogramme of energy (kgoe), a rise of about one third.

	GWP 10^{12} US$1990	TPE 10^{9TOE}	GWP/TPE US$/kgoe
1966	11.38	4.16	2.73
1970	13.81	5.17	2.67
1980	20.01	6.91	2.89
1992	27.99	7.85	3.56

Source: authors' calculations

The technical scope for lowering the ratios is not in doubt – as publications like *Factor Four* remind us (von Weizsäcker et al, 1997). What is of interest is how far this ratio can be manipulated by policy measures. For example, an environmental tax might force polluters to lower pollution per unit of their economic activity.

But economic systems seem to go wrong when it comes to providing the rest of the environmental functions listed above. Why?

As summarized above, one of the central messages of *Blueprint* 1 was that many environmental resources have no market. They are not bought and sold. Accordingly, there are no price signals to alert us to their scarcity or to induce discovery, substitution and technological change. The same feature of these missing markets also results in an uneven playing field between environmental conservation and the immediate factors which threaten conservation. To the slash-and-burn farmer there is little benefit in pointing to the many ecological functions served by the forest if he receives no income, in cash or kind, from those services. The fact that the trees act as a store of carbon is of no immediate consequence to the farmer, even though it is a matter of great concern if we believe in the science of global warming, for then the carbon is better stored in the biomass than released to the atmosphere as carbon dioxide through burning the trees. So it is with a great many environmental assets. The upstream polluter has little incentive to take account of the downstream river user, unless forced to do so. Manufacturers of chlorofluorocarbons had no incentive to be concerned about the effects of these chemicals on the stratospheric ozone layer and hence on excess skin cancers. European farmers have little incentive to take into account the loss of wildlife arising from hedgerow removal or pesticide and fertilizer applications. All of these cases are examples of externalities, uncompensated third-party effects. It is difficult enough to internalize the externality (that is to make the polluter regard the externality as a cost to himself or herself) when the externality results in cash losses to others. It is even harder when the losses show up as non-monetary losses, as for example in the loss of amenity or impaired health.

The missing-market phenomenon therefore biases our so-called economic development decisions against the environment and in favour of economic activity which harms the environment. Ultimately, some of the development in question will be worthwhile – this is a matter of comparing costs and benefits. But it should be fairly obvious that much development will be far more doubtful once we recognize that it is at the cost of ecological functions which themselves have economic value. That economic value is simply not realized because there are no markets through which its value can be expressed.

In this central theme we have three of the main features of environmental economics and the way in which environmental economists seek to find solutions to environmental problems.

First, we see that without markets there is a clear bias towards economic activity which, at best, downgrades the environment and, at worst, ignores it altogether. Hence there is a need to establish or create markets where none exist, or to modify markets where they exist but fail adequately to reflect environmental impacts. This conclusion is mitigated by the extent to which those creating degradation may themselves be unaware of the impact they are having and be willing to change their behaviour because they do have wider social and environmental concerns.

Second, we see that these missing or imperfect markets are a cause of environmental degradation. This is a major advance on most casual discussions of the causes of degradation, which tend to focus on the agents of destruction – the farmer, the logging company, the multinational company – rather than on the reasons for their behaviour. To devise a policy we first have to know the underlying causes. In this case, the solution lies in creating markets (see Box 1.4).

Third, while we could simply catalogue environmental impacts and show these alongside the economic benefits of the economic activity in question, it is far more forceful to put a money value on the environmental damage done. Then, costs and benefits can be compared directly, using the same monetary language that is used to justify economic development. Moreover, we have a substantial and lengthy experience of the former non-monetary approach in the form of environmental impact assessments (EIA). An EIA is a critically important activity, but it

---

Box 1.4 *The Pressure–State–Response Paradigm*

The pressure–state–response paradigm requires us first to inspect environmental problems and determine their importance (the state of the environment). Sometimes the paradigm operates by simply assuming an issue is important, but environmental economists prefer to assign measures of importance to environmental issues. Next, once the issue has been judged important enough to warrant attention, the causes of the problem are sought. Here again, the pressures tend to be stated as activities, such as pollution, but this is a seriously incomplete part of the analysis. It is essential to find the underlying causes of the problem, and these are likely to lie in the workings of the economy. Sometimes these are added to the paradigm as driving forces. Such driving forces will include market failures, for example, the fact that there are no markets for many environmental services. But governments are also fundamental causes of environmental problems, for example by subsidizing environmentally harmful activities. The Common Agricultural Policy is an example. The final response stage refers to the solutions and these may be found by looking at the fundamental causes and seeing what can be done to change them. If markets are missing, the solution is to create them by conferring property rights on the environmental resource. If government activity is causing the problem, governments need to rethink their approach.

Chapter 6 looks at the causes of environmental degradation in more detail.

---

is difficult to resist the view that much of it is cosmetic, more designed to say that the environment has been taken into account, than to overrule environmentally damaging developments. Going the one stage further and putting money values on environmental damage puts the environment on the same footing as the economic arguments in favour of development, provided, of course, that the exercise does not remain confined to the paper on which the analysis is written. There have to be incentives based on the monetary value analysis.

Posing the issue in terms of development versus conservation is a little dangerous. It implies that we can have one but not the other and, indeed, those who are opposed to economic growth see it in precisely those terms. We do not agree with that view. The comparison between development and environment has to be one of the types of economic development that can be secured at the same time as minimizing the risks to the environment, an issue we expand upon in Chapter 2. The reality is that the world has to accommodate at least 50 per cent more people than it has now and they will need space, food and water, shelter and infrastructure. That cannot be secured without environmental loss. While this may appear to lend support to those who argue against not only economic growth but also population growth, the population growth in question is unavoidable. A further 50 per cent on top of that is avoidable and everything that can be done that is humane and respectful of individual liberties should be done. But the first 50 per cent is demographically unavoidable. The debate has to be about the way in which we foster future economic development to meet the legitimate aspirations of people; that is, it has to be about sustainable development (see Chapters 2, 4 and 5).

Why is Monetizing the Environment so Controversial?

Blueprint 1 did place emphasis on the importance of placing money values on environmental assets and services. It proved to be probably the most controversial issue in terms of the popular discussion of the book in the media and in public forums. This perhaps diverted attention from the fact, also made clear in *Blueprint* 1, that the case for market-based approaches to solving environmental problems can be justified quite independently of whether valuation takes place. Nonetheless, we argued above that valuation is important because it places the environment in the same political dialogue as economic activity generally. Put another way, environment should be a core focus of a ministry of finance or industry as much as a ministry of environment. It is appropriate therefore to address the question of the validity of the money valuation approach. Actual developments in the theory and practice of valuation are discussed in Chapter 3.

Environmental economists have developed sophisticated techniques for measuring the total economic value of environmental assets (see Chapter 3). The rationale for applying these techniques lies in the need to ensure that environmental impacts are taken into account in decision making on the same basis as the conventional costs and benefits of economic activity. While there is an active debate about the reliability and validity of these techniques in eliciting money values, most of the controversy does not centre on the techniques, but on the very idea of monetizing the environment. Some of the criticism is embedded in so much misunderstanding and ignorance of what environmental economists actually do that it is difficult to separate what may be intellectually interesting arguments and criticisms from misconception. We can start by asking what economic valuation is all about.

Economists begin with the notion that economic value arises from meeting the preferences of individuals. Thus, the economic value of a commodity A is greater than a commodity B if A is preferred to B. Elevating human preferences to this high-level status is usually summarized in the notion of consumer sovereignty, that what people want, matters. In this naïve form it is of course similar in concept to a popular interpretation of democracy (see Box 1.5).

The motives that people have for their preferences are various. Whereas economists might once have said the motives were immaterial,

---

Box 1.5 *Preferences, Willingness to Pay and Economic Value*

The underlying value judgement in economics is that resources should be allocated according to what people want. This is the notion of consumer sovereignty or, as it might better be termed, individual sovereignty. These wants, or preferences, are revealed directly where there is a market place. People vote for a product by buying it. Some preferences are revealed in market places which do not appear, at first sight, to have much to do with the environment. For example, the housing market is about the demand and supply of houses. But houses are bundles of characteristics, and the environment surrounding the house is one such characteristic. So the demand for that environment is very likely to show up in the demand for houses. This is a form of indirect market. In many cases there may be no direct or indirect markets, so it is necessary to elicit preferences through hypothetical markets, for example by asking what people are willing to pay.

The motives for preferences can be varied and include:

- Pure self-interest: wanting something now;
- Future self-interest: wanting something to be conserved in case we wish to use it later;
- Altruism: wanting something to be conserved or made available because others want it;
- Bequest: a form of altruism, wanting something to be conserved so our children or future generations can use it;
- Existence: wanting something to be conserved even though we make no use of it now, nor intend to in the future. This motive will capture some of the intrinsic value of the environment since individuals may be judging what the environmental asset wants.

In principle, then we can measure preferences by what people are, or say they are, willing to pay. This willingness to pay is a measure of economic value.

---

they are now the subject of fairly extensive analysis because of arguments about the moral standing of various motives, and about the extent to which we can add up preferences based on different kinds of motives. But the essential point is that motives may vary. I may prefer A to B because it gives me personally more pleasure. I may prefer B because I think it is better for my children, for society as a whole, for all future generations, for other sentient beings, or for the good of the Earth. The reality is that motives vary enormously and more than one motive may be present for the choice of B over A. This is important, because some of the criticism of economic valuation rests on the idea that preferences have only one motive: self-interest. Self-interest quickly becomes equated with greed (even though they are not the same) and the misconceptions multiply rapidly. In fact it is extremely difficult to explain human behaviour on the basis of self-interest alone, although self-interest is very powerful. It would be hard to explain our attitudes to charities, or even our savings behaviour, if we were solely motivated by self-interest.

Preferences are revealed in various ways. When we vote for political parties and individuals we are expressing a preference. Economic decisions that affect the environment are sometimes the context for political votes, but the millions and millions of decisions that are made daily cannot be. We need another medium through which to identify preferences. The market is one such medium. In the market place preferences show up in our decisions to buy and not to buy goods or services. Since these goods and services have prices, the decision to buy can be equated with a willingness to pay at least the price that is asked. A decision not to buy is, conversely, equivalent to a willingness to pay less than the price. This is the link between preferences – the underlying tendency to vote 'yes' by buying the goods – and willingness to pay (WTP).

Political votes tend to be yes/no expressions. We either vote for or against something. In reality political systems also have other pressures which tend to reflect intensity of preference: lobbies and campaigns for example. Market-place votes also reflect intensity of preference in that we could be willing to pay an amount only just above the asking price or very much more than the asking price. Recall that everyone with a WTP less than the price will not buy it. Those with a WTP greater than the price will buy. But some will have a substantial excess of WTP over price – they would have been willing to pay a lot more than the price. Others will have only a small excess of WTP over price. This excess is like getting something for nothing, a benefit or gain of individual well-being that exceeds the price paid. It is known as the consumer's surplus. This concept is the central measure of the individual's net benefit from a good or service (see Box 1.6).

A moment's reflection will show that WTP depends on ability to buy. In general, the higher an individual's income the higher the WTP. The indicator that economists use for measuring preferences – WTP – is therefore biased towards whatever the prevailing distribution of income happens to be. If income is redistributed it is very likely that a different configuration of goods and services will be provided. We can now see another concern that critics of economic valuation have, but this time there is some reason to it. Whether or not environmental assets are conserved on the economic approach will depend on the distribution of income. If rich people favour the environmentally destructive activity, their WTP could be instrumental in bringing about that destruction, even though a show of hands (political votes) might be against it. Of course, it could work the other way round, and often does. Richer people may favour the environment more and may therefore be instrumental in saving it by expressing a strong WTP. But let us grant the potential criticism. Can it be overcome?

Box 1.6 *The Concept of Net Benefit*

The diagram shows a demand curve of the willingness of individuals to pay for the good in question. Thus, OX people are willing to pay OP or more for the good in question (we show numbers of people on the horizontal axis, whereas we would normally show the diagram in terms of units of the product). The heavy section of the demand curve shows that some people would have paid more than OP, so they get something for nothing. This is the consumer's surplus and it can be measured in monetary terms. The clue is to remember that willingness to pay reflects the well-being that individuals secure. If I am willing to pay OP, it means that it gives me OP units of well-being multiplied by the number of units I buy. In the case below, OP is the market price determined by the forces of supply and demand. So some people get the product for OP even though they were willing to pay more. This concept of consumer's surplus is also equivalent to a measure of net benefit. Essentially, willingness to pay is measured by the area under the demand curve, whereas actual payments are measured by the rectangular area of expenditure. The shaded triangle is therefore a measure of net benefit which equals total willingness to pay minus what is actually paid.

The income bias is of course present in all markets. In some cases, markets differentiate goods so that people on different incomes can secure the same good but at different levels of quality or packaging, for example. To some extent this can be done with environmental assets: some wildlife safaris, for example, are geared to the higher-income market, some to the lower end. But it still leaves an uneasy feeling that the natural environment should, somehow, be freely available to all, or be available to all at the same price. Of course, making it freely available immediately falls foul of the analysis as to why environments degrade. They degrade precisely because they often are free to all comers. They are, effectively, open access resources with no prices for their use. The absence of a price means the same thing as a zero price and when things cost nothing to the user they tend to be abused. If energy were freely available, a great deal more of it would be used, and there would be a consequent increase in pollution. Surprisingly, there still are people who believe that the environment should be free to all comers. They speak of rights to the countryside, for example, but with little awareness that free access spells certain disaster for the very thing they allegedly value.

In suggesting that environmental problems occur because of missing markets, and in noting that markets are biased in terms of the emphasis they give to those with higher incomes, one is effectively arguing that the environment should be allocated to users just like conventional goods. The next strand of criticism of the economic argument is that the environment is not like other economic goods. It is somehow different. Here the arguments vary but they might include reference to the fact that we all need the environment to survive: we need clean air and water, energy and even space and amenity. But we do not in fact allocate energy on a free-for-all basis: it is sold through markets. Some countries still adhere to the nominal idea that water should not be rationed by the market, but it is a fast disappearing idea precisely because it is widely recognized that water is often a scarce commodity. Why, then, should air or amenity be different? There is a source of debate here, but it is far from clear that the environment is so very different from other goods and services.

There are two further arguments for not rejecting economic valuation because of the income-bias issue. First, if we believe it is a problem it is possible to build a correction into the way we do the analysis. Indeed, the idea of weighting WTP for distributional or equity concerns was very popular in economics just a few decades ago (see Box 1.7). It fell into disuse mainly because it seemed an impractical way of correcting the cause of the bias, namely the prevailing distribution of income. And this provides the second reason for not being persuaded by the income-bias argument. The bias exists because of the nature of the prevailing income distribution. Seeking to correct the bias by rejecting economic valuation is a peculiar way of solving the problem. The correct approach is to change the distribution of income.

When economists monetize the environment, what they are actually doing is to place a money value on individual preferences for or against a given environmental change. It is preferences that are monetized, not the environment itself. But economists themselves tend to slip into the previous usage, speaking of the money value of a given asset. To that end we continue to use the same terminology here, so long as we are reminded from time to time about what it is that is being monetized.

Box 1.7 *Willingness to Pay and Ability to Pay*

Critics of economic approaches to environmental valuation often argue that willingness to pay is biased because it depends on ability to pay. Willingness to pay certainly does depend on income and wealth, so that what society is willing to pay, say, to conserve an environmental asset depends not just on tastes and concerns, but on the overall level of income in the economy, and on the distribution of that income. Even if the level of overall income (GNP) was kept the same, redistribution of that GNP would alter the willingness to pay for environmental assets. It is not always clear what the criticism of economic valuation is, given this fact. It could be that there is a bias in the type of environmental assets that will be provided because the rich will have a bigger say in what is provided than the poor. Or it could be that the rich will not demand environmental quality at all, condemning the poor to suffer environmental degradation they may not want. Or it may be that the rich can buy their way out of environmental problems, moving to cleaner and quieter areas with greater amenity, leaving the poor to occupy areas where there is little amenity and where there are risks to health and well-being. This last argument is part of what is known as the environmental justice issue, the view that the poor tend to locate in high risk, low quality areas because those areas are associated with lower house prices.

These are all serious issues and all need investigating carefully. But whether they should be allowed to influence environmental policy is a different matter. Pursuing the pressure–state–response paradigm of Box 1.4 we could just as well argue that policy should correct the underlying cause of this environmental inequality – the distribution of income. If it is difficult or impossible to do that, then modifying environmental policy to take account of distributional impacts is legitimate. But it is very much a second best argument and tends to divert attention away from the fundamental cause of the problem, which is income inequality.

Finally, if adjustments are to be made they are not difficult to make. Willingness to pay can always be scaled to account for income differences. There are various ways of doing this but one might be given by the formula:

$$AdjWTPj = (Y*/Yj).WTPj$$

where *adjWTPj* is the adjusted willingness to pay of social group *j*, *Y** is the average income of the population and *Yj* is the income of the social group *j*. Thus, suppose the affected group has an income of $15,000 per year per capita, and that the average income in the nation is $25,000. Let the willingness of group *j* to pay for some environmental asset be $5 per year. In conventional analysis we simply record the $5 as group *j* willingness to pay. In the modified, or equity-weighted approach, it is recorded as 25/15 x $5 = $8.3.

This is one of many approaches that can be used for equity weighting (see Pearce, 1986). Contrary to what is often said, economists have long known how to adjust willingness to pay for equity concerns, although few would argue it is a very sensible way of dealing with the problem of equity.

Monetization conjures up all kinds of picture thinking among critics. One, as we have seen, is equating money with greed, money as the root of all evil. But the pursuit of money as an end in itself is, of course, quite different to using money as a measuring rod of preferences. We are probably stuck with the misconception, but we should at least record its existence. Now suppose one is an ardent environmentalist and that what matters most is the conservation of the environment. From such a standpoint it is easy to see why monetization is a threat. For it could be the case that the money value of conservation (that is the money value of preferences for the environment) is less than the money value of the thing that threatens the environment. If we pursue the monetization logic, the sum of preferences for environmental destruction might exceed the sum of preferences against it. The environment should be dispensed with. That is, indeed, the logic of cost-benefit analysis which, in turn, is nothing more than a weighing up of monetized preferences for and against something. What the environmentalist is saying is that the analysis risks coming up with a dislikable answer.

Here we have another example of bad criticism, but in this case it is essentially disingenuous. For it means that any procedure for aiding decision-making is wrong unless it guarantees an outcome that the individual critic wants. On that basis democracy is wrong because it too cannot guarantee the outcome. Oddly, those who advance this argument also tend to advance the (false) view that economics is morally suspect because it is based on self-interest. Yet their own approach is based on a very stark form of self-interest: what they want is what should happen. We would argue that the vast majority of environmentalists are more enlightened than this, but some are not. They are, effectively, elites and their opposition to economic valuation has little to do with money at all. It has to do with the risks it poses for the self-importance of the elites in question. Criticism of this kind often masquerades under various guises. It is often said that we cannot trust people to make the right decisions because they are uninformed: an elitist argument and a view that could just as well be advanced against all democracy. (Notice, that the uninformed are always other people!). In any event, if informational deficiencies prevail, as they do, the solution is not to reject preferences based on limited information: it is to provide more information. There is also a subtle twist to the view that economic valuation places the environment at risk. Valuation may indeed show that a given asset has low economic value, but failing to value it at all in economic terms is far more likely to result in it being given an implicit economic value of zero, a result that guarantees it will not compete with some alternative developmental value.

A second argument is that the environment is beyond price and cannot, or should not, be brought within the purview of the measuring rod of money. It is not always clear what is meant by 'beyond price'. Sometimes, critics seem to think it means that the environment has an infinite value. In some ways this is correct: if we 'removed' the natural environment then no one would survive. In that sense the total environment does appear to have infinite value. But the only real sense that can be attached to this notion is that it is not meaningful to ask the question: what is the economic value of the total environment? The problem arises from a confusion over the difference between total and discrete or marginal change. This issue is addressed in Chapter 3. Another, related, interpretation of 'beyond price' is that the environment is somehow different to all other goods and services. The environment provides life-support functions without which we would not survive. In that respect it appears to be different. From this it is argued that we cannot allocate environmental services according to WTP. But a problem with this view is that energy is also a good without which we would not survive. Yet, as noted above, we allocate energy according to WTP since, by and large, energy is allocated through the market place. Much the same might be said of water, timber or building materials. The essentiality of the environment does not appear to provide a basis for removing it from the WTP context.

Sometimes, it is argued that views on the environment should be transformative – that we should have more environmental assets, regardless of what people say they want, because the provision of those assets will themselves change the preferences of those who initially do not want the environment (Brennan, 1992). Obviously, until everyone's view has been changed to fit in with the preconceived view of what is right, individuals should not have their preferences counted. This argument also risks being elitist, but it is true to say that societies often persist with the provision of services that people initially do not like in order to encourage transformation of those values. It is, of course, a perennial debate.

Finally, we are told that self-interested individuals should only have their votes counted when they act as citizens, thinking of others and the general good (Sagoff, 1988). As noted above, we have no reason to suppose that all monetized votes are motivated by individual self-interest, but even if they are, one wonders what conditions have to prevail before the critics accept that people may genuinely be telling us what they want, all factors taken into account. Nor is it very clear how one guarantees that everyone votes as a citizen rather than from a self-interested stance.

Valuation and Morality

But perhaps there are arguments, like the transformational one, which favour elitism. Perhaps there is some group of people who know better what is good for us than we do ourselves. They may even have an essential stewardship role on behalf of future generations that cannot express preferences for what they want because they are not yet here. Even this justification fades on analysis.

First, future generations are here already and we can talk to them. They are our children and grandchildren and they have voices. Generations overlap and all that is required is a set of overlapping contracts. We agree now with our children and grandchildren and they can agree with their children and grandchildren. The chances are that they will want very much what we want, but suppose they differ in their views? No one generation should be allowed to irreversibly deny what a future generation might want. That principle alone should make us cautious about depleting resources, but the rule quickly becomes stultifying if we are afraid to do anything at all simply because some future generation, perhaps 1000 years hence, might regret what we do today. Taking a precautionary approach is therefore sound advice, but it does not mean taking no risk at all.

Second, the elitist argument is self-defeating. What drives environmental degradation is the economic comparison between conservation and degradation. Economic systems are, as we have argued above, set up in such a way that these decisions are biased towards degradation. That is the reality, the way things are. It would be nice to think things will change and that, one day, everyone will wake up and say things should be different and that it is simply wrong to permit so much environmental degradation. The chances of this moral revolution are not zero, but they are not very high, and there are grave risks in waiting for this kind of millennial event. How far past 'revolutions' have changed matters is open to debate. Perhaps today we would not take environmental matters so seriously but for the emergence of environmental consciousness in the 1960s. But, if we take deforestation as a focal point of many of the campaigns, we find that rates of deforestation today are no less than they were in the 1970s. Of course, they might have been higher still but for the campaigns. But it is difficult to resist the judgement that, because the driving forces of deforestation lie with property-rights regimes, population change, and missing markets, the campaigns have done little to address those causes. Those who advocate the moral view have therefore to persuade us that they have been successful in the past before claiming that other approaches are worse. If, as we argue, economic factors drive environmental degradation, then economic factors have to be changed so as to reduce degradation. The elitist argument is then self-defeating, for it diverts attention away from the real causes of environmental degradation towards a solution based on what appears to be a cause, but where the solution has little or no chance of being realized. Even more oddly, the economic approach argues for a focus on economic causes and solutions, and economic valuation is part of that solution. But it does not argue that other approaches should also not be tried. In contrast, those who oppose the economic approach tend to argue that it has no role to play.

The genuine issue at the heart of what should be a real debate over economic valuation is the extent to which individuals have rights to see their preferences count, even if those preferences could ultimately be against their own well-being or the well-being of humans generally. This tension is, of course, at the heart of government and it would be silly to pretend that there is any easy answer. There are those who favour massive government intervention to act on behalf of people who may not judge 'correctly'. There are those who favour minimal government on the grounds that individuals should be free to choose, whether 'correctly' or not. The contexts in which this debate takes place extend far beyond theories of optimal government to everyday situations such as cigarette smoking, alcohol consumption, drugs and food safety.

2

The Meaning of Sustainable Development

Introduction

Blueprint 1 was ultimately concerned with how to make an economy more environmentally sustainable. That is, what are the various economic policies and instruments available for ensuring that the economy is able to meet the needs of the present generation without compromising the ability of the economic system, including its environmental resource base, to meet the needs of future generations? As noted in *Blueprint* 1, this concern has become the fulcrum for a new area of economic analysis now widely recognized as the economics of sustainable development.

Many of the conceptual and methodological issues concerning the analysis and measurement of sustainable development were first identified in *Blueprint* 1, and had an important influence on the academic and policy debates on incorporating sustainability as an economic goal. However, the economics of sustainable development has evolved rapidly in recent years, and the basic theory underlying economic thinking on sustainability has been greatly extended and applied in practice since *Blueprint* 1 was written.[1] In addition, new avenues of enquiry in economics, such as environmental Kuznets curves, endogenous or new growth theory, and ecological economics, also have something to contribute to our understanding of the economics of sustainable development. This

---

1 For summaries of these recent developments see, for example, Goldin and Winters (1995), Pearce and Atkinson (1995) and Toman, Pezzey and Krautkramer (1995).

chapter revisits the economics of sustainable development, noting both extensions to the theory and relevant developments elsewhere in economics.

The Contribution of *Blueprint 1*

Blueprint 1 was one of the first attempts to provide a synthesis of a growing interest in economics with the concern of sustainable development. One of the problems noted was the proliferation of definitions of the term – which were illustrated by providing a collection of such definitions in its appendix. Although diverse and wide-ranging economic interpretations of the concept of sustainability are inevitable given the broad nature of the term, a proliferation of definitions is unhelpful in developing policies for sustainable development. Moreover, a proliferation of definitions gives comfort to politicians who can always say they are meeting one definition or criterion as opposed to another. A major contribution of *Blueprint* 1 was an attempt to provide a consensus view of the theory of sustainable development, as interpreted by economists.

A second contribution was to point out that sustainable development represents an entirely unique objective, or development path, for an economy. Achieving sustainability is therefore different from other economic criteria, such as efficiency, and requires its own set of rules for managing an economy. This critical aspect of sustainable development is still often misunderstood, even by some economists.

For example, it is sometimes claimed that economic efficiency and sustainability are essentially the same objectives: attaining sustainable development – ensuring that future generations have at least the same economic opportunities as the current generation – is tantamount to ensuring intertemporal efficiency, ensuring that economic and environmental resources cannot be reallocated to make one or more individuals better off without making others, either of the same or of different generations, worse off. Hence, according to this view, there is no need for policy makers to consider additional criteria other than economic efficiency in deciding the optimal allocation of economic resources, including environmental resources.

However, as indicated in Box 2.1, this is not strictly true: the criteria for determining economic efficiency differ from that for ensuring sustainability. Although it is possible for development to be both economically efficient and sustainable, efficiency does not automatically guarantee sustainability. Consequently, if an economy is to be sustainable as well as efficient, then optimal allocation of both economic and environmental resources must satisfy the criteria for achieving both objectives.

Box 2.1 *Economic Efficiency and Sustainability*

Economists define an outcome as efficient if there is no change in the allocation of inputs (natural resources, labour and capital) or outputs (intermediate
products and final goods and services) that makes one individual in society
better off without making any other individual worse off. Well-functioning
markets generally promote efficiency by providing opportunities for individuals
to achieve mutually agreeable gains from trade.

However, underlying any state of the economy is what economists call
initial endowments. Each member of the economy holds some share of the
total natural, labour and capital resources with which to enter the market and
trade so that an efficient final outcome can be achieved. Including time and
multiple generations involves numerous complications. Today's initial resource
endowments and institutions will result in future time paths for endowments of
natural resources, capital and labour, which are used to produce flows of goods
and services over time. Depending on how complicated one wants to make the
analysis, technological progress can be added, affecting the productivity of
inputs over time and the degree to which they are substitutable.

Under ideal conditions, efficiency can still be achieved. Each possible
time path for endowments would lead, through market trade, toward a different time path for the economic well-being of current and future generations.
There are an infinite number of such outcomes, each of which is efficient in the
sense that there would be no way to reallocate inputs or outputs to make one
or more individuals better off without making others, either of the same or of
different generations, worse off. Under some time paths for endowments, the
generations may enjoy relatively egalitarian economic circumstances, while
under others some generations may be quite rich while others will not have the
capital and natural resources to live above poverty levels.

Although sustainability is more difficult for economists to define, we might
say that it is achieved if an economy is on a time path where future generations have economic opportunities that are at least as large as earlier
generations. Each generation's endowment may be taken to include its own
labour. Whether an economy is sustainable or not depends on the time paths
of natural resource and capital endowments and technological progress. Time
paths of endowments and technology that lead to constant or increasing
economic opportunities over the indefinite future are taken as sustainable.
Time paths where earlier generations leave later generations such poor endowments of resources and capital that economic opportunities decline over time
would be said to be unsustainable.

Thus, theoretically, there is potentially an infinite number of efficient time
paths, only some of which are sustainable. Efficiency does not guarantee sustainability. Some efficient paths are not sustainable. At the same time, there is no
reason in theory why an economy could not be both efficient and sustainable.

Source: Bishop, 1993 as adapted for Barbier et al, 1994

As argued in B*lueprint* 1, an important economic concept for understanding the role of the environment in sustainable development is to view the
way in which natural resources and environments provide economic
benefits as being similar to the way in which any valuable asset provides
'services' to an economy. Along with physical and human capital, environ-

Box 2.2 *The Total Capital Stock and Human Welfare*

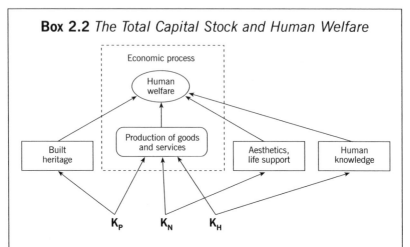

Human-made, or physical capital (K_P), natural capital (K_N) and human capital (K_H) all contribute to human welfare through supporting the production of goods and services in the economic processs. For example, K_P consists of machinery, equipment, factory buildings, tools and other investment goods that are used in production; K_N is used for material and energy inputs into production, acts as a sink for waste emissions from the economic process, and provides a variety of ecological services to sustain production, such as nutrient recycling, watershed protection and catchment functions, and climate regulation; and K_H includes the human skills necessary for advanced production processes and for research and development activities that lead to technical innovation. However, all three forms of capital also contribute directly to human welfare independently of their contributions through the economic process. For example, included in physical capital, K_P, is fine architecture and other physical components of cultural heritage; K_N includes aesthetically pleasing natural landscapes, and provides a variety of ecological services that are essential for supporting life; and increases in K_H also contribute more generally to increases in the overall stock of human knowledge.

mental resources should be viewed as important economic assets, which can be called natural capital (see Box 2.2) and also contributes to economic productivity and human well-being, both currently and over time. The value of natural capital could be measured in terms of its potential contribution to both present and future economic well-being.[2] Similarly, as with other assets in the economy, we can choose to use up or deplete natural capital today, or alternatively, we can choose to save or even expand these economic assets for future use. As shown in Box 2.2, the total capital stock available to the economy for producing goods and

2 Whether the actual welfare contribution of natural capital can be measured by an indicator of sustainable income is, of course, an important economic issue, which was addressed initially in *Blueprint 1* and will be discussed further in Chapter 4.

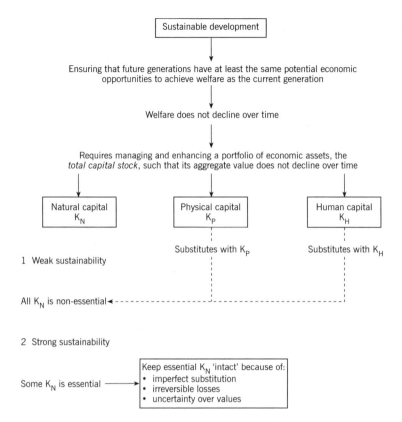

Figure 2.1 *Natural Capital and Sustainable Development*

services, and ultimately well-being, consists not just of human and physical capital but also of natural capital.

The importance of the total capital stock concept to sustainability is illustrated in Figure 2.1, which summarizes broadly the economic view of sustainable development as depicted in *Blueprint 1*. Most economic interpretations of sustainability take as their starting point the overall objective of sustainability as defined by the World Commission on Environment and Development (WCED, or Brundtland Commission). The WCED defined sustainable development as 'development that meets the needs of the present without compromising the ability of future generations to meet their own needs' (WCED, 1987).

Economists are generally comfortable with this broad interpretation of sustainability, as it is easily translatable into economic terms: an increase in well-being today should not have as its consequences a reduction in well-being tomorrow. That is, future generations should be entitled to at least the same level of economic opportunities – and thus at least the same level of economic well-being – as is currently available to present generations. Consequently, economic development today must ensure that future generations are left no worse off than present generations. Or, as Pezzey (1989) has succinctly put it, per capita well-being should not be declining over time.

As noted in Figure 2.1, it is the total stock of capital employed by the economic system, including natural capital, that determines the full range of economic opportunities, and thus well-being, available to both present and future generations. Society must decide how best to use its total capital stock today to increase current economic activities and well-being, and how much it needs to save or even accumulate for tomorrow, and ultimately, for the well-being of future generations.

However, it is not simply the aggregate stock of capital in the economy that may matter but also its composition, in particular whether present generations are using up one form of capital to meet the needs of today. For example, much of the recent interest in sustainable development has risen out of concern that current economic development may be leading to rapid accumulation of physical and human capital, but at the expense of excessive depletion and degradation of natural capital. The major concern has been that, by depleting the world's stock of natural wealth irreversibly, the development path chosen today will have detrimental implications for the well-being of future generations. In other words, according to this view, current economic development is essentially unsustainable.

While it is generally accepted by most economists that economic development around the world is leading to the irreversible depletion of natural capital, there is widespread disagreement as to whether this necessarily implies that such development is inherently unsustainable. From an economic standpoint, the critical issue of debate is not whether natural capital is being irreversibly depleted, but whether we can compensate future generations for the current loss of natural capital, and if that is possible, how much is required to compensate future generations for this loss (Mäler, 1995).

Finally, although the implications of environmental impacts for intergenerational equity is generally considered to be the main concern of sustainable development, environmental depletion and degradation can affect human well-being in a variety of different ways (see Box 2.3). These other implications of environmental deterioration can be significant, and were also addressed by *Blueprint 1*. They will be discussed further in later chapters of this book. The remainder of this chapter looks at recent economic thinking that has contributed to our understanding of the economics of sustainable development.

Box 2.3 *Environmental Deterioration and Economic Well-being*

One of the difficulties in determining whether environmental resources are being exploited sustainably and efficiently over time is that the implications of environmental degradation and depletion for human well-being are varied and complex. They include the following effects:

- The well-being of existing generations may be affected by any loss of environmental resources and ecological services today, if environmental values are not automatically reflected in market prices or in public decisions affecting the allocation of natural resources;.
- There may be additional implications for current well-being from environmental depletion and degradation if individuals are uncertain about their future demand for natural resources and ecological services and/or their availability in the future. For example, individuals may be unsure whether they will visit a site of natural beauty either today or in the future, but they may consider the possibility of a future visit to be a valuable option. However, irreversible development of the site would negate this option, thus affecting the choices and well-being of such individuals;
- Further complications also arise from ignorance, in that individuals today may not be aware of or recognize the full ecological and economic implications of environmental depletion and degradation;
- There may also be implications for intra-generational equity, or how the burden of natural resource loss and degradation today may be distributed unequally across different individuals, peoples, countries and regions;
- Finally, there are the implications for sustainability, or inter-generational equity, that is, how environmental depletion and degradation may affect the welfare of future as opposed to current generations.

Weak versus Strong Sustainability, Environmental Kuznets Curves and the Environment–Growth Debate

In *Blueprint* 1 we noted that economists are generally split into two camps over the special role of natural capital in sustainable development. The main disagreement between these two perspectives is whether natural capital has a unique or essential role in sustaining human welfare, and thus whether special compensation rules are required to ensure that future generations are not made worse off by natural capital depletion today (see Figure 2.1). These two contrasting views are now generally referred to as weak sustainability versus strong sustainability.[3]

---

3 In *Blueprint* 1 we also referred to these two interpretations of sustainable development as broad and narrow definitions of sustainability (Chapter 2). In addition, we demonstrated how the concept of weak and strong sustainability could be translated into criteria for project appraisal (Chapter 5). For further discussion of this distinction between weak and strong sustainability see Barbier, Markandya and Pearce (1990); Howarth and Norgaard (1995); Pearce, Barbier and Markandya (1990); Toman, Pezzey and Krautkramer (1995) and Turner (1993).

According to the weak sustainability view, there is essentially no inherent difference between natural and other forms of capital, and hence the same optimal depletion rules ought to apply to both. As long as the natural capital that is being depleted is replaced with even more valuable physical and human capital, then the value of the aggregate stock – comprising both human, physical and the remaining natural capital – is increasing over time.[4] Maintaining and enhancing the total stock of all capital alone is sufficient to attain sustainable development.

In contrast, proponents of the strong sustainability view argue that physical or human capital cannot substitute for all the environmental resources comprising the natural capital stock, or all of the ecological services performed by nature. Essentially, this view questions whether, on the one hand, human and physical capital, and on the other, natural capital, effectively comprise a single homogeneous total capital stock. Uncertainty over many environmental values, in particular the value that future generations may place on increasingly scarce natural resources and ecological services, further limits our ability to determine whether we can adequately compensate future generations for irreversible losses in essential natural capital today. Thus the strong sustainability view suggests that environmental resources and ecological services that are essential for human welfare and cannot be easily substituted by human and physical capital should be protected and not depleted. Maintaining or increasing the value of the total capital stock over time in turn requires keeping the non-substitutable and essential components of natural capital constant over time.

The debate between weak and strong sustainability is just as relevant today as when we originally wrote *Blueprint 1*. Recent extensions to the economic theory of sustainable development have not so much resolved this debate as sharpened its focus. Before reconsidering the weak and strong sustainability views further, we first explore a number of recent developments in the economics relevant to the key issues.

Since *Blueprint 1* was written, a new area of enquiry has emerged in environmental economics that has important implications for sustainable development. This recent literature is concerned with the analysis of environmental Kuznets curves (EKC) – the hypothesis that there exists an inverted U-shaped relationship between a variety of indicators of environmental pollution or resource depletion and the level of per capita

---

4 Note, however, that rapid population growth may imply that the value of the per capita aggregate capital stock is declining even if the total value stays the same. Moreover, even if the per capita value of the asset base were maintained, it may not imply non-declining welfare of the majority of people. These considerations also hold for the strong-sustainability arguments discussed below. Other population and distributional implications are discussed in more detail elsewhere in the book.

income.[5] The implication of this hypothesis is that environmental degradation should be observed initially to increase, but eventually to decline, as per capita income increases. Figure 2.2 shows a typical EKC estimated for sulphur dioxide (SO_2). One important interpretation of such EKC relationships is that general economic development will take care of the environment automatically, albeit at the expense of immediate and near-term losses in environmental assets.

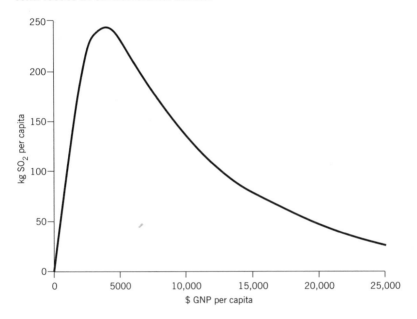

Figure 2.2 *An Environmental Kuznets Curve for Sulphur Dioxide*

---

5 The concept of an EKC relationship draws its inspiration from the income distribution theory developed by Kuznets (1955), who hypothesized that there is an inverted U-shaped relationship between an indicator of income inequality and the level of income. However, the exact origins of the EKC hypothesis are somewhat ambiguous, and appear to be the product of numerous studies conducted simultaneously in the early 1990s. Most sources point to the analysis by Grossman and Kreuger (1993) of air quality measures in a cross-section of countries for different years, which was part of a wider investigation into whether the claims that the economic growth accompanying the North American Free Trade Agreement might foster greater environmental degradation. Similarly, the study by Shafik (1994) was originally a background paper for the World Bank's enquiry into growth and environment relationships for the *World Development* 1992 (World Bank, 1992). Finally, Panayotou (1995) offers perhaps the earliest and most detailed explanation of a possible 'Kuznets type U-shape relationship between the rate of environmental degradation and the level of economic development' in analysis conducted for the World Employment Programme of the International Labour Office in 1992.

The above curve is the environmental Kuznets curve for SO_2 estimated across rich and poor countries of the world by Panayotou (1995). The peak or turning point level of per capita income where environmental degradation starts to fall is about US$5,000.

Taken to extremes, we do not have to regard the environment as anything special. As people get richer they will increase their demand for the environment and improve it, initially with public health legislation, then clean air, then conservation generally.

Although interest in the possibility of EKC relationships for a variety of environmental indicators has only really emerged in the 1990s, the debate over EKCs is likely to continue for some time. There are several reasons for this.

First, the EKC is a falsifiable hypothesis that can and will continue to be tested by a variety of empirical investigations. Thus an increasing number of studies are attempting to examine through different analytical methodologies whether the EKC hypothesis holds for a variety of indicators of environmental damage or resource depletion, both over time and across countries, regions, states, districts and even cities.

Second, the EKC hypothesis poses an important intellectual challenge. Explanations as to why environmental degradation should first increase then decline with income have focused on a number of underlying relationships, including:

- the effects of structural economic change on the use of the environment for resource inputs and to assimilate waste;
- the link between the demand for environmental quality and income referred to above; and
- types of environmental degradation and ecological processes.

It is not clear that we understand fully these critical relationships, nor is it clear which ones – if any – explain why we might observe an EKC relationship. For example, many of the original explanations of the EKC hypothesis focused on changes in the composition of goods and services due to structural shifts in the economy, the efficiency of resource use, the composition of inputs and technological innovation. However, it has increasingly been recognized that the effects of such changes on environment–income links are not exogenous processes – determined by factors outside the economy – but are influenced by policy choices (Panayotou, 1995; Stern et al, 1996; World Bank, 1992). Similarly, previous conjecture that the environmental quality is simply a luxury good – that the demand for improved environmental quality increases more than proportionately with income – is proving difficult to substantiate (McConnell, 1997). In addition, it has been suggested that

EKC relationships may hold only for certain types of environmental damage, such as pollutants with more short-term and local impacts versus those with more global and long-term impacts (Arrow et al, 1995; Cole et al, 1997; Selden and Song, 1994). Finally, and perhaps most importantly, the EKC hypothesis has revived interest in the long-standing debate over the environmental implications of economic growth (Ansuategi et al, 1998). Some commentators have argued that the empirical evidence on EKC relationships supports the general proposition that the solution to combating environmental damage is economic growth itself (Beckerman, 1992). Others have been more cautious, noting that conclusive evidence of an EKC relationship applies only to a few pollutants, thus making it difficult to use this evidence to speculate more generally about growth–environment linkages (Arrow et al, 1995). Still others have pointed out that, even for those pollutants displaying EKC characteristics, aggregate global emissions are projected to rise over time, demonstrating that the existence of an EKC relationship for such pollutants does not necessarily imply that, at the global level, any associated environmental damage is likely to disappear with economic growth (Selden and Song, 1994; Stern et al, 1996). Policy makers are following this renewed debate with interest: for them, the critical policy issue is whether economic growth should continue to be the main priority, with protection of the environment a secondary consideration to be addressed mainly in the future, or whether explicit policies to control environmental degradation at the local, national and global level are urgently required today.

Although recent EKC studies appear to have revived the wider growth versus the environment debate, these studies offer very little support for the view that economic growth alone is the solution to all environmental problems (see Box 2.4). Rather, it is clear from the EKC literature that specific policies to protect the environment are necessary to reduce environmental degradation problems that are imposing real welfare losses. As Arrow et al (1995) have succinctly put it: 'Economic growth is not a panacea for environmental quality; indeed it is not even the main issue.'

On the other hand, the EKC literature does offer some evidence that for certain environmental problems, particularly air pollutants with localized or short-term effects, there is an eventual reduction in emissions associated with higher per capita income levels, which may be attributable to the abatement effect that arises as countries become richer (Panayotou, 1997). Also, both the willingness and the ability of political jurisdictions to engage in and enforce improved environmental regulations, to increase public spending on environmental research and development, or even to engage in multilateral agreements to reduce emissions, may also increase with per capita income levels (Carson et al,

Box 2.4 *The Environmental Kuznets Curve: Reviewing the Evidence*

Empirical analyses of the EKC have focused on two key pieces of evidence:

- Whether a given indicator of environmental degradation displays an inverted U-shaped relationship with levels of per capita income; and
- the calculation of the turning point, the level of per capita income at which the EKC peaks – where a marginal change in the indicator of environmental degradation is zero. For example, in the EKC for sulphur dioxide depicted in Figure 2.2, the turning point on the curve appears to occur at just under US$5,000 per capita.

To date, most studies suggest that EKC relationships are more likely to hold for certain types of environmental damage, such as pollutants with more short-term and local impacts, than those with more global, indirect and long-term impacts (Arrow et al, 1995; Barbier, 1997; Cole et al, 1997; Selden and Song, 1994). In terms of types of localized environmental damage, the EKC hypothesis seems mainly to be valid for air pollution. In particular, studies that analyse EKC relationships across countries suggest that the strongest evidence in favour of this relationship is for sulphur dioxide, and to a lesser extent solid particulate matter (SPM). However, the results across all countries may not necessarily be valid for individual countries. For example, Vincent (1997) found SPM to be increasing with income in Malaysia, whereas Carson et al (1997) find that all major air pollutants decline with increasing levels of income across the United States. The evidence for other localized forms of environmental damage, such as water pollution, deforestation, urban waste and toxic metals, is more mixed.

However, even when an EKC relationship is estimated, often the turning point on the curve, where environmental degradation starts to decline with per capita income, proves to be very high relative to the current per capita GDP levels of most countries of the world (Barbier, 1997). For example, in the recent analysis by Cole et al (1997), none of the estimated EKC turning points for environmental indicators is below the minimum income level of the sample of countries analysed, and the turning points for nitrates, carbon dioxide, energy consumption and traffic volumes are well below the income range of the countries analysed. In the case of tropical deforestation, Cropper and Griffiths (1994) found that per capita income levels of most countries in Latin America and Africa were well to the left of the estimated turning point peaks. Overall, such results suggest that most countries have not yet reached levels of per capita income for which environmental improvement is likely to occur. The implications are a worsening global problem of environmental degradation as the world economy and populations expand, even for those environmental indicators that display EKC relationships (Selden and Song, 1994; Stern et al, 1996).

1997; de Bruyn, 1997; Komen et al, 1997). However, it is a great leap of faith to jump from these results to the conclusion that economic growth on its own will automatically foster environmental improvement. As Panayotou (1997) has concluded, 'when all effects are considered, the relationship between growth and the environment turns out to be much more complex with wide scope for active policy intervention to bring about more desirable (and in the presence of market failures) more efficient economic and environmental outcomes'.

This conclusion is even truer for low income and rapidly industrializing, developing countries, whose current per capita income levels are usually well below the levels associated with the turning points of most estimated EKCs. The implication is that, in the absence of national and multilateral policy interventions, environmental degradation will continue in these countries as per capita income increases, at least over the medium-term. In this regard, the observation of Vincent (1997) from his analysis of Malaysia is very apt:

> 'The lack of evidence of EKCs in Malaysia does not prove that EKCs do not exist anywhere. It does indicate, however, that policy makers in developing countries should not assume that economic growth will automatically solve air and water pollution problems.'

In sum, the implications of the EKC literature for sustainable development are fairly straightforward. Regardless of whether one is an adherent of the weak sustainability or strong sustainability view, the existence of EKC-relationships has very limited relevance to determining what actual policies are required in the economy to manage its total capital stock, including its stock of natural capital, to ensure that needs of the present are met without compromising the economic opportunities to meet the needs of the future. As Stern et al (1996) point out:

> 'policies to achieve sustainable development must incorporate explicit incentives to reduce environmental degradation, rather than assume that the problem will take care of itself as the global economy continues along its current development path ... EKC relationships offer very little in the way of guidance on the real policy choices concerning sustainable development.'

Economic Growth vs the Environment

At the heart of the environmental Kuznets curve debate is the issue of whether we can have economic growth and the environment together. The EKC literature suggests we can. But there are other issues that are relevant to the debate.

Some of the confusion about the compatibility of economic growth and environmental quality arises from a failure to define concepts and arguments. Thus, some writers regard economic growth as an increase in the materials and energy throughput of the economy. Defined in this way, the conflict between growth and the environment is not inevitable, but it is far more likely. It is not inevitable because, for example, we may have very large reserves of energy and materials, so that exhaustion is not a near-term issue, and because we may use more energy and materials but have less pollution because of abatement technology, technological change, and recycling. But defining economic growth as materials and energy throughput is not what economists would typically mean by economic growth. Economic growth is an increase in the level of real GNP over time. Now the link between growth and environmental degradation is far less certain because not only can the link between materials/energy throughput and pollution be broken, but so can the link between income growth and materials/energy throughput.

The second confusion arises because it is not always clear if the argument is about an empirical fact – we cannot have growth without environmental degradation – or whether it is a normative statement – we *ought* not to have economic growth. Such normative statements may be based in an 'if...then' statement: if we have economic growth, then we will have environmental degradation, and environmental degradation is morally bad. But the normative statement may have as much to do with the human values thought to underlie the pursuit of economic growth. Perhaps pursuing economic growth reinforces human greed, which is an intrinsically bad characteristic, a view discussed briefly in Chapter 1.

If economic growth is associated with environmental degradation, would it then follow that economic growth should be reduced? There are several problems in jumping to such a conclusion.

• Economic growth might be a cause of environmental degradation but there might be other causes as well and the other causes might be more important (see Chapter 6). Giving up, or reducing, economic growth might also be seen as incurring a social cost for many people who actually like the benefits of economic growth. Unless they are to be disenfranchised in some way, this means that we need to trade this social cost against the social cost of environmental degradation. Even if we take this to extremes, for example by arguing that environmental degradation involves huge social costs, even the end of the world as we know it, some people would argue that the social cost of interfering with individuals' rights to choose are also huge. Unless protecting the environment has super-moral status – it is morally much more important to conserve the environment than, say, to create employment – the issue becomes one of comparing costs and benefits. For some people, however, the environment does take on a super-moral status. As it happens, we know that there are many causes of environmental degradation – for example price distortions, lack of land tenure and resource rights, lack of credit access, subsidies, poor information and lack of education, and so on. So we may not even need to reduce economic growth: it would be odd to invite everyone to punish themselves when it might not be necessary.

• It tends to be assumed that economic growth is a policy variable, it is something that we can change. But is it? What we are interested in is long-term growth, not the kind of growth that preoccupies governments with their worries about short-run interest rates, budget deficits and inflation. Between 1885 and 1987 the average rate of economic growth in the UK was 1.8 per cent. This appears to be above that for England in the 18th century, perhaps 0.4 per cent per annum at the beginning of the 18th century and over 1 per cent at the end. Was economic growth in the 18th and 19th centuries a policy variable? Since systems of national accounts did not exist until well into the 20th century it seems odd to think that governments had full control of the economy before the development of the relevant statistics, although, certainly, there was a concern to regulate the supply of money. Governments did intervene, of course, and rising prices would have been one of the factors they did observe. But it is at least questionable that governments could act on a long-term economic growth variable .

• Suppose we decide that growth is something we can change. The modern theory of economic growth says that it is due mainly to endogenous technical change embodied in capital, including research and development and education, giving special emphasis to human capital. If this approach is correct then to lower economic growth means, amongst other things, the lowering of technical change and a reduction in education. Some would argue that this is a strange way to tackle an environmental problem, not least because we have good reason to suppose that increasing education is one of the best ways of solving environmental problems.

• What matters presumably is global growth – that is, the growth of the world economy. But even if one nation can control its growth rate, the chances that all countries would agree to control growth rates are small. One possibility, raised in some recent environmentalist literature, would be to control the volume of international trade, since this contributes to growth. But, as we argue in Chapter 6, this is not desirable in itself, nor is it relevant to solving environmental problems, even where those problems appear to be trade-related.

• Finally, consider what the growth hypothesis is: it is that the *change* in GNP is causing the problem. But GNP is a flow concept, so it is not just the growth of this flow that should be the focus of attention, but the flow itself. If reducing growth were the right policy, we should not be worrying about increments to GNP; we should be trying to reduce GNP. While there are some intellectual antecedents of this view, the practical question is whether there is anything sacred about zero economic growth. On the basis of the thought experiment, the answer has to be 'no': we should drive GNP down, who knows, even to zero or to some subsistence level. Once we argue for zero growth we are logically involved in arguing for negative growth. The anti-growth view is therefore illogical in many respects. Far more fruitful is to pursue the idea that the composition of GNP can be changed. What matters is not economic growth as such, but the way economic growth is secured. It is essential that growth be secured at lower and lower ratios of materials and energy input to economic output.

Endogenous Growth Theory

Another recent advance in the economics literature with implications for sustainable development is the emergence of endogenous or new growth theory.

Essentially, endogenous growth theory has resulted from a vigorous debate about the role of technological innovation in long-term economic growth. In conventional neoclassical models of economic growth, the process of technological innovation is not generally explicitly modelled. Instead, it is assumed that the rate of technological progress is determined exogenously of the economic system. However, this view has been challenged by the more recent models of endogenous growth theory (Romer, 1990; Lucas, 1988; Rebelo, 1991). A key feature of these models is that technological innovation – the development of new technological ideas or designs – is endogenously determined by private and public sector choices within the economic system.

Two important implications emerge from the endogenous-growth literature (Barro and Sala-I-Martin, 1995). First, as the level of technology in an endogenous-growth economy can be advanced perpetually through public and private investments, such as research and development expenditure and increases in human capital skills, and since the effect of technical innovation is to augment the physical capital used in production, then potentially the economy can sustain growth rates indefinitely. In other words, if public and private sector investments in human capital and innovation are optimal then it is possible for an economy to attain a perpetually constant rate of growth in output and consumption. The latter is referred to an economy's long-run or steady-state level of growth. Second, as in the case of neoclassical growth models, some endogenous growth models still display the property known as conditional convergence; that is, as the economy develops, its growth rate should eventually diminish until it reaches its steady-state growth rate (see Box 2.5). The importance of conditional convergence is that an economy grows faster the further it is away from its own steady-state growth rate, and also it is no longer the case that the growth rate of poor countries should exceed that of rich countries.[6]

Economic Growth Rates across Countries

The recent debate in economics over the role of innovation in economic growth has fostered empirical investigations across countries and regions to determine the factors underlying long-term economic growth (Barro and Sala-I-Martin, 1995; Mankiw et al, 1992; Pack, 1994; Romer, 1994). Unexpectedly, these comparisons of growth rates have pointed to an important but unresolved issue for analysts: why is it that the long-term economic growth rates of poor countries as a group are not catching up with those of rich countries? (see Box 2.6).

Some economists have argued that the property of conditional convergence does not necessarily mean that poorer countries should display higher rates of growth than richer countries (Barro and Sala-I-Martin, 1995; Mankiw et al, 1992). For example, a rich country may actually be further from its long-run rate of growth than a poorer country, because the rich country may have a higher rate of savings or more effective institutions, including better developed markets, property rights systems and government institutions. Given these conditions, the long-run growth rates of the rich country would be much higher than for a poor country (see Box 2.5).

Empirical evidence seems to support this notion: for example, Barro and Sala-I-Martin (1995) show that once the adverse effects on growth of government distortions and poor institutions across countries are accounted for – as represented by such indicators as the ratio of government consumption to gross domestic product (GDP), the black-market premium on foreign exchange, political instability and the lack of

---

6 To facilitate comparison with endogenous growth models, it is convenient to think in terms of the neoclassical model with exogenous labour-augmenting technological progress. In the latter model, per capita consumption, physical capital and income will grow in the steady state at the exogenous rate of technical progress. Endogenous growth models also display steady-state rates of per capita growth, but of course in these models long-run growth will be affected by the endogenous determinants of technical progress. However, as demonstrated by Barro and Sala-I-Martin (1995), the key point is that the long-run growth conditions predicted by both endogenous and neoclassical growth models conform to the properties of conditional convergence.

Box 2.5 *Absolute and Conditional Convergence in Long-run Economic Growth*

In neoclassical growth theory, the hypothesis that poor economies tend to grow faster than richer countries is referred to as absolute convergence. It is based on the assumption that there is a long-run constant, or steady state, level of income per capita (y^*) that is common to all economies, and since poorer economies

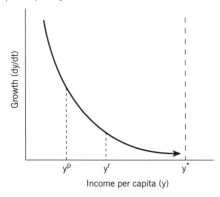

are further from this equilibrium compared to rich ones, the former must grow more to reach the steady state. The hypothesis of absolute convergence is indicated in the figure (left), where y^p indicates the current income per capita of a representative developing country and y^r current income per capita of an industrialized economy.

However, neoclassical growth theory, as well as some endogenous growth models, can also be consistent with the property known as conditional convergence. According to this hypothesis, rich and poor countries differ in their structural characteristics, and therefore will not have the same long-run steady state. Thus each type of economy has its own

unique long-run income level (neoclassical theory) or steady state growth rate (endogenous growth theory). For example, under conditions of endogenous growth, the economy's growth rate should eventually diminish until it reaches its long-run, or steady-state, growth rate, dy^*/dt. The main implications of conditional convergence are that an economy grows faster the further it is away from its own steady-state growth rate, and also that poor countries do not

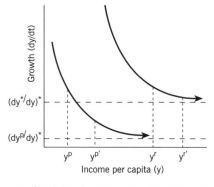

necessarily grow faster than rich ones. Conditional convergence is illustrated in the lower figure, which depicts endogenous growth rates that are higher for a rich country than for a poorer country.

Further discussion of absolute and conditional convergence, as well as the differences between endogenous and neoclassical growth theory, can be found in Barro and Sala-I-Martin (1995).

enforcement of contracts – then growth does appear to be negatively correlated with the initial level of per capita income. The implication is that persistently bad government policies and ineffective institutions are

Box 2.6 *Comparing Long-term Growth Performance across Countries*

As noted in Box 2.5, the hypothesis of absolute convergence of neoclassical growth theory maintains that poor economies should grow faster than rich ones, as the former eventually catch up in development. However, the first figure (left) shows that, for a sample of 118 rich and poor countries, average rates of growth during the period 1960–85 have, if anything, a slightly positive relation to the 1960 level of per capita GDP. This suggests that, contrary to the absolute convergence hypothesis, countries that were initially richer in 1960 grew at a faster rate than countries that were initially poorer.

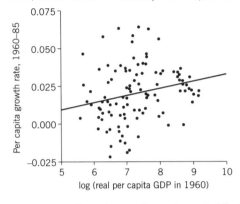

In comparison, the next figure shows that for the 20 original Organisation for Economic Co-operation and Development (OECD) countries, the average growth rates for the 1960–85 period are negatively related to the initial level of per capita income in 1960, as the absolute convergence hypothesis predicts. Given that OECD countries are all advanced industrial nations with relatively similar economic institutions, policies and structures, this has led many economists to consider how differences in these factors across all countries have affected their relative long-term growth performance.

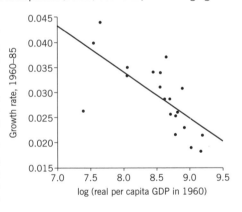

Source: Barro and Sala-I-Martin, 1995

inhibiting the long-run growth prospects of low-income countries, and explain why their growth rates are consistently lower than those of rich countries.

Such empirical findings are wholly consistent with both neoclassical and endogenous theories of growth, so it is not surprising that there is widespread support for this view in the modern growth literature. For example, according to the endogenous growth school, the lack of stable

economic polices and institutions in poor countries inhibits the generation or use of new technological ideas to reap greater economic
opportunities, thus constraining economic growth and development.
That is, poor countries fail to achieve higher rates of growth because
they fail to generate or use new technological ideas to reap greater
economic opportunities:

> 'The feature that will increasingly differentiate one geographic area
> (city or country) from another will be the quality of public institu-
> tions. The most successful areas will be the ones with the most
> competent and effective mechanisms for supporting collective inter-
> ests, especially in the production of new ideas.' (Romer, 1993)

Even critics of endogenous growth theory concede that institutional and
policy failures are important reasons for the inability of poor countries
to harness technological innovation to attain higher rates of economic
growth. For example, Pack (1994) argues that 'the potential benefit of
backwardness is that, if countries could capitalize on their backwardness, they could enjoy a rapid spurt of catch-up growth'. However, he
also states that:

> 'the benefits from backwardness do not accrue automatically but
> result from purposive activities on the part of individual firms within
> a general favourable policy environment. This includes a stable
> macroeconomic policy and institutions designed to facilitate the
> identification and absorption of technology.'

Consequently, the inability of poor countries to take off economically
'can be attributed to failed policies and weak institutions'.

Resource Dependency in Low-income Countries

Although institutional and policy failures in poor economies are important determinants of their inability to innovate sufficiently to achieve
higher long-term growth rates, another important factor may be the
structural economic dependence of these economies on their natural
resource endowments.

Barbier (1994) shows that many low-income and lower middle-
income economies – especially those displaying low or stagnant growth
rates – are highly resource dependent. Not only do these economies rely
principally on direct exploitation of their resource bases through primary
industries, such as agriculture, forestry and fishing, but also over 50 per
cent or more of their export earnings come from a few primary commodi-

ties (see also Chapter 7). These economies tend to be heavily indebted and are experiencing dramatic land use changes – especially conversion of forest to agriculture – as well as problems of low agricultural productivity, land degradation and population carrying-capacity constraints. A recent analysis by Sachs and Warner (1995) has confirmed that resource-abundant countries – countries with a high ratio of natural resource exports to GDP – have tended to grow less rapidly than countries that are relatively resource poor.

Recent explanations as to why resource dependence may be a factor in influencing economic growth point to a number of possible fundamental linkages between environment, innovation and long-term growth relevant to poor economies. Matsuyama (1992) shows that trade liberalization in a land-intensive economy could actually slow economic growth by inducing the economy to shift resources away from manufacturing (which produces learning-induced growth) towards agriculture (which does not). Sachs and Warner (1995) extend the Matsuyama model to allow for full 'Dutch disease' influences of a mineral or oil-based economy; that is, when an economy experiences a resource boom, the manufacturing sector tends to shrink and the non-traded goods sector tends to expand. The authors' theoretical and empirical analyses support the view that a key factor influencing endogenous growth effects is the relative structural importance of tradeable manufacturing versus natural resource sectors in the economy.

Environmental Change, Innovation and Social Ingenuity

On the whole, endogenous growth theorists have not been concerned with the contribution of natural resources to growth or with the role of innovation in overcoming resource scarcities.[7] However, for some years resource economists have explored the effects of an economy's dependence on natural resources and its long-run growth (Dasgupta and Heal, 1979; Stiglitz, 1974). They have usually employed neoclassical growth models that assume exogenous rather than endogenous technological change. The results have been generally optimistic: even under conditions with exponential population growth and with exhaustible and limited supplies of natural resources that are essential for production, sustained growth and a long-run steady-state level of positive per capita consumption are attainable (Stiglitz, 1974).

---

7 Recent studies in extending endogenous growth models to incorporate environmental considerations have generally focused on the short- and long-run implications of including the accumulation of pollution and its disutility in an endogenous growth context (see, for example, Bovenburg and Smulders 1995; Musu and Lines 1995).

Barbier (1999) extends this analysis to an endogenous growth economy. He combines the exhaustible resource model developed by Stiglitz (1974) and the endogenous growth model developed by Romer (1990) to determine whether an economy's dependence on an exhaustible natural resource is necessarily a binding constraint on long-run growth. The results of the analysis are fairly conclusive: although technological change is endogenous, it is still effectively resource-augmenting. Sufficient allocation of human capital to innovation will ensure that in the long run resource exhaustion can be postponed indefinitely, and the possibility exists of a long-run endogenous steady-state growth rate that allows per capita consumption to be sustained, and perhaps even increased, indefinitely.[8]

However, Homer-Dixon (1995) points to another potential relationship between innovation and resource availability. He argues that an economy's supply of ingenuity – the stock of 'ideas applied to solve practical social and technical problems' – may itself be constrained by resource scarcities, especially in low-income countries. In this analysis, an increase in the level of technical ingenuity is similar to the technical innovation discussed by endogenous growth theorists. These theorists, he notes, 'are mainly interested in technical ideas such as manufacturing techniques, industrial designs, and chemical formulae, especially those developed and applied within the firm'. But the supply of this technical ingenuity depends on an adequate supply of social ingenuity at many levels of society.

Social ingenuity, according to Homer-Dixon, consists of ideas applied to the creation, reform and maintenance of institutions 'such as markets, funding agencies, educational and research organizations, and effective government'. If operating well:

> '*this system of institutions provides psychological and material incentives to technological entrepreneurs and innovators; it aids regular contact and communication among experts; and it channels resources preferentially to those endeavours from and necessary for technical innovation.*'

Therefore, in agreement with the institutional arguments of Romer (1993) and Pack (1994), Homer-Dixon identifies social ingenuity as a precursor to technical ingenuity.

---

8 However, Barbier (1999) also develops a further version of the model that shows negative feedback effects between the rate of resource utilization and innovation, along the lines suggested by Homer-Dixon (1995). Although it is possible to sustain per capita consumption over the long run in this model, the conditions under which this occurs are much more stringent and again assume that the economy is able to build up sufficient human capital and innovate.

He further describes two mechanisms by which resource scarcity can limit both the total supply and the rate of supply of ingenuity. First, increased scarcity often provokes competitive action by powerful elite groups and narrow social coalitions to defend their interests or to profit from the scarcity through rent-seeking behaviour.[9] These actions – which Homer-Dixon calls social friction – can hinder efforts to create and reform institutions and can generally make it harder to focus and coordinate human activities, talents, and resources in response to scarcity. Moreover, severe scarcity sometimes causes social turmoil and violence, which can directly impede the functioning of ingenuity-generating institutions, such as markets (Homer-Dixon, 1994 and 1995; Homer-Dixon et al, 1993). Second, endogenous growth theory notes that capital, especially human capital, is essential to the generation of innovation (Romer, 1990). Yet, Homer-Dixon argues, resource scarcity often reduces the availability of human and financial capital for the production of ingenuity by shifting investment 'from long-term adaption to immediate tasks of scarcity management and mitigation'.

Figures 2.3 and 2.4 illustrate the contrast between the conventional and alternative views of the innovation process proposed by endogenous growth theory and Homer-Dixon respectively (Barbier and Homer-Dixon, 1999). According to the conventional view (Figure 2.3), market responses to natural resource scarcity automatically induce endogenous technological change that leads to resource conservation, and in turn, to the amelioration of scarcity. However, as noted above, this view assumes that stable economic policies and social institutions exist to facilitate endogenous innovation. This assumption may not be valid for many poor economies.

According to an alternative view based on Homer-Dixon's analysis (Figure 2.4), in some poor countries resource scarcity itself contributes to an unstable social and policy environment at local, regional and even national levels. Scarcity exacerbates social friction and conflict, which results in an undersupply of social ingenuity. Social frictions and conflict interfere directly with the smooth functioning of markets, while the reduced supply of social ingenuity perpetuates market, policy and institutional failures. These failures in turn undermine the innovation process,

---

9 If increasing resource scarcity is reflected in market prices, than the value of the depleted scarce resource will rise relative to the costs of depletion. The result is that increasing scarcity generates higher economic profits, or rents. If property rights are well defined and maintained, and in particular if the resource is under sole ownership, then economic theory suggests that the resource will be depleted to maximize long-term economic rents, and thus generally conserved for as long as possible. However, these conditions rarely hold in developing countries for scarce resources, and often there is competitive rent-seeking by many powerful interest groups to extract maximum rent in the short run through resource depletion (Barbier, 1994).

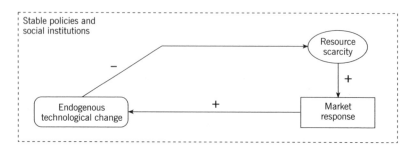

Source: Barbier and Homer-Dixon, 1999

Figure 2.3 *Endogenous Technological Change and Resource Scarcity:*
the Conventional View

in particular by disrupting the ability of poor economies to generate
sufficient human capital, develop research and development capacity,
utilize existing technological knowledge, and to produce and dissemi-
nate new technologies throughout the economy. In short, while resource
scarcity often induces mitigating market and endogenous technological
responses, it can also disrupt the stable policy and social environment
necessary for these responses to occur automatically.

There is some evidence that in many poor economies depletion and
degradation of natural resources – such as agricultural land, forests,
fresh water and fisheries – may be a contributing factor in social
processes that destabilize the institutional and economic conditions
necessary for innovation and growth (Barbier and Homer-Dixon, 1999;
Homer-Dixon, 1995). Most of these instances appear to occur at the
regional or local level. For example, in Bangladesh increasing scarcities

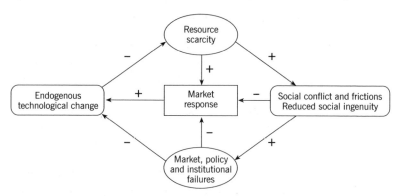

Source: Barbier and Homer-Dixon, 1999

Figure 2.4 *Endogenous Technological Change and Resource Scarcity:*
an Alternative View

of land and water have aggravated social struggles over the distribution of power and wealth, which have in turn limited innovations to control flood and irrigation necessary for boosting productivity (Goletti, 1994; Boyce, 1987). In Haiti, depletion of forest and soil resources has led to significant rent-seeking behaviour by powerful elites such as wealthy landowners, who have blocked reforestation projects, land improvements and other innovations in rural areas that would have threatened their highly profitable monopoly of forest and arable land resources (Wallich, 1994). Finally, Deacon (1994) has found evidence that across a wide cross-section of low- and middle-income countries social and political instability is highly correlated both with low levels of productive investments and resource scarcity (in this case deforestation). Thus Deacon suggests that the overall results of his analysis 'are broadly consistent with the hypotheses that deforestation results both from population growth – and the increased competition for land and natural resources that accompany it – and from political environments that are not conducive to investment'.

In sum, recent applications of endogenous growth theory suggest that resource dependency ought not to be an absolute barrier to low-income resource dependent economies achieving both long-term growth and sustainable development. However, as discussed in Box 2.7, it is not sufficient for these economies to focus exclusively on policies and institutions to foster improved innovation in their more advanced economic sectors. Instead, the take off into higher growth rates and sustainable economic development will be directly related to the ability of these economies to manage their natural resources efficiently and sustainably over the medium to long term.

Ecological Economics: a Preview

Another recent development in environmental thinking that has influenced views on sustainability has been the emergence of ecological economics (see Chapter 10): here the implications for the sustainability debate are briefly discussed.

One of the major difficulties in assessing the body of literature that could be described as ecological economics is that there is no one agreed definition of the term. Some authors have argued that ecological economics is essentially trans-disciplinary – a new discipline that has emerged out of the old disciplines of economics and ecology (Costanza et al, 1991). Others have been more cautious, suggesting that 'ecological economics is not a new discipline as such, but a new category of analysis or synthesis of approaches, for tackling problems of economic-environmental interaction where a single discipline approach will not suffice' (Barbier et al, 1994).

Box 2.7 *Endogenous Growth, Innovation and Natural Capital: Implications for Sustainable Development*

Recent developments in endogenous growth theory and empirical investigations into the factors determining long-term growth are inherently optimistic. Provided that countries can foster both effective policies and institutions, including the necessary public and private investments to enhance research and development and human capital skills, then the resulting advances in technical innovation ought to allow economies to achieve high and sustainable rates of long-term growth. Moreover, there is no inherent reason why poorer countries cannot also sustain higher rates of long-term growth than they currently achieve. The main obstacles appear to be persistent policy distortions, political instability and institutional failures. Even dependence on natural resources may not necessarily be a problem. If in the long run an economy allocates sufficient human capital to innovation so as to reduce its dependence on a declining natural resource base, then per capita income can be sustained indefinitely (Barbier, 1999).

In the case of low-income countries, correcting problems of chronic policy failures, social instabilities and poor institutions that inhibit innovation and long-term growth prospects should also enhance the ability of these economies to reinvest the rents from natural resource exploitation into more dynamic and advanced sectors of the economy (Barbier, 1994; Matsuyama, 1992; Sachs and Warner, 1995). However, focusing simply on policies and institutions to foster improved innovation in the advanced economic sectors of low-income economies may not be sufficient. As these economies are highly dependent on their natural resource base for economic growth and development over the medium term, the take off into higher growth rates and economic development will be directly related to the ability of these economies to manage their natural resources efficiently and sustainably over the medium to long term. Unfortunately, in most low-income countries current economic policies and investments in agriculture, forestry and other resource-based sectors have led to rapid changes – frequently with adverse economic consequences – in resource stocks and patterns of use. Demographic trends have often worsened the relationship between population and resource carrying capacity in many regions. Continuing agricultural extensification into marginal lands has increased the susceptibility of economic systems and livelihoods to environmental degradation. Statistical evidence of these trends for resource-dependent poor economies can be found in Barbier (1994). For a theoretical exploration of how poor initial resource endowments can lead to unsustainable growth paths, see Barbier and Markandya (1990).

Thus the continuing dependence of most of the world's poorest economies on their resource bases suggests that environmental management should be given a higher priority as a development concern. A major factor affecting the long-term development prospects of poor economies is their failure to place a higher priority on policies for efficient and sustainable management of the natural resource base to maintain the capital required for the transition to and achievement of long-term sustainable economic development goals. Moreover, there is some evidence in poor economies that chronic environmental degradation may itself be contributing to social conflict and political instability, thus undermining the social and economic conditions necessary to foster long-term innovation and development (Barbier and Homer-Dixon, 1999; Homer-Dixon, 1995).

As will be discussed further in Chapter 10, we take the latter view. It is premature to suggest that there is a new paradigm of scientific thinking that has emerged which can be called ecological economics. Nevertheless, there is a growing body of literature that consists of inter-disciplinary collaboration in the fields of economics, ecology and other social and natural sciences in order to analyse complex problems of ecological degradation. Such problems are highly diverse, ranging from the sustainability of farming systems subject to soil loss, drought and other stresses and shocks to the global problem of biodiversity loss, and require more than one discipline to analyse and deduce implications for policy. Perhaps it is this latter body of literature which could be identified as ecological economics.

Possibly the most important contribution of the inter-disciplinary literature comprising ecological economics has been to draw on the work, mainly of ecologists, to point out the important implications of ecological functioning and resilience for human welfare.

By ecological functioning, ecologists usually mean those basic processes of ecosystems, such as nutrient cycling, biological productivity, hydrology, and sedimentation, as well as the overall ability of ecosystems to support life. As indicated in Box 2.8, ecologists consider the collective range of life-support functions to be the key characteristic that defines an ecosystem, as well as the source of the many key ecological resources and services that are important to human welfare.

Whereas economists tend to focus only on those ecological resources and services provided by ecosystems that appear to contribute directly to current and future welfare, ecologists point out that such natural capital is an integral part of a much more broader array of life-support functions that characterize ecosystems.

Although there is some dispute in the ecological literature over precise interpretations of the term ecological resilience, ecologists generally use this term to mean the capacity of an ecosystem to recover from and thus absorb external shocks and stresses, whether they be natural (such as drought, fire and earthquakes) or human-induced (such as pollution and biomass removal). As the health of an ecosystem is usually determined by its capacity to deliver the life-support functions appropriate to its stage of ecological succession, then the ecological resilience of the system is inherently linked to its ecological functioning. That is, if an ecosystem is resilient, then it should recover sufficiently from any human-induced or natural stresses and shock and function normally.

As will be discussed further in Chapter 10, the ecological-economics literature has called attention to the important role of ecological functioning and resilience in sustaining human livelihoods and welfare.

Box 2.8 *Life-support Functions and the Generation of Ecological Resources and Services*

The life-support functions of ecosystems are the continuous interactions between organisms, populations, communities and their physical and chemical environments. These interactions generate many ecological resources and services that are of fundamental value as they sustain human societies and existence. Many key ecological resources and services can be traced to specific life-support functions of ecosystems. Some are indicated below as regulation, production, carrier and information functions.

Regulation functions	*Production functions*	*Carrier functions*	*Information functions*
Providing support for economic activity and human welfare through: •protection against harmful cosmic influences •climate regulation •watershed protection and catchment •erosion prevention and soil protection •storage and recycling of industrial and human waste •storage and recycling of organic matter and mineral nutrients •maintenance of biological and genetic diversity •biological control •providing a migratory, nursery and feeding habitat	Providing basic resources, such as: •oxygen •food, drinking water and nutrition •water for industry, households, etc. •clothing and fabrics •building, construction and manufacturing materials •energy and fuel •minerals •medicinal resources •biochemical resources •genetic resources •ornamental resources	Providing space and a suitable substrate for: •habitation •agriculture, forestry, fishery, aquaculture •industry •engineering projects such as dams and roads •recreation •nature conservation	Providing aesthetic, cultural and scientific benefits through: •aesthetic information •spiritual and religious information •cultural and artistic inspiration •educational and scientific information •potential information

Sources: de Groot, 1992; Ehrlich and Ehrlich, 1992; Folke, 1991; and Odum, 1975

The maintenance of some degree of ecological functioning and resilience appears to be necessary for generating certain biological resources (such as trees, fish, wildlife and crops) and ecological services (such as watershed protection, climate stabilization and erosion control) on which economic activity and human welfare depend. However, if ecosystems are insufficiently resilient to recover from persistent problems of environmental degradation, for example those arising from land use conversion, pollution and over-exploitation of resources, then the ability of ecosystems to function normally and deliver important biological resources and ecological services will be affected. Ecosystems that are subject to persistent environmental degradation and disruption begin to malfunction, breakdown, and ultimately, collapse.

At some stage, the loss of ecosystem functioning and resilience will translate into a decline in the availability of some economically important biological resources and ecological services, for example, the loss of fish stocks as the result of pollution impacting on marine systems, the inability of rangeland pastoral systems to recover from drought, and the decline of the watershed protection function of degraded forests. At first these ecological and welfare impacts may be localized, but if they occur on a sufficiently large scale, they may generate wider national, regional or even global effects. Although the scale of such impacts and their ultimate effects on human welfare are difficult to determine, the irreversible loss of key biological resources and ecological services through the disruption and breakdown of ecosystems could constitute a growing problem of ecological scarcity.[10] As natural environments and ecosystems deteriorate, ecological resources and services that are abundant today may not be available tomorrow. At the very least, the rising scarcity of ecological resources and services will mean that they will increase in value relative to human-made goods and services produced in economic systems. Over the long term, the danger is that persistent and rising ecological scarcity may be an indicator of more widespread and frequent disruptions to the functioning and resilience of ecosystems, thus increasing the likelihood of ecological collapse and catastrophe on ever-widening scales.

Finally, as noted in Box 2.9, the ecological-economics literature clearly endorses the strong sustainability view. As will be discussed further in Chapter 10, the implication of this point of view is that ensuring sustainable development will in turn require, first, identifying those essential ecological resources and services that are most at risk from

---

10 The term 'ecological scarcity' is used here in the same context as defined by Barbier (1989), who developed this concept of 'an increasing relative scarcity of essential environmental services and ecological functions' as a means of distinguishing ecological scarcity from more conventional economic problems of natural resource scarcity. For example, he argued that 'this alternative approach may be particularly applicable to cases where cumulative resource depletion and degradation through economic over-exploitation lead to severe ecological disruption and the collapse of livelihoods', that is 'conditions under which present patterns of resource exploitation have transgressed ecological thresholds'. For further discussion see Chapter 10 and Barbier et al (1994).

Box 2.9 *Ecological Economics: Implications for Sustainable Development*

The ecological economics literature clearly endorses the strong sustainability view. If this literature is correct, then many components of our natural capital stock are based on ecological processes and functions that we know very little about. Moreover, global ecological disruption as a result of the cumulative impacts of pollution, habitat modification and over-exploitation of some biological resources, may be undermining the ecological functioning and resilience upon which many important ecological resources and services depend. Thus not only are we in danger of depleting essential ecological components of natural capital, but the widespread disruptions to the functioning and resilience of ecosystems may mean that these essential components are being irreversibly lost.

The implication is that ensuring sustainable development will in turn require, first, identifying those essential ecological resources and services that are most at risk from current patterns of economic activity and development; second, taking appropriate policy measures to protect these irreplaceable components of natural capital; and finally, recognizing that the protection of these ecological resources and services will also require maintaining the functioning and resilience of the key ecosystems on which they depend.

Needless to say, such an approach would require a fundamental rethinking in the way in which countries currently manage their environments, as well as the relative importance of policies for environmental protection in the process of economic development. The additional costs required to adjust current patterns of economic activity and development could be significant, especially in the short- and medium-term. It is safe to say that, despite the concerns raised by the ecological economics literature on the need for such fundamental policy shifts to achieve sustainable development and protect the interests of future generations, the vast majority of governments are still too concerned about the likely economic costs arising from such policy prescriptions to adopt them comprehensively.

current patterns of economic activity and development; second, taking appropriate policy measures to protect these irreplaceable components of natural capital, and finally, recognizing that the protection of these ecological resources and services will also require maintaining the functioning and resilience of the key ecosystems on which they depend. Such an approach clearly involves a fundamental rethinking in the way in which countries currently manage their environments, as well as the relative importance of policies for environmental protection in the process of economic development.

Weak and Strong Sustainability Revisited

Although the recent literature on environmental Kuznets curves, endogenous growth and ecological economics is unlikely to resolve the debate between weak and strong views of sustainability, the contributions in these three areas do provide some important insights into the overall sustainability of our current economic development path.

The EKC literature offers some evidence that for certain environmental problems, particularly air pollutants with localized or short-term effects, there is an eventual reduction in emissions associated with higher per capita income levels. However, there is little empirical justification from this literature for the view that environmental degradation will lessen as economies develop and become richer. If anything, recent analyses of specific pollutants, countries and regions suggest that local, national and even multinational policy interventions appear to have a large impact on influencing the reduction in pollution and other types of environmental degradation. Unfortunately, for at least two major global environmental problems – SO_2 emissions and deforestation – existing policy interventions do not appear to be enough, as projections of estimated EKC relationships for SO_2 and forest cover confirm that these problems will continue to worsen on a global scale (Selden and Song, 1994; Stern et al, 1996).

On a more optimistic note, endogenous growth theories offer the hope that investments and human capital and innovation can sustain economic growth, even if an economy is dependent on exhaustible natural resources. The key appears to be developing effective policies and institutions, including the necessary public and private investments to enhance research and development and human capital skills. Endogenous growth theory could possibly be interpreted as offering some support for the weak sustainability view. Provided that obstacles such as persistent policy distortions, political instability and institutional failures can be overcome, any economy – even a low-income and resource-dependent developing country – should be able to foster endogenous innovation to substitute human and physical capital for a declining natural capital base in order to sustain economic opportunities and welfare indefinitely.

However, there are two caveats to this optimistic conclusion. First, in the case of the world's poor economies, there is increasing evidence that their prospects for economic take off are being adversely affected by the lack of efficient and sustainable management of their natural resource bases. In order for these economies to reinvest the rents from natural resource exploitation into more dynamic and advanced sectors of the economy, they need to ensure that their natural capital is being both efficiently and sustainably exploited over the medium and long term. The extent to which poor economic policies and investments are leading to over-exploitation and degradation of the resource base of these economies is a major factor affecting their sustainable development. In addition, there is some empirical evidence that processes of environmental degradation in developing countries may in turn contribute to social conflict and political instability, thus undermining the social and economic conditions necessary to foster long-term innovation and development.

The second caveat arises out of the ecological economics literature. The type of resource-saving innovations envisioned in most endogenous growth models are likely to be technologies to abate pollution and other waste products, and to conserve the use of raw material and energy inputs. However, the type of ecological resources and services identified in the ecological economics literature, such as biodiversity, amenity services and ecological functions, are less amenable to substitution by the conventional resource-saving innovations developed in the economic process. Thus while it is possible that innovations fostered by the economic process might lead in the long run to the substitution of human and physical capital for one type of natural capital – raw materials and energy inputs from exhaustible and renewable resources – such innovations are less likely to lead to the substitution for the more unique, and possibly essential, range of ecological resources and services of concern to ecology and ecological economics, including the general life-support functioning and resilience of ecosystems. Of course how essential these ecological resources and services are to current and future human welfare, and how costly it might be for society to maintain and protect them, remain important empirical issues that still need to be addressed.

Conclusion

Regardless of whether one follows the strong or weak viewpoint on sustainability, there are nevertheless some important areas of common ground between the two views that are important starting points for making progress towards sustainable development. For example, in *Blueprint* 1 we argued that, as there exists considerable scope for substituting human and physical capital for natural capital through conservation and substitution of resource inputs, reducing pollution and improving environmental protection, then designing policies for sustainable development must begin with these basic objectives in mind. To do this, however, requires progress in three areas.

First, many of the resources and services of our natural capital endowment are either unpriced, meaning that unlike other goods and services in our economy there are no markets for them, or they are underpriced, meaning that where markets do exist for some environmental goods and services the prices in these markets do not necessarily reflect their true contribution to human welfare. As long as we allow environmental goods and services to continue to be unpriced and under-priced, then we are effectively undervaluing their contribution to human welfare relative to other goods and services in the economy.

Thus the first step in promoting better policies for sustainable development is to determine the correct economic values that should be placed on the various goods and services provided by natural capital, and to develop a variety of economic tools for assessing these values. In the next chapter, we discuss this key first step of valuing the environment in more detail.

Second, improving our efforts in environmental valuation is in turn important for assessing the economic consequences of natural capital depletion and degradation. In order to consider how well our economies are substituting physical and human capital for natural capital, we have first to measure how much the value of the natural capital stock has been depreciated through current efforts to use environmental resources and services to promote greater levels of consumption and investment in the economy. Determining the sustainable level of income and consumption, that is, accounting for the increases in the total available goods and services in the economy net of the depreciation in the value of the natural capital stock, is an important economic approach to measuring sustainability. Equally, determining the ecological limits to exploitation of the natural capital stock, including ecological thresholds, carrying capacities and key ecological goods, services and natural environments that might be considered essential, is an important ecological contribution to measuring sustainability.

Thus the second step in promoting policies for sustainable development is to derive approaches to measuring the economic and ecological consequences of depletion and degradation of the natural capital stock. Recent advances in these approaches are the subjects of Chapters 4 and 5.

Third, determining the appropriate mix of human, physical and natural capital to ensure sustainable development is ultimately about designing appropriate incentives, institutions and investments for efficient and sustainable management of the natural environment. The fact that many of the goods and services provided by the environment are currently unpriced or underpriced in our economic system is an indication of how poorly current institutions, including markets, reflect the true economic value of these goods and services. This in turn suggests that, in making decisions that affect the depletion and degradation of natural capital, governments and individuals are not responding to the correct incentives for efficient and sustainable management of our environmental assets. As a consequence, incorrect private and public investment decisions are made, which not only lead to the excessive loss of natural capital but also fail to generate sufficient substitution of human and physical capital to compensate for this loss – even where it is both technically feasible and economically efficient to do so. Thus the third step in promoting sustainable development is to determine the causes of environmental degradation, particularly where the failures of institutions, markets and government policies are the main contributing factors, and to demonstrate how correcting these failures can lead to improved incentives and investments for efficient and sustainable management of natural capital. Chapters 6 to 9 discuss this critical step in designing policies for sustainable development.

Finally, an important issue raised in this chapter is the view of some proponents of ecological economics that the way in which current disciplines, such as economics and even ecology, approach environmental problems is unhelpful for designing a blueprint for sustainable development. What is needed instead to make genuine progress towards sustainable development, it is argued, is a new discipline that transcends the outmoded thinking of the conventional social science and science disciplines. In Chapter 10 we assess the argument for a new paradigm based on ecological economics, and whether such a paradigm shift in academic and policy analysis is indeed required before we can truly usher in an era of sustainable development.

3

Valuing the Environment

Introduction and Basic Theory

Chapter 1 addressed some of the controversial features of placing monetary values on the functions and services of environmental assets. In this chapter we look at some of the ways in which money values can be ascribed, and at the ways in which monetary valuation is used in practice. The general arguments are that there is an internally consistent set of procedures for determining the economic values that can be attached to environmental assets, and that monetary valuation is far more widely used than might be realized. In particular, there has been a substantial growth in the practical use of monetary valuation since *Blueprint* 1 advocated its use.

Chapter 1 sets out some of the basic assumptions underlying monetary valuation. The concept that is sought is the willingness to pay to secure an environmental asset, and this willingness reflects individual preferences. As we saw, the motivations for those preferences vary, and some considerable research effort has gone into seeing how important the different motivations are. As we shall see, particular interest has attached to a category of economic value called non-use value (NUV), which is a willingness to pay to conserve an asset even though the individual expressing this makes no use of the asset now, nor intends to make use of it in the future (in Chapter 1 this was termed 'existence value').

Willingness to pay is not the only relevant concept for monetary valuation. Just as it is possible to seek the willingness to pay for an environmental service, so it is possible to ask what people are willing to accept (WTA) to go without the service of the environmental asset. Which one should be used?

For a long time, economic theory suggested that there should be little difference in the two concepts. Typically the range of error was thought to be within 5 per cent. The reason for this is that both are essentially measuring the same thing. The chart below summarizes and assumes that there is some project that either improves or reduces the well-being of a given individual. For 'project' it is just as correct to substitute 'policy'.

Technical name of the measure of consumer's surplus	Context: the project benefits the individual	Context: the project makes the individual worse off
Compensating variation	WTP for the project	WTA for tolerating the project
Equivalent variation	WTA to forgo the project	WTP to avoid the project

The terms 'equivalent' and 'compensating' surplus are technical terms for gains and losses and are introduced here simply to show that willingness to pay and accept reflect an underlying economic theory. When an individual gains (gets a benefit) the two relevant measures are what that individual is willing to pay for the benefit or what they are willing to accept to forgo the benefit. Given that the increment (the benefit) is the same in each case we should not expect the difference between the two to be large. Where the project confers a cost, the individual will be willing to accept compensation for putting up with the project or be willing to pay to avoid it. Again, the two should not differ much. In each case, the idea is that the measures reflect what is required to make the individual no worse off before or with the project.

In practice, we do observe differences in the two concepts that are significant. Willingness to accept will often exceed willingness to pay by a factor of 4–15 times. Clearly, if the former is used it might substantially alter the estimate of project benefits compared to the situation when the latter is used. Why might the two differ?

- The 'one-short' phenomenon. Most of the evidence suggesting the two concepts differ comes from contingent valuation studies where individuals are asked directly whether they are willing to pay or to accept a sum of money (see later in this chapter). Contingent valuation tends to be a one-off valuation: respondents are asked once about their valuations, but they are not asked again. (Where respondents are asked again, there is evidence that they tend to lower their estimates of willingness to pay. This is known as giving respondents time to think.) But contingent valuation tries to mimic the market place and most market transactions are not one-off transactions –

they are repeated several times. The issue arises therefore as to whether willingness to pay or accept differ so much simply because the respondent is faced with a one-off situation which is unlike most market transactions. There is some evidence from experimental work that the two initially diverge and then converge as questions are repeated (Coursey et al, 1987). If this is correct, it would be wrong to use the large values obtained from the initial situation. It might be better to average the estimates of both.

- Lack of substitutes. The second feature of contingent valuation studies is that they often relate to assets with few substitutes such as significant rivers, major wetlands and well-known scenic landscapes. In such contexts it has been shown that we can expect willingness to pay or to accept to diverge (Hanemann, 1991). The supposition, then, is they will not diverge much if the asset in question does have substitutes.
- Prospect theory. Some commentators argue that willingness to pay or to accept will diverge even when there are substitutes. This is because people regard losses as being conceptually distinct from gains. Our willingness to pay to improve, say, water quality by one unit may well not therefore be the same as our willingness to accept compensation to tolerate a reduction in water quality by one unit. Individuals may adopt a benchmark of the situation they are in now. This becomes the reference point (Knetsch and Sinden, 1984). Moves that reduce well-being compared to the reference point are treated quite differently to moves that improve well-being relative to the reference point. Psychological prospect theory suggests this phenomenon is widespread and is not confined at all to environmental contexts.

Given that the two estimates might differ significantly, which is the one to choose? In many cases the issue is resolved by seeing who has the property rights. If individuals have some defined right to a clean environment, then, in a context where the environment is to be put at risk, the correct concept if willing to accept, since they are being asked to forgo something to which they have a right. In other contexts, there are several reasons for preferring the willingness to pay estimates:

- Theory suggests they should not differ when there are substitutes – recorded differences may well be an artefact of the techniques used to elicit values;
- Willingness to pay estimates in contingent valuation studies are generally supported by other valuation techniques based on revealed preference, so that the higher willingness to accept estimates become outliers (Carson et al, 1996);

- Adopting willingness to pay amounts to adopting conservative valuations and this may be important if there is reason to expect that respondents exaggerate their willingness because of the hypothetical context of contingent valuation studies.

The Uses of Monetary Valuation

Blueprint 1 called for more use to be made of monetary valuation approaches in the field of public policy. We identified several uses.

Cost-benefit Analysis

In such analysis costs and benefits are measured, as far as possible, in monetary terms. CBA can be applied to investment projects and to policies. An investment project might be something like a road or a dam, a power station, a tunnel or bridge. In principle, the project can be in the private or public sector, but since the analysis has traditionally been defined in terms of what the gains and losses are to society, project-oriented analysis tends to be confined to public sector projects. The idea of using CBA to evaluate policy is more recent. In principle, the techniques and considerations are exactly the same. Policies have costs and benefits. The basic rule is not to sanction anything where the costs exceed the benefits. If benefits exceed costs then the project or policy is potentially worthwhile, but may still not be the best choice. This is because there may be some alternative where the ratio of benefits to costs is even higher. To say benefits exceed costs is therefore to adopt a screening rule only. Typically, we aim to choose the option that maximizes the difference between benefits and costs (Box 3.1).

Monetary valuation is required for all those benefits and costs that can be valued in credible terms. Note that benefits will include anything for which people are willing to pay, and costs will be anything for which they are willing to accept compensation or willing to pay to forgo. Thus all environmental costs and benefits are included.

Modified National Accounts

Blueprint 1 drew attention to the potential of using monetized costs and benefits in a more expanded measure of GNP. Although it did so, we cautioned that this was probably not a priority use of monetary valuation and that drawing up these accounts would be expensive. Surprisingly, attempting to find a measure of a 'greener' national product has become big business. The basic aim is to take GNP and observe that it is made up of output which is truly additional and output which is needed to cover the depreciation of the capital base of the economy.

Box 3.1 *The Elements of Cost-benefit Analysis*

CBA tries to reduce an investment project or a policy to a comparison of the money value of costs and a money value of benefits. While few people object to costs being measured in money terms, they may not always realize that costs should measure opportunity cost. Opportunity costs is what people would be willing to pay for the alternative they go without because a particular project or policy is chosen. Opportunity cost is nearly always a positive sum, simply because resources are scarce and we cannot have everything we want. But this means that opportunity cost is measured in terms of willingness to pay. The rationale for cost-benefit analysis, then, is that benefits should also be measured in units of willingness to pay. (Those who object to benefits being measured in such units might like to reflect on the inconsistency in then accepting a money measure of costs.)

Costs and benefits accrue over time. So, we could simply add up costs over time and see if they are greater or smaller than benefits similarly added up over time. But recall from Chapter 1 that the fundamental principle in environmental economics is that individuals' preferences count. Individuals are known generally to prefer benefits now rather than later. Similarly, they regard costs in the future as being less important than costs now. We say that people discount the future. The rate at which they discount the future is known as the discount rate. It is usually convenient to assume that discount rates are constant over time – that individuals do not discount the future at different rates in different time periods. In reality, it is doubtful if this is true and there is an emerging literature on variable discount rates. Because it makes the presentation easier, we keep to the idea of a constant discount rate here. These rates of discount are presented as a percentage – for example we say we discount the future at, say, five per cent per year.

Now the basic rule for (provisionally) adopting a policy or project is given by the formula:

$$t \ (Bt - Ct)/(1+s)^t > 0$$

where the t reminds us that we are measuring benefits B and costs C in each time period, and s is the discount rate. Notice that discounting is like compound interest upside down.

Since there will be alternative policies to address the same problem, and alternative investment projects, the formula above has to be estimated for each option. In each case we are estimating the net present value (NPV), and, depending on the context, we will tend to choose the project with the highest NPV (the biggest difference between discounted benefits and discounted costs).

This is usually summarized by saying that GNP = net national product (NNP) + depreciation. It is obvious that it is NNP, not GNP, which comes closest to measuring the goods and services that are potentially available for individuals to consume. Perhaps because depreciation measures are somewhat uncertain, nearly all economic commentary uses GNP, not NNP. But if we deduct depreciation on machinery and roads, for example, from GNP to get NNP, why not deduct depreciation on other assets, including environmental assets? This is the essence of a modified accounting framework. But to measure depreciation on environmental assets we need monetary measures of depreciation. Once again, what is being measured is the willingness to pay of individuals to avoid that depreciation (or the compensation they require to tolerate it). So, monetary valuation is integral to a proper estimate of GNP. Chapter 4 addresses the issue in more detail.

Proper Pricing

Chapter 1 showed that the essential feature of many environmental problems is the absence of a market for the environmental goods and services in question. In the market place, prices are determined by the interaction of supply and demand. But if there is no market place we cannot know the demand for environmental services. It will appear as if it is zero and hence the price that we can expect to get for those services also appears to be zero. If we have a given piece of land which can be used for a national park or for mining, it will have positive economic value as a mine but zero value as a national park. This, albeit exaggerated case, explains the uneven playing field spoken of in Chapter 1. Now we apply our non-market valuation techniques. What they are doing is estimating the demand curve which, as Chapter 1 showed, is in fact a willingness to pay curve. Once we know the curve we can estimate the total willingness to pay for the national park and this can be compared to the opportunity cost of having the park, namely the mining profits forgone. This is the cost-benefit approach above. But we can also use the demand curve to find a price for entering the national park, a price which would maximize the revenues or profits from the park. In this way we can capture the willingness to pay for the park in the form of entry prices, using the revenues to invest in conservation of the park.

Non-use Value

Probably one of the most contentious features of economic valuation has been the role played in environmental policy, project and damage liability studies by the concept of non-use value. Suppose we are considering the conservation of a wetland area. Birdwatchers are willing to pay to conserve the wetland area because they derive enjoyment from watching birds: they make use of the wetland. Wildfowlers will also be willing to pay for their use of the area, as are boaters, hikers and general recreationists and tourists. But there may well be people who are willing to pay to conserve the wetland even though they may never use it. Such individuals are said to have a non-use value (previously also known as existence value, and now also known as passive use value).

Differentiating use and non-use is not easy. Does someone who does not visit the wetland, intends never to visit it, but who enjoys watching television films about it have non-use or use value? Most economists would argue that this is use value because the individuals in question leave a behavioural trace in the markets for television films. Compare this to just contemplating the beauty of the wetland and feeling satisfied that the flora and fauna are there. This would appear to be non-use. The dividing line between use and non-use value is fuzzy but has something to do with whether or not we can identify changes in behaviour associated with the utility derived from the thing being valued.

Non-use value is a public good, a term that has a special meaning in economics. A public good has two attributes. First, it is one that can be consumed by one individual without reducing the consumption by any other individual – it is said to be non-rivalrous. Clean air is a non-rivalrous good: your consumption of it does not reduce my consumption of it. So it is with non-use value: any pleasure you get from contemplating the wetland in no way detracts from my pleasure from the same act of contemplation.

The second feature of a public good is that it is non-excludable: you cannot exclude me from the benefits of clean air once clean air is provided. The same goes for non-use value.

The relevance of the public good nature of non-use value is that care needs to be taken when determining how much people are willing to pay for it and over what population it should be aggregated. It is often thought that public goods attract free riders, people who deliberately understate their willingness to pay in the expectation that others will secure the good or service. The free rider problem suggests that public goods will be under-provided because real demand for it will be greater than the revealed demand. Looked at from a different point of view, people will not be willing to supply the good if they think that a substantial portion of the market will be able to get the good for nothing.

The practical importance of non-use value can be partly determined by looking at available estimates of it in relation to use value, but only partly because there are disputes about the validity of some of the estimates. In other cases, it is clear that what is estimated is some mix of use and non-use value.

Not many studies have attempted to separate economic value according to use and non-use elements. Box 3.2 reports a number of available studies, ignoring those studies where total values are estimated without attempts to separate them by types of value, and ignoring those studies where only non-use value is sought (famous examples of which are the *Exxon Valdez* and the Kakadu conservation zone in North Australia – see Carson et al, 1995, and Carson, 1994).

Box 3.2 Non-use Values

Study	Nature of good being valued	Non-use value as percentage of total value
Kaoru, 1993	Water quality in Massachusetts	59
Loomis et al, 1993	Forest protection in Australia	67+
Stevens et al, 1991	Endangered wildlife in US Atlantic salmon Bald eagle, wild turkey, coyote	85 (existence) 82 (intrinsic + bequest)
Walsh et al, 1984	Wilderness in Colorado	42 (existence + bequest)
Sutherland and Walsh, 1985	River water quality in Montana	72 (existence + bequest)
Greenley et al, 1981	River water quality in Colorado	34 (existence + bequest)
Brookshire et al, 1983	Grizzly bears and bighorn sheep	Existence values close to user WTP for grizzly bears and about one third for bighorn sheep
Madariaga and McConnell, 1987	Water quality in Chesapeake Bay	70% of users and 69% of non-users said they would prefer improved water quality even if access denied
Fredman, 1994	White-backed wood-pecker in Sweden	No monetary estimate but existence value 'important'
Garrod and Willis, 1996	Alleviating low flow in R Darent, UK	91% NUV/TV for non-users within 60 km of river
Willis et al, 1996	Wildlife enhancement scheme on Pevensey Levels, E Sussex, UK	NUV = 75% TV for non-users within 60 km radius NUV = 97% TV for non-users extrapolated to all UK households
Bateman et al, 1992	Conservation of the Norfolk Broads	76–91% or 57–6%*
Willis, 1990	3 SSSI	75–80%

* percentage depends on range of use values and the treatment of 'near Broadland' mail respondents. In the latter case, these people could be visitors or potential visitors and hence not 'non-use'. In the figures shown, they are first excluded altogether and then included in use values.

Both the US and UK studies suggest that non-use values can be very important, with fractions of total value being anything from 50 to 98 per cent. However, there are several reasons to be cautious about this initial impression. One main one is that the vast majority of benefit or damage estimation studies make no attempt to measure non-use value. This could be because it was not intended to be part of the study design, or because the investigators felt that such separation was not valid or important. There is a fairly firm suggestion in the literature that non-use value is only likely to be significant when the object of value is itself scarce or unique in some way. As with any good, values are likely to be smaller, the greater the availability of substitutes. The caveat here is that more empirical tests for non-use value are needed before we can be very confident about this statement.

Second, the size of non-use value in some studies is open to question. Two UK studies illustrate the point: the River Darent study (Garrod and Willis, 1996) and the Pevensey Levels study (Willis et al, 1996). In the former case, which considered the willingness to pay to enhance river flows to improve the river environment, non-use value was found to be 91 per cent of total willingness to pay. Since the River Darent is not known outside of the local region, Garrod and Willis truncated the aggregation process so that only those within a 60 km radius had their non-use value willingness to pay recorded. This would appear to be a conservative procedure and if the sample of non-users is random it would appear to be correct. But the study does not record the relationship between distance from the site and willingness to pay, which would have been helpful. In the Pevensey Levels study a similar procedure is used, with non-use values being truncated at 60 km. Here the study does record that there was 'little detectable decline' in non-use value with distance, that is the 60 km truncation would appear to result in underestimation of benefits. As it happens, use and non-use values within the 60 km area failed to exceed the costs of the environmental improvement so that non-use values outside the area become very important. As the Pevensey Levels are an internationally renowned site, there is some rationale for extending non-use value over a wide population.

These studies are highlighted not to cast doubt on their findings, but to show the sensitivity of aggregated non-use value to the assumption about the population over which aggregation is to take place. Small values over very large groups of people may account for the substantial size of the estimates. But this does not mean that the process of aggregating is incorrect: it is important to remember that this is one of the features of public goods as defined above.

The obvious way to set a realistic limit to the geographical boundary for non-use value is to observe how it varies with distance. One would anticipate that willingness to pay will decline with distance both for users (as confirmed by the travel cost method) and non-users: this is spatial discounting. The rationale for spatial discounting is that:

* People's interests in, and knowledge of, the site are less the further away is the site. Bateman and Langford (1997) confirm that there is a lower survey response rate as distance increases, indicating that people are less motivated to complete questionnaires the further away they are from the site in question;
* Even among respondents, people's willingness to pay is less likely to be greater than zero the further away they are from the site;
* Among those respondents who are willing to pay sums greater than zero, there is a lower willingness the further away the respondent is from the site.

Bateman and Langford (1997) conducted a detailed investigation of distance-decay in willingness to pay for the conservation of the Norfolk Broads, perhaps Britain's most famous wetlands site, with a mailed questionnaire to people across Great Britain. The essential findings are:

* The analysis was able to determine user and non-user value rather than use and non-use value. That is, the willingness to pay estimates come from those who visit (use) the site and from those who, at the time of the questionnaire, did not visit the site. But it is clear that some users had non-use values – they would have been willing to pay for something even if they did not visit; and non-users also had some use value because they had visited in the past. The suspicion that the latter is true is revealed in the high self-selection in the responses to the mailed questionnaire: more than a quarter of respondents had previously been in the Broads. This is too high to reflect a random sample of the population. Nonetheless, those who had never visited the site had significantly lower willingness to pay than those who had visited the site;
* Non-user value definitely declined with distance, although there is the suggestion of a constant willingness to pay beyond 150 km;
* While the values elicited are per annum, it is important to understand that respondents varied in the extent to which this annual sum would be committed over time. That is, some were willing to pay the sum for just one year, some for two to five years and some for a lifetime.

There is a debate within the economics profession as to whether non-use values should be included in cost-benefit appraisals. Those in favour tend to argue that they appear to be wholly legitimate components of human well-being: many people disapprove of and are genuinely upset by losses to environmental assets they do not personally use. As such they should be included in any cost-benefit analysis, since cost-benefit analysis is defined as the procedure for aggregating gains and losses in human well-being. Those who argue against say that non-use values arise out of some form of altruism and this is not consistent with the self-interest that is thought to underlie the individual's valuations in a cost-benefit analysis. This is sometimes expressed as saying that what people get is some form of warm glow, moral satisfaction, or impure altruism. People are willing to pay to feel good about something and this is not the same as being willing to pay for the good in question.

Against this, economists have been quick to point out that what motivates the individual could be self-interest, concern for others or concern for non-human species amongst other things. Warm glow is not precluded simply because it is warm glow. Moreover, warm glows as motivations for charitable donations show that they are not peculiar to hypothetical markets such as those used to estimate non-use value. Warm glows could, however, result in embedding in questionnaire responses, the phenomenon whereby the respondent appears to give the same value for something regardless of how much of it there is. Embedding can, however, be avoided by careful questionnaire design.

Commitment occurs when the motivation for non-use value is simply that something is right or the outcome of some moral imperative. If the source of this value is commitment, should this be included in a cost-benefit analysis? If the value is the result of some moral imperative, one implication is that individuals expressing this value are not willing to trade-off the environmental value against any other monetary sum. They cannot, in fact, be compensated. Yet, the concept of compensatable losses is fundamental to cost-benefit analysis. The issue is often put in terms of lexicographic (or lexical) orderings – preference orderings which are always dominated by one object of value, just as a dictionary orders words according to the alphabet. It is often thought that these committed individuals show up as protest votes in a contingent valuation study – as people who refuse to cooperate with the questionnaire. The reasons for protest votes vary substantially and it cannot be assumed that all protests are due to lexical orderings.

A further problem is that the evidence for lexical preferences is very ambiguous. A few contingent valuation surveys have found that a minority of respondents have indicated intrinsic value as their motivation whilst simultaneously being unwilling to pay anything at all for conservation. But these studies are open to several criticisms. First, they may not have made the trade-off context realistic. Some studies have shown that the percentage of people refusing to make the trade-off changes dramatically the clearer it is made that the environmental assets in question can only be conserved at some real economic cost. Arguably, rights may be easily assigned and defended when they cost nothing. Second, they may not in fact be identifying lexical preferences at all. Foster and Mourato (1997) conducted a questionnaire exercise on pesticides and bread. Respondents were asked to rank various combinations of attributes: price, health (of consumers) and birds (the environmental impact). A lexical algorithm would then rank all options on a single attribute, say price, and then decide any equally ranked option on the basis of, say, health. Eighteen per cent of respondents appeared to respond according to a lexical algorithm. While this appears to give support to the presence of lexicality, Foster and Mourato note that conformity with the algorithm is not necessarily conformity with lexical preferences. They show that the 18 per cent of respondents could simply have very strong preferences for a particular attribute of the options.

Non-use value is important because, in the contexts where it is relevant, it is seen to dominate the outcome of cost-benefit studies. It is important, however, to understand that in a great many contexts, it will not be relevant. But in situations where the asset in question has some unique attributes, and these are often precisely the subject matter of cost-benefit studies, it will be relevant. At the moment, there seems no logical reason to exclude non-use value from cost-benefit studies and this could add greatly to the power of such studies to act in favour of the environment. What matters most, then, is ensuring that it is properly estimated and properly aggregated.

The Techniques of Monetary Evaluation

Since whole volumes have been devoted to the theory and practice of monetary valuation of environmental impacts, here we can do no more than offer a brief sketch. For more detail, the reader is recommended to consult the excellent text by Garrod and Willis (1999).

Valuation techniques can be broadly divided into:

- Revealed preference approaches in which values are obtained by looking at willingness to pay in market places that involve the environmental impact in question. For example, the demand and supply of houses, and hence the price of houses, is affected by noise and air pollution;
- Stated preference techniques in which values are elicited through some form of questionnaire approach.

Notice that we do not discuss direct market approaches here. For example, the economic value of air pollution damage on crops can be estimated by looking at a dose-response relationship between pollution and crop loss, and then valuing the crop losses in market value terms. This is in fact a widely used technique, but the focus here is on those impacts where no direct market exists. Table 3.1 summarizes the main methodologies, omitting some that are included in more comprehensive analyses.

Table 3.1 *Summary of Valuation Methodologies*

Revealed preferences	Stated preferences
Hedonic pricing:	Contingent valuation
Housing markets	Conjoint analysis
Labour markets	
Travel cost method	
Random utility (discrete choice)	
Market prices (direct markets)	

Hedonic Price Method

The hedonic price method (HPM) uses surrogate markets – markets which are affected by the asset in question – to determine values of a non-marketed good. This method is based on the idea that a good can be viewed as a bundle of characteristics, each with its own implicit price. Some of the characteristics may have no direct market. Thus, a house can be thought of as a bundle of characteristics – number of rooms, proximity to public transport and closeness to amenities, for example. Individuals express their preferences for a particular non-market attribute by their selection of a particular bundle of characteristics. These preferences will be reflected in the differential prices paid for the good in the market. For example, a house in a noisy area will, other things being equal, be less expensive than a house in a quiet area. The hedonic pricing approach then applies econometric techniques to data on house prices and their characteristics to derive the relationship between the attributes of the good and its market price. From there, implicit prices for non-market characteristics can be estimated. Even when properties differ in many ways, not just in environmental or cultural quality, it is still be possible to uncover the implicit prices if the data and statistical techniques are good enough.

When fully implemented, the hedonic approach comprises two main stages. First an equation is estimated to explain house prices or rents as a function of a number of housing and neighbourhood characteristics, including any environmental attributes of interest. This gives a hedonic price function from which the implicit price of the environmental or cultural attribute can be estimated for each level of the attribute. The second stage expresses the implicit prices faced by each household as a function of the respective attribute levels and various social and economic characteristics. This second equation is known as the (marginal) willingness to pay function.

The hedonic approach has a number of limitations. It relies on the assumption that the housing market is freely functioning and efficient where individuals have perfect information and mobility so that they can buy the exact property and associated characteristics that they desire. The resulting willingness to pay measures reflect only those impacts of which individuals are aware. For example, if the particular housing location produces a health effect that residents are not aware of, that effect will not be captured by the hedonic price approach. Notice that it will also only capture the use values of residents. It will not capture any of the benefits from visitors to the area, nor any non-use value.

Travel Cost Method

The travel cost method (TCM) uses differences in travel and other costs to individuals making use of a recreation site to infer the recreational value of the site (Clawson and Knetsch, 1966). The method takes advantage of the fact that, in most cases, a trip to a recreation site requires an individual to incur costs in terms of travel, entry fee, on-site expenditures and time. Different individuals incur different costs to visit different sites, and these implicit prices can be used in place of conventional market prices as the basis for estimating the value of recreation sites and changes in their quality.

Simple travel cost models attempt to estimate the number of trips to a site or sites over some period of time. There are two variants of the model. The first can be used to estimate representative individuals' recreation demand functions. This is done by observing the visitation rate of individuals who make trips to a recreational facility, as a function of the travel cost. The value of a recreation site to an individual is measured by the area under his or her demand curve, so that the total recreation (use) value of a site is simply the area under each demand curve summed over all individuals. This individual travel cost model requires that there is variation in the number of trips individuals make to the recreational site, in order to estimate the demand function. One particular problem therefore arises from the fact that such variation is not always observed, especially since some individuals do not make any trip.

A different approach is known as the zonal travel cost method. The unit of observation is now the zone, as opposed to the individual. The visitation rate used is the number of trips per capita from each zone. Zones are constructed by dividing the region around a site into areas of increasing travel cost. The observations of trips are then allocated to their zone of origin, and the population of each zone. The visitation rate is calculated by dividing the number of trips from each zone by the population in the zone.

In both variants of the simple model, the demand curves are estimated by undertaking statistical regression analysis, relating visitation rates to socio-economic characteristics (for example income), estimates of the costs of visiting a site, and some indicator of site quality. The area under the demand curves provides a measure of consumer surplus. Unless the site being valued is unique, most individuals will have access to a range of substitute sites that they could use for the same or similar activities. Omitting these substitute sites will lead to bias in benefit estimates, although there is no simple way of incorporating substitutes into the simple travel cost model. Including all possible substitutes is obviously impractical, so judgement is needed on the part of the researcher. Multi-site models vary in their complexity and their ability to explain substitution behaviour. Other problems of the methods are the valuation of travel and on-site time, establishing the true purpose of the journey and insufficient variation in site quality, apart from a number of potential statistical problems.

Random Utility or Discrete Choice Model

Whilst the traditional travel cost technique focuses on the choice of the number of trips an individual takes in a year (a continuous choice), the random utility model (RUM), also known as the discrete choice model, goes to the other extreme. It narrows the decision time-frame down to the period in which the individual chooses between recreational sites for a given trip (a discrete choice). Recreationists are not seen as maximizing their own well-being by choosing the number of trips they intend to take in a year, but by choosing the alternative which offers them the highest level of satisfaction out of the options available to them on each separate choice occasion. Random models are particularly suitable for cases where the major component of recreation behaviour is substitution between sites that are differentiated from each other in terms of quality, and to estimate the value of particular features or assets of the site which may be of interest.

In the random utility framework it is assumed that on each choice occasion an individual, having decided to take a trip, is faced with a set of possible alternative sites that differ in their characteristics. For example, each locality may provide different types of cultural experiences and imply different travel costs. Different people faced with the same set of alternatives may make different choices since they may attach different values to the characteristics of the alternatives. An individual will choose the alternative which provides the highest level of satisfaction. The probability that a particular individual will visit a specific site is equal to the probability that the satisfaction derived from a visit to that site is greater than the satisfaction that would be derived from a visit to any other site. Making various assumptions, this probability can be obtained by econometric procedures.

Contingent Valuation Method

The contingent valuation method (CVM) is a survey-based technique. By means of an appropriately designed questionnaire, a hypothetical market is described where the good in question can be traded. The approach is akin to market research for a new product. This contingent market defines the good itself, the institutional context in which it would be provided, and the way it would be financed. A random sample of people is then directly asked to express their maximum willingness to pay (or willingness to accept) for a hypothetical change in the level of provision of the good. Respondents are assumed to behave as though they were in a real market.

Although still controversial, this direct survey approach to estimating household demand for public goods has been gaining increased acceptance amongst both academics and policy makers as a versatile and complete methodology for benefit estimation in the case of environmental improvements and other public goods. In recent years, the contingent valuation method has been extensively applied in both developed and developing countries to the valuation of a wide range of non-market goods and services. Much of the impetus to this acceptance derived from the conclusions of the special panel appointed by the US National Oceanic and Atmospheric Administration (NOAA) in 1993 (Arrow et al, 1993) following the *Exxon Valdez* oil spill in Alaska in 1989. The oil spill resulted in claims for damages and some of those claims were assessed using contingent valuation (Box 3.3). Since many hundreds of millions of dollars were involved, it is not surprising that this method became very controversial. The US government established the NOAA panel precisely because of this. The panel concluded that, subject to a number of recommendations, such methods could produce estimates reliable enough to be used in a judicial process of natural resource damage assessment. The panel recommended certain rules of the game for conducting such studies (Box 3.4). Furthermore, contingent valuation is the only technique able to capture all types of benefits from a non-market good or service including non-use values.

There are three basic parts to most contingent valuation surveys. First, it is customary to ask a set of attitudinal and behavioural questions about the good to be valued as a preparation for responding to the

Box 3.3 *Contingent Valuation in Practice: the* Exxon Valdez

Probably the most famous contingent valuation study relates to the oil spill damages caused by the oil tanker *Exxon Valdez* when it ran aground in Prince William Sound in South East Alaska in March 1989. Some 11 million gallons of crude oil were discharged from the ship. In the US the concept of passive use value (what we have called non-use value) was already familiar, and its use in assessments of damages in compensation claims had already been cautiously adopted. The CVM was used in the law suit brought against the Exxon company which owned the ship by the State of Alaska.

After some preliminary attitudinal questions, the questionnaire began by indicating the background to the survey, namely the *Exxon Valdez* spill. Respondents were shown photographs of the area where the spill occurred and a map of the extent to which the spill travelled. They were shown photographs of the wildlife that was put at risk and were told how many seabirds etc. had been killed or damaged. Respondents were then given a scenario in which future oil spills in Prince William Sound would be prevented by having tankers accompanied by escort ships (the *Exxon Valdez* had strayed outside shipping lanes to avoid icebergs). Respondents were told that this scheme would be paid for by a fund partly financed by oil companies and partly by a one-time tax on households. Notice that respondents were told they would have to pay some of the cost. Sometimes in CV studies, respondents answer that it is not their responsibility and that someone else (often the government) should pay. Respondents were then told how much the avoidance programme would cost per household, with the amounts and the form of the elicitation question being varied. Respondents were asked if they were willing to pay this initial amount. If they answered 'yes', they were asked if they would pay a higher sum. If they answered 'no', they were asked if they would pay a lower sum. This is an example of the close-ended elicitation format. Respondents were then asked follow-up questions on socio-economic information and attitudes, for example. Interviews were face-to-face and there was a 75 per cent response rate.

With several different question formats and a number of ways of econometrically interpreting the results, the analysts chose what they regarded as the most robust estimates of willingness to pay. WTP estimates were also related to the various attitudinal and socio-economic variables. The model performed well, with estimates generally varying with the variables, such as income, in the manner expected. WTP also varied with scope – the expected scale of the damage, which is important because it signals that there is unlikely to be embedding.

The median household WTP was found to be US$49, which, when aggregated across all households, came to US$2.8 billion. This was the lowest conservative estimate, with other estimates ranging up to US$9.3 billion. Note that the estimate was based on willingness to pay, whereas if we think of all individuals as having some sort of property right in Prince William Sound, then WTA should be chosen and the sums would probably have been higher. The use of WTP is consistent with the NOAA recommendations. Finally, note that the estimates are of non-use value and exclude the damages to local fishermen and residents.

In the event, Exxon paid about US$1 billion in damages. The legal case sparked an enormous controversy over the use of CVM, with Exxon fighting back by sponsoring studies to show that this method produces unreal results. The debate continues, but CVM has become established in the US as a means of estimating damages from resource disasters, big and small.

Source: Carson et al, 1995

Box 3.4 *The NOAA Panel Recommendations on Conducting Contingent Valuation Studies*

Use personal interviews
Use a dichotomous choice format
Carefully pre-test any photographs used
Favour a conservative design (more likely to under- rather than over-estimate WTP)
Use a representative sample (rather than a convenience sample)
Remind respondents of budget constraints
Include follow-up questions to the valuation question

Use a WTP measure rather than WTA
Adequately pre-test the survey instrument
Use an accurate scenario description
Deflect warm glows (overstatement of WTP to appear generous)
Check temporal consistency of results
Remind respondents of undamaged substitutes
Provide a 'no' answer or 'don't know' option
Cross-tabulate the results
Check respondents' understanding

---

valuation question, and in order to reveal the most important underlying factors driving respondents' attitudes towards the public good.

Second, the contingent scenario – the object to be valued, along with its context – is presented and respondents are asked for their monetary evaluations. The scenario includes a description of the commodity and the terms under which it is to be hypothetically offered. Information is also provided on the quality and reliability of provision, timing and logistics, and the method of payment. Then respondents are asked questions to determine how much they would value the good if confronted with the opportunity to obtain it under the specified terms and conditions. The elicitation can be asked in a number of different ways – see Box 3.5. Respondents are also reminded of substitute goods and of the need to make compensating adjustments in other types of expenditure to accommodate the additional financial transaction.

Third, questions about the socio-economic and demographic characteristics of the respondent are asked in order to:

- Ascertain the representativeness of the survey sample relative to the population of interest;
- Examine the similarity of the groups receiving different versions of the questionnaire; and
- Study how willingness to pay varies according to respondents' characteristics.

Econometric techniques are then applied to the survey results to derive the desired welfare measures such as average willingness to pay.

A number of factors may systematically bias respondents' answers in a contingent valuation study. These factors are not specific to the method but are common to most survey-based techniques and are mostly attributable to survey design and implementation problems. Possible types of bias include:

* Strategic behaviour (such as free-riding) whereby respondents make false willingness to pay statements because they think others will pay more than them and secure the good anyway;
* Embedding, where the valuation is insensitive to the scope of the good. Scope refers to the fact that the good may vary in size. Embedding exists when respondents make the same willingness to pay statement regardless of how much of the good they hypothetically purchase;
* Anchoring bias, where the valuation depends on the first bid presented;
* Information bias, when the way the question is framed unduly influences the answer; and
* Hypothetical bias, which refers generally to the fact that the context is hypothetical rather than real so that answers may not be the same as those that would occur if respondents really had to pay.

Despite the continuing debate, the contingent method is the most flexible and powerful of all the valuation techniques. It is applicable to almost all public goods and can measure non-use values. Box 3.6 deals with some of the more common criticisms of the method.

Conjoint Analysis

Currently, valuation practitioners are increasingly developing a predilection for conjoint analysis techniques which have some advantages over contingent valuation method designs.

Conjoint analysis applies to a family of survey-based methodologies that have been used extensively in the marketing and transport literature to model preferences for bundles of characteristics of goods, and to isolate the value of individual product characteristics typically supplied in combination with one another. Conjoint analysis presents respondents with sets of two or more alternative options. Each option is characterized by a number of attributes, which are offered at different levels across options. A price or cost variable is typically one of the attributes. Respondents are then asked to rank or rate the options according to their preferences or simply to choose their most preferred alternative. Willingness to pay can be indirectly inferred from the choices made.

The method has two principal attractions: first, its unique ability to deal with situations where changes are multi-dimensional and trade-offs between them are of particular interest; second, its avoidance of an

---

Box 3.5 *Value Elicitation Questions in Contingent Valuation*

Open ended	What is the maximum amount you are willing to pay?
Payment card	Show a card with a selection of prices and ask respondents to choose the one that best depicts their maximum WTP. Can be seen as a variant of the open-ended method. Cards may be anchored to show actual household expenditures or taxes, or unanchored.
Single-bounded dichotomous choice	Are you willing to pay $X? Yes or no. The price $X (bid level) varies across randomly selected individuals in the sample.
Double-bounded dichotomous choice	Same as above with follow-up. Are you willing to pay $X? Yes or no. If yes: are you willing to pay $Y>X? Yes or no. If no: are you willing to pay $Z<X? Yes or no.
Iterative bidding game	Full sample with same questionnaire: are you willing to pay $X? If yes, raise price until some stopping point. If no, lower price until some stopping point. Split sample: start one group at low price and raise prices for all yes responses. Start other group at a high price and lower prices for all refusals.

---

explicit elicitation of respondent willingness to pay by relying instead on the ranking, rating or choice of a series of alternative packages of characteristics. Being essentially a variant of the standard contingent valuation format, conjoint analysis can also measure all forms of value. Its main limitation is the difficulty respondents might have with complex choices between bundles with many attributes and levels.

What Practical Use is Made of Monetary Valuation?

Monetary valuation and cost benefit analysis have entrenched themselves into practical policy appraisal far more than ever before in UK, European and American history. This section provides a brief overview of the various contexts. More detail can be found in Pearce (1998b).

Cost-benefit Analysis in the US

In the US cost-benefit analysis has developed beyond the 1950s focus on water resources, extending into most areas of public policy including education and health. A major impetus came within weeks of President Reagan taking office in 1981 and issuing Executive Order 12291 requiring a cost-benefit analysis for all new major regulations. The order required,

Box 3.6 *Some Common Issues with Economic Valuation*

Because the contingent valuation method is now widely used, much of the debate on economic valuation has centred on its validity. To some extent this is unfortunate because it probably remains the case that other valuation techniques are more widely used. They attract less controversy and hence valuation per se might attract less controversy.

But there are interesting issues within the debate. Critics often argue that the method is not reliable because it asks hypothetical questions about hypothetical scenarios, and that people will not, in practice, pay what they say they will pay. In part this criticism rests on a confusion. If a real payment mechanism existed, it would not be necessary to resort to hypothetical procedures. It is precisely because they do not exist that the contingent valuation method is required. Nonetheless, the criticism has some foundation because the method 'hangs by a bootstrap': we cannot know if the answers are truthful.

There are various ways of testing for this potential hypothetical bias. First, willingness-to-pay answers from questionnaires could be compared with what people actually do pay. In so far as these comparisons are meaningful (there are not many cases where people actually do pay), they do suggest an upwards bias in hypothetical answers. So long as the nature and degree of bias are known, of course, hypothetical answers can be adjusted.

Second, answers from contingent valuation studies can be compared to answers from the less controversial revealed preference studies. Carson et al, (1995b) report a comparison of 83 studies and revealed preference estimates on a comparable basis. They show that the ratio of contingent-valuation willingness to pay and revealed-preference willingness to pay is 0.77 to 0.92, which is remarkably consistent. This test is known as convergent validity.

Third, the underlying assumption of contingent valuation is economic rationality. We would therefore expect willingness-to-pay answers to be consistent with the predictions of economic theory. If willingness varies inversely with income, for example, this would not be consistent with theoretical expectations. In the same way we can test for internal consistency. Someone saying he or she doesn't care at all about the environmental asset in question but who is willing to pay a large sum to conserve it, would be treated with suspicion. These kinds of internal and construct validity tests help determine if the method is sound or not.

Source: Carson et al, 1995b

among other things, that 'regulatory objectives shall be chosen to maximize the net benefits to society', and that, for given regulatory objectives, 'the alternative involving the least net cost to society shall be chosen'. This did not mean that analyses were carried out consistently or universally. Substantial areas of regulation are not subject to an analysis. Indeed, some regulations explicitly forbid an appraisal of costs and benefits. Court rulings have also established that where the original enabling legislation does not mention costs and benefits, agencies may not consider them (for a detailed description of which environmental legislation is subject to cost-benefit analysis, see Morgenstern, 1997). Nonetheless, cost-benefit analysis plays a significant role in regulatory assessment. In contrast, as we shall see, there has been a cautious trend in the UK towards a general requirement for some sort of regulatory analysis, but nothing as precise as the US legislation. Much of the stimulus to cost-benefit analysis in the US came, as it had in the 1950s, from a concern about efficiency in government. But whereas the earlier concern related to a real scarcity of government funds and political concerns with major investments, the 1980s and 1990s focus was on regulation. In particular, there was a political backlash against perceived excessive regulation and against clear inconsistencies and irrationalities in public controls. In the view of those concerned about regulation, cost-benefit analysis would help to prevent over regulation. In the environmental arena, several attempts had already been made to test the consistency of environmental policy with a cost-benefit test. Freeman (1982) found that air and water pollution controls resulted in unrecorded gains in the US GNP of a little over 1 per cent. Put another way, the US GNP was understated by 1 per cent because of unmarketed gains. Portney (1990) suggests that US air quality control policy had benefits in excess of costs in the early 1980s. Freeman (1990) found water pollution control to have costs in excess of benefits for the mid-1980s. By far the most detailed benefit-cost assessment of US regulation has been produced by Robert Hahn (1996). Hahn first uses the regulatory agencies' own numbers to see which 1990–95 regulations pass a cost-benefit test. He concludes that around 50 per cent of final and proposed regulations would pass such a test and about 50 per cent would fail. Focusing on the Environmental Protection Agency regulations Hahn finds aggregate net benefits of some US$70 billion across 40 final regulations, and US$18 billion across 21 proposed regulations. But only 12 out of the 40, and 9 out of the 21, pass a cost-benefit test. More detailed analysis suggests that only regulations relating to clean air and safe drinking water have benefits greater than costs. Turning to the quality of the estimates of benefits and costs, Hahn considers that agencies have an incentive to exaggerate benefits, while some regulations quite explicitly forbid a balancing of costs and benefits, thus providing no incentive to consider a cost-benefit analysis. Some costs might be overstated, however. On balance he concludes that, if the estimates were to be recomputed by a neutral economist, they would significantly reduce net benefits.

It is interesting to note these several attempts to compare costs and benefits across the whole of regulatory activity. No such exercise can be found elsewhere, and certainly not in the UK or Europe generally. Indeed, such an exercise would be immensely difficult precisely because no formal requirements existed to carry out a cost-benefit analysis prior to enactment or *ex post*. Sporadic assessments have taken place, but usually at the behest of Parliamentary Select Committees (see House of Lords, 1994–95, on bathing water quality).

The other stimulus to the use of cost-benefit analysis in the US came from legal actions for damages. The US has a greater proclivity to use the courts than in Europe. Monetary valuation of damages is a natural means to determine court settlements and they have been widely used for this purpose, ranging from liability assessments under the Superfund legislation (which deals with clean-up of hazardous waste sites) to probably the most well known settlement for pollution damages, the *Exxon Valdez* case of 1989 in which an Exxon tanker spilled oil into Prince William Sound in Alaska (Carson et al, 1995) – see Box 3.3. In contrast, Europe has only some environmental liability legislation and there is no tradition of 'taking CBA to court' (Kopp and Smith, 1989).

Cost-benefit Analysis in the UK: the Emergence of Regulatory Appraisal

Cost-benefit analysis has had a chequered history in the UK. Its first application was project-based and was to road transport. Britain's first motorway was the M1 from London to Birmingham. The application of the analysis was in fact experimental rather than an integral part of the assessment. Had the analysis shown excess costs, the motorway would still have proceeded. Costs of construction were compared with the benefits in terms of working and non-working time saved, reduced accidents, and changes in fuel consumption and vehicle wear and tear (Coburn et al, 1960). A little later the London Victoria underground railway was evaluated in cost-benefit terms (Foster and Beesley, 1963), an interesting study because the line was not justified in purely financial terms but was found to be profitable from a social standpoint once all time savings had been included. A consistent feature of these early studies was the total neglect of environmental impacts. The COBA *Manual* (Highways Agency, 1997a) for using cost-benefit analysis continues to exclude environmental impacts, although these are treated in extensive detail in non-monetary terms in a separate extensive publication (Highways Agency, 1997b).

The past resistance of the Department of Transport (now merged with the Department of the Environment) to extending cost-benefit analysis to environmental impacts has never been easy to explain, not least because the revealed and stated preference techniques required for monetizing environmental impacts – which are excluded from COBA – are the same as those used to value travel time savings and accidents, which are included in COBA. The Standing Advisory Committee on Trunk Road Assessment, which advises the Department of Transport, consistently advised against monetization (eg SACTRA, 1991). Nonetheless, opposition to the use of monetization has slowly eroded.

Part of the slow progress in the Department of Transport was probably due to an unwillingness to embrace these techniques in contexts where political opposition at public inquiries was likely to be highest. In part, this reluctance was reinforced among the older generation of civil servants by the experience of the massive public inquiry – the Roskill Commission – into the siting of London's third airport in 1969–71 (Commission on the Third London Airport, 1971). A government-appointed research team concluded that an inland site was preferred on cost-benefit grounds. Most significantly, apart from savings in air and ground travel time (which together dominated the analysis) the team attempted to value noise nuisance and the reduction in amenity value through an estimation of impacts on house prices (the hedonic property price approach). By today's standards, the study was primitive, but it was the first significant attempt to estimate environmental impacts in monetary terms. Environmental opposition to the study was intense and it is easy to see why when it is observed that environmental costs amounted to less than a half of 1 per cent of total social costs at the preferred site, and only 1.5 per cent at the worst site. Moreover, the analysis took place against a totally contrary political backdrop since the Commission's least preferred site – Foulness on the coast – was the only one supported by any of the county authorities. The Commission was subject to some ridicule for allegedly placing a fire insurance value on an historic Norman church at one site. In fact this was only a suggestion at one stage and never appeared in the final report, despite continuing erroneous comment that it did. (see, for example, Grove-White, 1997). Nonetheless, the damage was done. Not only did the Commission's least preferred site become the government's chosen site, but cost-benefit analysis suffered consequently from the adverse criticism (for a full discussion see Pearce, 1970, and Dasgupta and Pearce, 1972).

As in the US, cost-benefit analysis began with project applications, reflecting the way in which the underlying theory itself developed, and only later came to be applied to policy. Although some bodies such as the House of Lords Select Committees had for some time been putting pressure on government to indicate the costs and benefits of European directives, the modern period of cost-benefit analysis in the UK dates from the late 1980s with the first effective environment White Paper (UK Government, 1990). While there had long been pressure to put environmental concerns further up the political agenda, most of the argument has been along traditional conservationist lines. In 1987 the United Nations had produced the Brundtland Report on sustainable development (World Commission on Environment and Development, 1987). The report was extremely influential. Whilst failing to recognize many of the inevitable trade-offs between environment and economic development, the Commission nonetheless established environment as a key element of economic policy. Basically, all economic activity affects environment, and many environmental policies positively affect the economy, for example through improved health and productivity. While these were familiar messages to environmental economists, they secured a world-wide platform with the Brundtland Commission's report. Since countries were obliged to respond to the report, the UK Department of the Environment commissioned a report to interpret the meaning of sustainable development and to define the outlines of a coherent environmental strategy. The resulting 'Pearce Report' – *Blueprint for a Green Economy* (Pearce et al, 1989) – secured massive media coverage for its emphasis on market-based instruments, especially pollution taxes, and on monetization of environmental impacts. The report was generally sympathetically received within government, in part because – as is now evident – some internal efforts had been made several years previously to secure adoption of a similar agenda.

Several factors were at work which explain the change, some of which were not peculiar to environmental policy.

First, the sheer weight of research in applied environmental economics had grown to such proportions in the late 1980s that it would have been difficult for anyone to ignore it. Arguably, policy would have had to respond sooner or later.

Second, there was a renewed emphasis on efficiency in public expenditure in an effort to meet overall macroeconomic objectives of controlling public expenditure generally, and because of continuing publicity over waste in local and central government. As in the US, cost-benefit analysis appeared to hold out the prospect of delivering some of that efficiency.

Third, there was the continuing underlying theme of deregulation in an effort to reduce the perceived costs of regulation on business and on competitiveness. Indeed, deregulation units were subsequently established in government departments, with a central unit in the Cabinet Office, and guidance was issued on regulatory appraisal. In 1995 a deregulation task force recommended that:

> '*no regulatory proposal affecting business should be entertained by a Minister without a proper CCA (compliance cost assessment). Ministers should be required to personally sign off all CCAs and risk assessments. No regulatory proposal should be considered collectively by Ministers without a certificate signed by the responsible Minister that he has read both the risk assessment and CCA, and that he believes that the balance between costs and benefits has been appropriately struck.' (Cabinet Office, 1996)*

Echoing Presidential Executive Order 12291 in the US, regulatory appraisal became a requirement for all regulatory proposals affecting business. Such appraisals might include a risk assessment (construed as an assessment of uncertainty) but would always include a CCA indicating the costs to UK industry of complying with the regulation. In fact, since April 1993 CCAs had been required for all legislation that might have an impact on business. In 1994 this was extended to the impacts on small businesses. Essentially, what began as a narrowly focused exercise, estimating only the costs to business, was broadened in 1996 to include economy-wide costs and some effort at estimating benefits. It remains the case that regulatory appraisals vary substantially in the information they contain and few would qualify as a comprehensive cost-benefit appraisal.

Fourth, and perhaps less significantly, the European Commission had begun to embrace formal cost-benefit appraisal of proposals for directives and amendments to directives. This they had done in light of Article 130R(3) of the Single European Act which, while not explicitly referring to cost-benefit analysis, clearly mandated some form of cost-benefit appraisal. The UK probably cannot be thought of as a follower in this respect, however, since it had been instrumental in getting the clause included in the Act because of growing concerns about the cost of regulations. The decision contrasts with an earlier refusal by the Commission to estimate costs and benefits, despite an explicit request from the European Parliament to do so (Environmental Data Services, 1980).

Fifth, as we have seen, environmental issues had risen up the political agenda because of the stance adopted towards sustainable development. One of the central features of sustainable development is the pervasive role of environment in all decisions. Environment had therefore to be treated seriously and formally: there was a need to know how it could be incorporated into decision making. The advances in project appraisal and monetary evaluation of environmental impacts held out considerable promise in this respect.

Cost-benefit Analysis in the UK: Official Guidance on Environmental Appraisal

One outcome of these changes was the publication of Policy Appraisal and the Environment (Department of the Environment, 1991). This document sought to give guidance on environmental appraisal techniques for project and policy evaluation, and the guidance includes monetary evaluation, along with risk assessment (which was the subject of separate subsequent guidance: see Department of the Environment, 1995), and multicriteria analysis. Although unstated, there was a presumption that monetization and cost-benefit analysis were more favoured. This is consistent with guidance from the UK Treasury which had long published a *Green Book* for guiding government departments in their appraisal work. The latest issue (UK Treasury, 1997) is couched mainly in terms of monetized costs and benefits, although explicit attention is paid to situations where monetization is thought not to be possible. In 1997 the then Department of the Environment issued a discussion paper on costs and benefits in the context of environmental policy and competitiveness (Department of the Environment, 1997a). This signalled a concern not to identify environmental regulations only with drag effects on the economy, but with opportunities as well, for example in the abatement technology sector.

Some indication of the commitment to more rigorous approaches to policy was the follow up to *Policy Appraisal and the Environment*. Consultants were hired to see how far the guidelines were being implemented. The indications were that the guidance was too long and detailed for those who need to provide rapid guidance on the environmental implications of policy initiatives and too short for those requiring technical guidance (Department of the Environment, Transport and the Regions, 1997). An investigation into what guidance was in fact available revealed that there were numerous manuals and guidelines on cost-benefit analysis for sectoral use, especially in the water sector (EFTEC, 1998), but most related to projects rather than policies. Policy appraisal might differ because of the scale and pervasiveness of the effects of policy – errors could be catastrophic politically whereas project failure can usually be confined. Policy appraisal also faces many more uncertainties than project assessment, although the problems are far from fatal as the US experience shows.

Brief guidance on policy appraisal was issued in 1998 by the Department of the Environment, Transport and the Regions (DETR) (1998). It advises that several steps are required to assess the possible environmental impact of a policy:

- Impacts can be broadly assessed by screening;
- Only significant impacts matter and significance should be tested with the screening process;
- Screening involves checklists based on the likely implications of the policy for the consumption of natural resources: water, greenfield land, materials, energy; the creation of waste; the creation of emissions to air and effluent to water, and the increase in global pollutants;
- Attention should be paid to second and higher order impacts – the creation of one effect may exacerbate another effect (such as the loss of greenfield sites, which may increase biodiversity loss);
- Quantify costs and benefits where possible. While the guidance reaffirms the role to be played by formal assessment techniques,

and by cost-benefit analysis in particular, it offers no guidance on how a significant impact is to be measured or what significance means. More to the point, the guidance is little more than the bare bones of any rational approach to policy making. The fact of its issue suggests that the need to impose some sort of elementary order on decision making is still needed, despite the decades of work on cost-benefit and other appraisal procedures.

Cost-benefit Analysis in the UK: the Record

The consultants' report on the use of the *Policy Appraisal* guidelines (Department of the Environment, Transport and the Regions, 1997, op cit) revealed that there was a long way to go before cost-benefit analysis was widely adopted across government departments. This is especially true in contexts where policy is primarily non-environmental but has environmental consequences. For overtly environmental policy, however, the analysis has secured a much stronger foothold. Monetary valuation has been applied to issues relating to the National Air Quality Strategy, agricultural issues such as pesticides, waste management (fairly extensively), the pricing of energy, chemicals management, water resources, forestry, and rural amenity (Pearce, 1998b). Full cost-benefit studies are rare: most deal either with the cost side or the benefit side. Some general conclusions are:

- In some areas, especially waste, monetary benefit estimation has been extremely influential in determining policy. Notably, the initial setting of the UK landfill tax was based on monetary estimates of environmental costs;
- Benefit and damage studies are also being used to inform decisions about possible market-based instruments, notably a pesticides tax and a tax on extraction of aggregates from quarries;
- The setting of environmental standards is still determined by considerations unrelated to benefit estimates, such as critical loads and avoidance of health impacts. Nonetheless, cost-benefit analysis is being used indirectly to substantiate those targets and to help determine the time-paths for their achievement;
- Some agencies, such as the Health and Safety Executive and the Forestry Commission, routinely use cost-benefit analysis. This use extends beyond project appraisal to the role of costs and benefits in setting risk standards in the former and in the justification of afforestation in terms of non-timber benefits in the latter;
- The Environment Agency has shown considerable interest in cost-benefit analysis, reflecting the requirements of the Environment Act of 1995 to take into account the likely costs and benefits of its actions,

and to be excused from this requirement only if it is 'unreasonable' to do so. While the requirement does not formally mandate any particular form of analysis, considerable effort in the Act has gone into devising guidelines on the use of unit monetary values for assessing schemes and policies based on benefits transfer – the borrowing of money values from one context for application in another context;

*   Overall, substantially greater use is made of cost-benefit analysis and benefit estimation than is probably realized.

Obstacles to the Further Use of Cost-benefit Analysis

If cost-benefit analysis and benefit estimation are more widely used than is realized, it remains the case that there is substantial ambivalence both within government and among regulatory agencies towards its extended use. The sources of this resistance are several.

First, there continue to be doubts about the reliability of such studies, and especially about benefit estimation. There is substance to these doubts by the very nature of the environmental economics research process in Europe. The formal requirements to engage in cost-benefit analysis are not rigid, as with the Environment Act's mandate to the Environment Agency, or the new Regulatory Appraisal process for government departments. As such, the analysis has developed from a mix of studies prepared unilaterally by academics for research interest, and by academics and consultancies for individual agencies and government departments. While the number of studies is surprisingly large, it is not large enough to provide a statistical base for benefits transfer. Combined with the fact that the science of economic valuation has evolved and still is evolving, uncertainty is endemic in the estimates. This uncertainty presents government with several problems. First, if policy was directly related to benefit estimates, then it is conceivable that the policy could be subject to legal challenge. This prospect is discounted by some experts because policy is, ultimately, whatever politicians decide it is. Only judicial review relating to unreasonable behaviour could challenge it. Nonetheless, there is some explanation here for the distancing of policy from cost-benefit analysis results.

Second, there is hostility within some parts of government to some aspects of the analysis, whatever the official guidance. Some of the traditional arguments against monetization are often emotive and irrational, but some coherence is afforded to these views from the belief that environmental assets are somehow different and should not be subject to trade-offs (see Chapter 1). Academic studies which claim that individuals do not trade-off environment and other goods – the so called lexical preferences – give some comfort to this view, even though, as noted above, they are suspect.

Third, it is often argued that cost-benefit analysis is not transparent. Highly varied and different costs and benefits are reduced to single numbers, giving the impression of a black box approach to policy. This is a valid criticism which could be surmounted by showing the sensitivities of the cost-benefit analysis outcome to various factors and by showing clearly which stakeholders gain and which lose. Sensitivity analysis tends to capture most of the former, but the latter is not a feature of most modern analyses and should be. This may also help overcome the reasonable objection that most analyses fail to identify the incidence of costs and benefits on different groups when, in most cases, this could easily be done. Trying to build a consensus among stakeholders about a policy change clearly explains the divergence of many policy outcomes from what would appear to be rational on cost-benefit grounds. This also explains some of the emphasis on process which, taken to the limit, implies that, so long as the main stakeholders are assembled round a table, whatever is the outcome is for the best. Arguably, however, cost-benefit analysis reaches stakeholders who tend to be excluded from process – not everyone has a well organized lobby or voice.

Fourth, cost-benefit analysis tends to present results in a reasonably cut-and-dried manner, subject to the uncertainty of the estimates. Benefits exceed or do not exceed costs. But decision makers may place as much importance on flexibility of decision. An analysis that, in effect, removes that flexibility will not be welcome. At its worst, this view says that politicians will do whatever they want, and that they do not want to be troubled by cost-benefit studies that might produce the opposite answer: an analysis crowds out flexibility.

Fifth, as noted previously, cost-benefit analysis works best when the goal of policy is economic efficiency. Distributional considerations can be accounted for (see Chapter 1), but their incorporation probably raises the level of discomfort that critics feel. Other goals such as employment creation, protection of competitive position and the desirability of the process of decision making tend to be omitted from many studies. While calling for more use of cost-benefit analysis in Europe, Navrud and Pruckner (1997) argue that the more formalized use of such analysis in the US owes more to the tradition there of emphasizing economic efficiency when compared to Europe. This may be true but raises the issue of how best to accommodate multiple objectives if that is the desired goal. It is far from clear that other approaches fare any better. Cost-benefit analysis is readily supplemented with an analysis of effects on competitiveness and employment, and modern practitioners of the contingent valuation approach emphasize its role in securing public participation. Nonetheless, these broader concerns may explain the current interest in the UK in multi-criteria techniques which have been popular for some time in the Netherlands. The Environment Agency has experimented with multi-criteria techniques for ranking project options. The focus of multi-criteria approaches (although limited) does reflect the fact that cost-benefit analysis is efficiency oriented, whereas policy goals are often wider than efficiency alone. This offers one explanation for the apparent gap between the current widespread practice of cost-benefit analysis and the fact that decisions appear not to be heavily influenced by it. If decision making is rational, and efficiency was the only goal, then the analysis should show up as being influential. But efficiency is not the only goal, nor are decisions always made rationally. It would therefore be surprising if the analysis dominated actual decisions.

Sixth, the science of benefit estimation changes very rapidly. It is hard enough for academics specializing in the subject to maintain pace with the large published and even larger 'grey' literature. Busy civil servants are even less likely to be at the cutting edge of developments. Understandable ignorance of the literature does account for some continuing hostility to monetization.

Finally, cost-benefit analysis is practised with varying degrees of sophistication. If it is poorly executed, critics will use poor practice as a basis for criticizing the technique *per se*. The risks of poor practice are highest in benefits transfer since the temptation to use existing studies to provide estimates for new sites is a strong temptation: it saves the costs of an original study and is highly suited to approaches based on guidelines and manuals of practice. An interesting illustration of the problems arose with the public inquiry into Thames Water Company's proposal to extract borehole water from near the River Kennet. The proposal was opposed by the Environment Agency on the grounds that the abstractions would affect the flow of the Kennet, which is a valuable chalk stream, is located in an Area of Outstanding Natural Beauty and is a Site of Special Scientific Interest (SSSI). The Agency chose to use benefit assessment as its main case against Thames Water, adopting economic valuations recorded in a benefits manual prepared by the Foundation for Water Research (1997). No original study was carried out with respect to the Kennet. Since the issue was the effect of low flow on users and non-users, the relevant part of the FWR manual was that relating to studies of low-flow alleviation. In this case there was only one such study and it related to the River Darent in Kent (Willis and Garrod, 1995; Garrod and Willis, 1996). The Darent study was itself of interest because non-use values, that is the willingness to pay for flow improvement by individuals who did not visit the Darent at all, amounted to just under 90 per cent of the total benefits. The public expenditure part of the Darent low-flow alleviation was not fully authorized by government, even though they had received the Darent benefit assessment study which showed benefits greatly exceeding costs. Garrod and Willis (1996) speculate that failure to secure the full authorization arose from scepticism about the non-use value estimates in the Darent study. Despite this experience, the Environment Agency borrowed the Darent study estimates for both use and non-use values and applied them to the Kennet. The risks in such an exercise are considerable, and the problem was compounded by multiplying the individual non-use values per person by an arbitrary population defined as the population served by the Thames Water Company. The end result was that Thames Water's appeal against the Agency's original restriction on abstraction was upheld by the public inquiry. The inquiry inspector reduced the non-use value component of the Kennet benefits by 98 per cent to just £0.3 million compared to £13.2 million as estimated by the Agency. The adjustment reflected the reduction of the affected non-use population from the 7.5 million people in the Thames Water area to just 100,000.

For some, the Kennet decision was a serious blow to cost-benefit analysis. But an alternative view is that the Agency was pursuing a risky misuse of an analysis by borrowing figures from a manual which in turn had to rely on just one, albeit well-executed, study of a single river. Benefits transfer is controversial in its own right and few practitioners adopt it without reservations. Misusing benefits transfer is not a criticism of the analysis in itself. The proper course of action in the Kennet case should have been an original benefit assessment. But the controversy has focused attention on an important issue of how to define the relevant population for non-use values.

Conclusions

Cost-benefit analysis has gone through cycles of favour and disfavour in the UK. Currently, it is in favour. This may not be obvious from a casual inspection of government and regulatory agency activity, but it is clear that such analyses are multiplying and that they are exerting some influence. There are more studies and they are having more bearing on individual pieces of legislation than might be thought. But their role should not be exaggerated. There is a much smaller tradition of using cost-benefit analyses for regulatory appraisal and for damages settlements in Europe than there is in the US. In the UK, notable developments that are leading to a change in that situation are the development of formal regulatory appraisal for all new regulations, and the requirements upon the Environment Agency to use cost-benefit analysis. In mainland Europe, a similar stimulus has come from Article 130R of the Treaty on European Union (Pearce, 1998). If damage legislation was ever to develop in Europe, there would be further stimulus to benefit estimation. One area where benefit estimation could be expected to develop is in the public inquiry process. Surprisingly, few public inquiries are informed by benefit estimates, an issue that requires a separate explanation on some other occasion. Obstacles remain. Monetization is controversial. Much of the controversy is misplaced and reflects on poor understanding of what monetization is about, but some of it has substance and needs to be addressed. In some cases the obstacles can be overcome by improving the way in which cost-benefit analysis is presented and carried out. In other cases the ethical debate is to the fore and in many cases it raises many pertinent issues. Arguably, advocates of cost-benefit analysis have overstated their case, making it sound as if such an analysis substitutes for decision-making. It can, at best, inform decision-making and it is important that it does so since economic efficiency is all too easily forgotten in the political process. Finally, the issue is whether we have anything better as a decision aid. Here there has to be doubt. Cost-benefit analysis still seems 'the best game in town'.

4

Measuring Sustainable Development: Economic Approaches

Introduction

Chapter 2 introduced the concept of sustainable development and showed that it can be interpreted in various ways. Nonetheless, a consistent definition, first suggested in *Blueprint* 1, is that sustainable development is about increasing the per capita level of well-being over time. How that well-being is measured is open to debate, but we offer the further suggestion here that the focus should be on the conditions for achieving sustainable development, and that these conditions are not likely to change much however sustainable development is defined. In all cases, what matters is the capacity of coming generations to generate well-being from the resources that we leave them. It is hard to see how those resources will differ much in nature regardless of how sustainable development is defined. Of course, it is open to anyone to define sustainable development. Indeed, this probably accounts for the huge literature on the subject. We argue that our own approach is internally consistent – that is we have a theory of sustainable development. Chapter 2 showed how this theory revolved round the notions of different kinds of capital and technology. Armed with these concepts, we now show that it is possible to measure sustainable development. Probably the most important feature of any measure should be its ability to identify when an economy (a corporation, a city, an economic sector, a

Box 4.1 *Environmental Indicators and Sustainability Indicators*

Since *Blueprint 1* was published in 1989 vast efforts have been devoted to developing indicators of sustainable development, or so-called sustainability indicators. In reality, the great majority of these indicators are not indicators of sustainability, but environmental indicators which show trends in the environment and, sometimes, in social and economic conditions. Such indicators are often very valuable but they do not constitute measures of whether an economy is on or off a sustainable development path. For that to be the case they would first have to be rooted in some theoretical construct of what sustainable development is, and, second, would have to have some origin that is a point on the scale below which the economy is declared unsustainable, and above which it is sustainable. Very few of the environmental indicators so far developed meet these tests.

A good example is the set of indicators produced for the UK by an interdepartmental working group of UK ministries (Department of the Environment, 1996). Some 21 indicators are produced, beginning with economic indicators, sectoral trends, changes in natural resource endowments and changes in environmental quality. For example, sustainable development involves producing a healthy economy, so the indicator chosen is GDP per head. To capture a little of the demands that the economy places on the environment, it is noted that the structure of the economy has moved away from heavy industry towards lighter industry and services. So, the structural composition of GDP is also shown. Other economic indicators include savings ratios, consumers expenditure, the rate of inflation, employment and government borrowing. But by themselves, or even together, these indicators tell us little or nothing about future sustainability.

Just as troublesome are the sectoral indicators. Sustainable development requires an effective transport system but the challenge is to bring it into balance with its effects on the quality of life. The indicators chosen are passenger miles, number of short journeys, the cost of travelling (but excluding all social costs) and the amount of freight traffic. To find if these changes in transport use have affected the quality of life one would expect to see indicators of the quality of life, for example the number of households exposed to traffic noise. There is no indicator of noise nuisance. But there are indicators of air pollution from freight and passenger traffic. Even here, however, they show emissions rather than population exposure to air pollution.

One other example is expenditure on environmental pollution control. But this could go up because the environment is getting worse, or because it is already very clean and the (marginal) cost of making it cleaner still is very high. In the first case, it is a response to a bad state of affairs, and in the second case to a good state of affairs. Little can be inferred from such indicators.

The examples illustrate the problems of trying to use partial indicators on their own to measure an aggregate concept like sustainable development. If air pollution emissions go up, we can perhaps say that, on this one indicator, we are getting less sustainable or increasingly unsustainable. But if other emissions go down what would we then say? The information contained in the indicators data is immensely valuable, and some of it could be used to help construct a proper sustainability indicator. But it does not of itself tell us anything about sustainability. Much of the problem arises from not having any theory of sustainability, so that available data determine what is selected.

nation, the world as a whole) is on or off a sustainable development path. This important feature helps distinguish true sustainability indicators from the vast number of indicators which have evolved and which purport to be about sustainability, but which are not (Box 4.1).

Taking the theory of Chapter 3, this chapter explores various ways of constructing economic indicators of sustainable development. The three indicators chosen follow automatically from the discussion in Chapter 3:

- *Wealth* Chapter 3 suggested that an economy with rising stocks of capital assets was *prima facie* likely to be more sustainable than one with constant or declining levels of assets. By placing a money value on capital assets we can aggregate them to produce a measure of the stock of wealth, comprising man-made capital, human capital and environmental capital. Social capital presents another challenge, as we shall see;
- *Green national product* Chapter 2 noted that one of the driving forces for measuring environmental assets in monetary terms was the construction of a revised GNP measure. By estimating the depreciation on different types of assets, the estimates can be deducted from GNP to secure a modified 'green' GNP;
- *Genuine savings* We introduce a variant of the green GNP measure which we term genuine savings. As we shall see, this has the advantage that it has a point of origin below which economies can be said to be unsustainable and above which they are sustainable.

Measuring Wealth

Chapter 3 argued that an economy was potentially on a path of sustainable development if its stocks of capital assets were rising over time. Since population could well be rising at the same time, a better indicator of sustainability is that the per capita stocks of assets should be rising over time. The indicator, then, is:

$$W = (Km + Kn + Kh)/POP$$

where Km refers to man-made capital, Kn to natural capital, Kh to human capital and POP to population. W is overall wealth.

The only available measures of overall wealth come from work at the World Bank (Kunte et al, 1998). Table 4.1 shows the results for selected countries.

Table 4.1 reveals some surprises. The traditional history of economic growth theory has tended to suggest that a nation's wealth is very much dominated by its stock of man-made capital assets, such as roads and

Table 4.1 *Estimates of Overall Wealth for Selected Countries, US$000/capita*

Country	Total Wealth US$000	% due to Kh	% due to Kn	% due to Km
Haiti	13	76	8	16
India	20	70	7	22
Benin	25	76	8	16
China	37	77	7	16
Egypt	52	64	5	31
Peru	59	67	8	25
Indonesia	60	75	12	13
South Africa	83	75	5	20
Thailand	117	79	6	14
Malaysia	137	73	9	18
Saudi Arabia	171	40	42	18
UK	266	79	2	19
US	401	77	4	19

Source: Kunte et al, 1998

machinery. Yet the wealth data suggest that this type of capital accounts for only 10–30 per cent of overall wealth. Second, natural capital appears to be relatively unimportant except for those nations with significant energy reserves (for example Saudi Arabia and Indonesia). Third, the role played by human capital is dominant at about 70–80 per cent for most countries. In part some of these findings may reflect the way in which the estimates are derived (Box 4.2). But, otherwise, they tend to be consistent with the way that modern theories of economic growth have developed, with a focus on skills, technology and knowledge. The disparities in wealth tend to mirror those for income: the US has 30 times as much wealth per capita than Haiti, for example.

Can these estimates be used to measure sustainability? If the estimates are repeated for different years, and if the coverage is extended, then the answer is probably yes. As they stand, they tell us little about sustainability. Nor can we say that wealthier countries are more sustainable than less wealthy ones, although there are some reasons for thinking this might be the case. As an example, a country with more assets can withstand shocks and stresses better than one with few assets, so long as the stress or shock does not affect all assets at once. At the moment, the estimates are exploratory, providing a stimulus for others to improve the data on which they are based.

Modifying GNP

Probably the largest effort has gone into estimating a modified or green measure of national product. While there remain sometimes highly technical disputes about the best way of making these modifications,

Box 4.2 *Estimating Overall Wealth*

There are formidable problems in estimating wealth as shown in Table 4.1. The World Bank's procedures can be summarized as follows:

Mineral and energy reserves are estimated. They are then valued by looking at the net profits that could be achieved from those reserves. The net profit is basically the price obtained for the resource ex mine minus the costs of extraction, where costs include the depreciation on conventional capital used to extract the resource. The flow of net profits is reduced to a present value (see Chapter 2) and this is the value of the reserve.

Much the same procedure is used for timber, but if the resource is sustainable then the annual flow of profits is estimated to infinity (since the resource can be renewed for ever). Few of the world's resources are, however, sustainably harvested.

Crop and pasture land is also similarly treated. It yields a flow of revenues over time, revenues that should increase if there is evidence of productivity increases. Revenues are measured by using the world price of the crop. Costs are deducted to obtain profits (or rentals).

The approach to protected areas should be based on what people are willing to pay to protect them. But data problems make this difficult so the land is valued at its opportunity cost, that is at what it would obtain in some alternative use such as pasture land.

Km is based on what is known as a perpetual inventory model which enables flows of investment expenditures to be converted into values for individual man-made assets.

Kh, the largest item and the most difficult to estimate, is derived as a residual. The procedure is to calculate the following:

(a) add up the economic returns to labour in the agricultural sector, estimated as 45 per cent of the overall returns (agricultural GNP). This nets out the returns to land.
(b) Add non-agricultural GNP to (a)
(c) Deduct depreciation in (a) and (b)
(d) Deduct any rentals to minerals and energy reserves.

Steps (a) to (d) give an estimate of the overall returns to labour and man-made capital. Hence man-made capital should now be deducted, to give the return to human capital in GNP per annum. These annual returns are summed over the remaining life expectancy of the relevant population and discounted to give the present value of the future returns to *Kh*.

Data limitations are severe, but will be become less daunting as the research expands.

there is growing acceptance of the procedure outlined below. It is necessary to present the material algebraically but there is an intuitive explanation for each stage.

First, we define GNP as the sum of all the incomes in the economy. Those incomes are either spent on goods (consumed) or saved. Writing C for consumption and S for saving we have:

GNP = C + S

Net national product (NNP) is traditionally defined as GNP minus the depreciation on man-made assets K*m*. Essentially, this is the income left over after we put money to one side for the depreciation of assets. Note that failure to put this money to one side would one day mean finding, for example, that machinery has worn out and that there are no funds to replace it. This is a truly unsustainable position. So, we can also write:

NNP = GNP − *d*K*m*

where *d*K*m* is depreciation on man-made capital.
Putting the two equations together we have:

NNP = C + S − *d*K*m*

But there are other assets in the economy, the depreciation on which is ignored by this formula, namely the depreciation on K*h* and K*n*. Putting K*h* to one side for the moment, we can modify the above equation to be:

NNP* = C + S − *d*K*m* − *d*K*n*

where *d*K*n* is now the loss in value of natural assets. The * on NNP reminds us that we are now measuring a modified version of NNP.
Finally, we can investigate *d*K*n*. Suppose K*n* consists of two kinds of assets: non-renewable ones, like oil, and renewable ones, like fisheries or timber. For non-renewable resources each year there are discoveries D of new resources and there is an extraction rate Q. So, the net loss of these resources each year is given by:

Loss of non-renewables = Q − D

For renewables the same considerations hold but the discovery rate is replaced by the natural rate at which such resources grow (the biological growth rate, B) and the extraction rate is replaced by the harvesting rate H.

Loss of renewables = H − B

In each case we need to value these losses (and of course, the losses could be gains if, for example harvests are less than natural growth). We therefore multiply each of the net changes by the profit (more strictly, something called the rental which is measured by price minus the marginal cost of extraction. In economics, the rental is a measure of resource scarcity, hence its use as an indicator of depreciation) which is the price minus the cost of extraction (harvesting). Call this Rn for non-renewables, and Rr for renewables. Then the depreciation on natural resources is given by:

$$dKn = R_n(Q - D) + R_r(H - B)$$

Finally, we need to bear in mind that there is also pollution and this affects the environment too. We can treat this analogously with resources above by thinking of the environment as suffering from pollution due to emissions E but with the environment having some capacity to assimilate pollution A. Then the net change in the environment is given by E–A and we have to value that. The valuation is in fact the willingness of the population to pay to avoid that pollution WTP.

So, the overall depreciation on natural resources and the environment is given by:

$$dKn^* = R_n(Q - D) + R_r(H - B) + WTP(E–A)$$

The final equation looks a little daunting:

$$NNP^* = C + [S - dKm - dKn^*]$$

Or:

$$NNP^* = C + S - dKm - R_n(Q - D) - R_r(H - B) - WTP(E-A)$$

We have taken the trouble to spell the equation out because it will have another use in the next section. While it looks complicated we can rewrite it in words as follows:
Remembering that:

$$C+S = GNP$$

we have:

> NNP^* = GNP – depreciation on man-made capital – depreciation of natural resources and the environment.

The long version shows what kind of information we need to collect in order to estimate NNP^*, the green national product. A calculation of green national product for Costa Rica is given in Box 4.3.

Box 4.3 *Modified National Product for Costa Rica*

Solózarno et al (1991) used the procedures discussed in the main text to estimate a revised national product for Costa Rica. Costa Rica has three significant environmental problems: deforestation, soil erosion and overfishing. Remote sensing and geographical information systems were used to estimate the physical changes in forest cover and mangroves, and such systems were also used to estimate rates of soil erosion. Sampling of fisheries was used to estimate the relationship between biological yields of fish and rates of harvest.

For economic valuation the procedures were also sophisticated. For forests the procedure was to estimate the economic value of the change in standing timber for different types of timber. The relevant unit value that is applied to the timber is known as the stumpage value. Stumpage value is defined as the difference between the market price of the timber and the cost of harvesting, transport and milling (processing the tree into timber). Stumpage value can be thought of as the most that a timber concessionaire would be willing to pay for the right to harvest the trees. As the formula in the main text shows, if harvests exceed natural growth (and managed replanting), the forest is potentially unsustainable. Hence, the depreciation on the forest equals the change in the standing timber multiplied by the stumpage value.

Soil erosion was estimated using the universal soil loss equation which relates soil loss to topography, rainfall, soil management and erositivity. The resulting volume of eroded soil was converted to the units of fertilizer needed to offset that erosion, together with the labour costs that would be involved. Since fertilizer has a price, this gives an economic value of the erosion. While quite widely used, this procedure is somewhat doubtful, since it assumes that the value of erosion is measured by what it costs to compensate for it. But it may not be worthwhile to do this: the replacement costs may, for example, be higher than the actual crop losses.

Finally, fishery losses from overfishing were valued according to the market price of the fish minus the costs. Once again, the relevant depreciation of the fishery is measured by the difference between catch rates and biological regeneration rates.

The end results for 1988 are as follows:

Million colones (1984)	Minus dKn 21,163
GDP 207,816	forest depreciation 17, 890
Minus dKm 5,301	soil erosion 2,623
=NDP 202,515	overfishing 650
	= greenNDP 181,352

GDP is conventionally measured (GDP rather than GNP) but the difference is not important here). We get to net domestic product (NDP) by deducting depreciation on *Km*. Then we deduct the depreciation on *Kn*. Note that depreciation on *Kn* is considerably larger than the depreciation on *Km*. The end result is green net domestic product. The depreciation on *Kn* is some 10 per cent of the original GDP sum, revealing the magnitude of resource depreciation in Costa Rica. For 1970–89 annual depreciation varied between 3.5 and 10.2 per cent. Added up over the whole period, resource depreciation equalled one year's entire GDP.

Source: Solózarno et al, 1991

How useful is green national product? In *Blueprint* 1 we advocated the measurement of green national product but did not regard it as a high priority. There were several reasons for this and they remain valid today, ten years later. First and foremost, by itself green national product does not tell us whether we are sustainable or not. It fails the test introduced earlier of there being an origin, a point below which the indicator shows non-sustainability and a point above which the indicator says we are sustainable. But green national product measures do not tell us much about sustainability. The fact that, as is usually the case, green national product lies below conventionally measured national product does not mean the economy is unsustainable. It certainly points that way, because it is telling us that we are depreciating the asset base of the economy and we cannot do that for ever. But the linkage is not very explicit. A second reason derives from the exaggerated expectations that people had for green measures of GNP. Many argued that because GNP is so firmly embedded in our financial and economic reports, people have come to believe it is a good measure of economic performance and of changes in human well-being. If only we had a changed measure, then, people would start to change their minds and would pay as much attention to what is happening to the environment (dKn) as they would to the economy. We doubted this view and our doubts have been borne out. There is very little evidence that modified measures of NNP have led to any change. By and large this is because there is little in such measures to induce behavioural change.

Overall, then, green product measures ask the right questions and produce interesting results, but not so interesting that they are likely to induce behavioural change on the part of decision makers. At the time we wrote *Blueprint* 1, however, we had nothing to offer by way of an alternative. Since then we have found a simple modification of green product – genuine saving.

Genuine Saving

Genuine saving was first introduced in Pearce and Atkinson (1993). Today, the concept of genuine saving has been adopted by the World Bank, who have estimated it for over 100 countries.

The concept is easily explained because it has already been derived in the discussion on green national product. We repeat the basic equation for green net national product, which is:

$$NNP^* = C + [S - dKm - dKn^*]$$

We define the expression inside the square brackets as genuine saving. It is the amount that is saved in the economy, minus the depreciation on capital assets. Intuition tells us that if our economy is a firm, and the firm fails to put resources to one side (savings) at least equal to the depreciation on factory and machinery, then the day will come when the machinery needs replacing and there will be no funds to finance their replacement. The firm might borrow the money, but this is simply postponing the day when replacement is impossible, because the borrowing itself has to be repaid. A firm that fails to engage in this proper kind of saving activity is going to go bankrupt, or, to rephrase it, it is unsustainable. So it is for an economy – exactly the same logic applies.

This intuition also points the way towards a simple indicator of sustainability, namely:

$$Sg = S - dKm - dKn^*$$

where Sg means genuine savings. We can see that the indicator has been extracted from the basic equation for green national product, but the Sg measure overcomes one of the main problems with green national product: it has an origin. An economy that is potentially sustainable will have $Sg > 0$ and one that is potentially unsustainable will have $Sg < 0$. (In reality, there are some technical complications, but the basic rule is robust.)

Moreover, we can rank countries according to their genuine savings. The value of ranking is that it draws political attention to performance. No country wishes to have negative genuine savings, and countries with positive genuine savings rates will tend to prefer to be higher up the Sg index than lower down. Ostensibly, the modified national product measure could have done this, for example, by ranking countries according to the ratio of dKn to GNP, but the savings indicator appears to be powerful in this respect.

Two further changes need to be made to the genuine savings formula. We have focused on depreciation of two capital stocks, Km and Kn. What of human capital? It is of course possible to destroy knowledge – think of the loss of indigenous knowledge when ethnic groups are forced to migrate. But in general, Kh increases, it does not decrease. We therefore need to add the appreciation of human knowledge. One, admittedly simple, indicator for this is to add in the current expenditure on education. This makes the Sg measure:

$$Sg = S - dKm - dKn^* + aKh$$

where a is the rate of appreciation.

The second change is more of a tidying-up factor, and allows for the fact that many countries borrow abroad to finance domestic investment expenditure. An economy's gross saving is equal to its gross domestic investment minus any foreign borrowing, simply because it is financing some of the investment from foreign borrowing. Before computing genuine savings, then, we need to calculate gross savings where:

Gross domestic investment – net foreign borrowing = Gross savings

and

Gross savings – dKm – dKn = genuine savings

Table 4.2 shows the World bank's estimates of Sg for various regions of the world. The estimates are normalized by expressing each component as a percentage of GNP – the formula:

$$Sg = S - dKm - dKn*$$

Is rewritten:

$$Sg/GNP = S/GNP - dKm/GNP - dKn*/GNP$$

Recall that a negative Sg suggests unsustainability and a positive Sg suggests sustainability.

Table 4.2 *World Region Estimates of Genuine Savings (percentage of GNP)*

Region	Average 1970–79	Average 1980–89	1993
Sub-Saharan Africa	7.3	–3.2	–1.1
Latin America and Caribbean	10.4	5.5	6.1
East Asia and Pacific	15.1	18.6	21.3
Middle East/North Africa	–8.9	–8.8	–1.8
South Asia	7.2	7.6	6.4
OECD	15.7	15.7	13.9

Source: World Bank, 1997

Table 4.2 shows two regions with negative genuine savings: sub-Saharan Africa and the Middle East/North Africa. Africa tends to have low gross savings rates to begin with, but deducting depreciation pushes it into unsustainability, even allowing for investment in human capital through education. The Middle East picture is more complex. What happens here is that the outcome is heavily influenced by the fact that these countries have large oil reserves. Taking oil out of the ground constitutes depreciation. But, of course, sustainability is ensured if these revenues (rentals) are reinvested in other forms of capital. Table 4.2 suggests that at least some Middle East countries have consumed a large part of the proceeds of oil wealth rather than reinvesting it.

The genuine savings measure also has the capacity to surprise, as we showed in *Blueprint* 3 (Pearce, 1993). There the genuine savings indicator revealed that the UK was pursuing an unsustainable development path throughout most of the 1980s. A significant feature was the fact that revenues from North Sea oil were being consumed rather than reinvested. Air pollution damage also plays a significant role in creating unsustainability (Hamilton and Atkinson, 1996). While not unsustainable, a similar picture is revealed for the US where gross savings rates are low to begin with. The effect of deducting resource and environmental depreciation has been to make the US marginally sustainable (S*g* is just above zero).

Technological Change

A moment's reflection on the underlying theory of sustainable development reveals the neglect of an important feature in the development process: technological change. We argued in Chapter 3 that capital stocks (per head) should be rising over time to ensure sustainability. But each unit of capital could be made to work more productively through time. If so, we could even have declining capital stocks, but with increasing ability to generate well-being because each unit of capital stock is more productive. This rising productivity of capital stocks is a feature of technological change. Moreover, technological change will attach to Kh – that is, humans themselves become more productive; to Km – traditional capital becomes more productive; and even to Kn since a unit of oil or copper, for example, may become more productive.

Hamilton et al (1998) show that the Sg formula needs a further modification to allow for technological change:

$$\text{S}g = \text{S}g = \text{S} - d\text{K}m - d\text{K}n^* + a\text{K}h + \text{PV(T)}$$

Where the term PV(T) is the present value of future technological change, that is the flow of well-being from technological change all discounted back to the present. Clearly, what matters is the scale of this effect. Some authors have suggested that PV(T) is very large indeed. Weitzman and Löfgren (1997), for example, suggest that GNP in the US is understated by some 40 per cent because of the failure of the accounts to reflect future gains from technological change. If this is right, then making adjustments for dKn (perhaps of the order of 2–10 per cent of GNP) would appear to be a waste of time. The adjustments are swamped by the huge gains from technological change.

The academic argument continues and is fairly technical. But the literature is beginning to suggest that what matters is the nature of technological change. Is it exogenous or endogenous? Exogenous technical change falls like manna from heaven. No one has to do anything about it, it simply occurs. Endogenous change is embodied in the various forms of capital and comes about from explicit decisions within the economy. In this case, the creation of new technology uses scarce resources that could otherwise be employed elsewhere in production.

By and large, it would appear that if all technological change is exogenous, then PV(T) is potentially huge. If all technological change is endogenous, PV(T) tends towards zero. Hamilton et al (1998) suggest that, in practice, most technological change is endogenous and that a typical adjustment for PV(T) is about 3 per cent for an advanced economy. If so, the genuine saving calculation remains very relevant. Additionally, calculating PV(T) in the US is one thing, but it is far less clear that poor countries can expect such rates of change. Even in rich countries, it is as well to bear in mind that not all technological change is benevolent. Chlorofluorocarbons were hailed as a great technical breakthrough in the 1930s only to be the subject of a major international agreement to phase them out at the end of the 20th century because of their role in depleting the stratospheric ozone layer. Some might argue that genetic modification through biotechnology is going the same way.

Social Capital

There is one other form of capital that needs consideration in the discussion about sustainability: this is social capital. Putnam (1993) speaks of social capital as comprising certain features of social organisation – norms of behaviour, networks of interactions between people and between institutions, and trust between people. Empirical studies of economic growth have shown that conventional growth-accounting models (stressing labour, capital, technology) explain only a limited amount of the difference between growth rates in different economies. Studies of the Asian 'miracle' economies, before the recent crisis, suggested that institutional arrangements for cooperation and information exchange may be as, if not more, important than conventional factors. But close inter-personal and inter-institutional arrangements may not always be good for sustainable development. After all, price-fixing cartels are a form of social arrangement, as is the Mafia. This suggests that social capital may have positive and negative aspects.

On the positive side it is suggested that social capital contributes to economic development in the following ways:

- Flows of information between economic agents are better and higher if there are closer social relationships. Such flows may relate to anything from price information, information on the availability of materials or labour, through to information on the credit worthiness of individual agents;
- Trust reduces the need to search out information in order to make a transaction: that is transaction costs can be reduced. Trust may also result in behaviour which avoids the need to make laws and hence to intervene via government;
- Social links between individuals and organisations and government also reduce the need for overt public control. Governments may find it easier and more efficient to operate via established social links than to legislate. The rise of voluntary agreements as a means to control environmental problems may be a case in point. Polluters simply agree to self-regulate and, in turn, self-regulation will be all the more efficient if the polluters have social arrangements whereby they trust each other.

Also on the positive side, social capital contributes to environmental improvement by:

- Substituting for other forms of capital, especially man-made capital. Arrangements to share machinery (eg tractors, harvesters) mean that fewer tractors are needed;
- Reducing the high discount rates that often imperil the environment. This happens because individual insecurity is reduced by ganging together to fight particular causes and by spreading risks among the social group;
- Reducing external effects, – the spillover effects of one agent's actions on the well-being of another. Effectively, such behaviour is inhibited by the concern for neighbours and third parties arising from social norms of behaviour;
- Resolving the risks arising from common property. Common property involves a whole community owning and managing a resource, a situation that has risks of environmental destruction if the resulting communal management system breaks down. The stronger the social ties, the less likely the management system is to collapse;
- Inhibiting antisocial behaviour that damages the environment, whether it is simply the dumping of illicit waste, litter or perverse destruction of wildlife.

Social capital could have negative results by keeping contracts to those within the social circle, when those outside are more efficient. Examples include price-fixing, closed-contract award systems, and even the requirement that small firms institute some social welfare system to look after those in the social group, imposing costs that impair productivity. One might summarize these problems as the creation of rent by restrictive activity and through lobbying of government and others.

Can social capital be measured? Studies are in their infancy but there are promising directions. First, the breakdown of social capital will be revealed in various social indicators such as crime and violence, and perhaps the break-up of the family. Such negative indicators offer some scope for analysis. On the positive side, Foster et al (in press) conducted major surveys to elicit both the public's willingness to pay and the willingness to pay of voluntary sector users for voluntary sector services. The public were asked their willingness to pay to avoid the closure of voluntary sector activities on the hypothetical assumption that the charities had to close for lack of government support. The study revealed that, on average, the general public were willing to pay around 40 per cent more for the charities than they actually gave in donations. The total willingness to pay can be thought of as a measure of concern for others – a major dimension of social capital.

Social capital therefore presents a new and challenging dimension of sustainable development. It may, as some have argued, account for the dynamism of some economies and even for lower environmental damage than might otherwise occur. For those concerned with the breakdown of traditional social values, social sustainability indicators will also be important.

Weak and Strong Sustainability Again

All of the indicators in this chapter relate to weak sustainability, that is they all assume that there is some form of substitution between capital assets. Several criticisms have been advanced against this view of sustainability.

On the technical side, it has been observed that positive genuine savings do not necessarily indicate sustainability. Atkinson et al (1997) suggest that genuine saving is a one-sided test for (weak) sustainability. What is proposed is a more cautious test for unsustainable behaviour rather than sustainability *per se*. Even so, the empirical evidence that is emerging indicates many countries appear to fail this apparently simple test, as we observed above.

Martinez-Alier (1995), Victor et al (1996) and Cabeza-Gutés (1996) have pressed the case for indicators that effectively deny the range of substitution possibilities embodied in genuine savings. In other words, their critique is that weak sustainability is not strong sustainability. These are largely negative criticisms in that no actual alternative indicators are presented but perhaps serve to make the important point that genuine savings – or for that matter any single sustainability measure – is not exclusive as a means to evaluate progress towards sustainable development. Nonetheless, these critiques overlook the fact that strong sustainability is not a unique measure of sustainability either. Indeed, strong sustainability has to be supplemented with weak sustainability, since one cannot focus narrowly on improving just one capital asset if others are depreciating. Nor has empirical evidence been advanced to the effect that substitution is the wrong assumption. The problem for advocates of strong sustainability is that assertions of non-substitutability do not constitute evidence on non-substitutability. Those who criticize weak sustainability for assuming substitutability therefore commit at least a parallel fallacy in assuming non-substitution, much as we may sympathize with the emotional basis of strong sustainability.

Martinez-Alier (1995) notes that countries failing weak sustainability tests tend to be located in the developing world, although, as we have seen, developed countries can also fail the genuine savings test. Many developing countries are highly dependent on resource extraction activities and the depletion of these assets often means that high levels of savings need to be generated if aggregate real wealth is not to be run down. Given that these resources are often traded with developed countries, a frequent criticism is that this resource trade works to the disadvantage of poor countries. Put another way, rich countries can import their sustainability at the expense of the unsustainability of poor countries. The general argument appears to be about responsibility in that developed countries are to a large extent reliant on foreign resources to support their domestic economies. Indeed, several of these developed countries (eg the Netherlands and Germany) have expressed concern over their responsibility for resource depletion in other countries.

There is, in principle, nothing to stop any importing country assisting a developing country upon whose resource it is dependent in its efforts to avoid persistently non-negative genuine savings via, say, bilateral aid. Indeed, there are existing schemes to stabilize the export earnings of primary producers. However, the extended rationale would be to secure sustainability in these countries rather than to maintain security of supply. Presumably, any assistance, if forthcoming, would be targeted toward those low-income countries where the potential for saving out of income is severely restricted. In this respect, indicators of these dependencies would be useful.

Cabeza-Gutés (1996) has questioned the use of genuine savings where countries such as Japan and the US appear to pass this weak sustainability test. The popular perception is that these countries ought not to be sustainable. To some extent, however, there is little point in developing indicators simply to confirm preconceived views, although, as we noted, the US does not emerge from the genuine savings analysis as unconditionally sustainable, whilst the UK exhibited significantly negative genuine savings in the years 1980–86.

It is worth noting that the genuine savings indicator is able to capture a significant feature of pollution problems, namely transboundary pollution flows. The rationale for adjusting measures of national income, in the presence of transboundary effects, is an extension of the polluter-pays-principle to the domain of national accounting. This means that the estimates of the unit damage costs of pollution in a given country should include all costs, including those in other nations. The argument for this treatment of transboundary pollution in the case of savings rules is, if anything, even stronger. Some portion of a given country's total savings should, at least notionally, be set aside in order to compensate the recipients of the pollution emitted and transferred across international boundaries.

We suggest that a good part of the weak versus strong debate is misguided since weak sustainability is common to both approaches. Nonetheless, crucial issues remain. Perhaps we have reached a stage in human development when additional environmental depreciation does have such high costs that it constitutes *de facto* non-substitutability. This is what many ecologists have been saying for some time. But advocates of strong sustainability have been strongest in assertion and weakest in offering empirical substance for their views. That does not make them wrong, but it does suggest they have yet to be proved right.

The remaining challenge is to turn sustainability indicators, such as genuine savings, into *ex ante* decision-guiding measures. At the moment, most sustainability indicators have an *ex post* characteristic, that is they are useful in finding out whether a country, a sector, or a corporation has been sustainable or is currently sustainable. *Ex ante* indicators would enable a decision maker to look forward in time and answer questions such as: is this policy going to contribute to sustainability? Several suggestions can be made for this important policy research agenda.

First, all policy, whether it is aimed at environmental goals or not, must be appraised for its environmental impact. The environmental effects of policies are uncertain, difficult to quantify and even difficult to identify.

Second, the monetization of environmental impacts needs to be encouraged and broadened.

Third, in common with modern economic growth theory, work on sustainability indicators suggests that investment and technological change are key measures for sound and sustainable economic development. Investment in human capital clearly becomes a priority, but there has also now to be a stronger emphasis on investment in social capital as well. As far as the environment is concerned, the genuine savings approach clearly shows that it cannot be treated as a dispensable item in economic development policy. It is now clear that whole regions of the world – sub-Saharan Africa in particular – have impaired their development prospects by depleting natural capital.

5

Measuring Sustainable Development: Ecological Approaches

Introduction

Ecologists have proposed several indicators of sustainability. Unlike economic valuation approaches, ecological indicators are not concerned with measuring the impacts of environmental degradation on human welfare. Instead, they are generally used to measure either the overall state of the environment or the health of specific ecosystems. Such ecological approaches may be just as vital as economic valuation approaches for the design of sustainable development policies.

We focus on those ecological approaches that relate to the ability of the environment to sustain essential ecological resources and functions. These include various measures of ecosystem health, functioning and threshold limits, such as biological diversity indicators, estimates of species loss, carrying capacity, ecological footprints, and indicators of ecosystem stability, resilience and sustainability. As discussed in Chapter 2, since there may be limits on the ability of any economy to substitute human and physical capital for certain key resources and services of ecosystems, then ecological indicators may have an important role in providing information on those irreplaceable components of natural capital that may be critical to sustaining human welfare.

We start with the concept of biological diversity and the construction of biodiversity indicators.

Biodiversity indicators

Just as many economists consider measures of sustainable income to be important indicators of the welfare generated by economic systems, ecologists have generally agreed that an important indicator of the state or health of any natural environment is the degree of diversity that it contains. Biological diversity – or biodiversity for short – refers to the range of variation or differences in living organisms and their environments. The diversity of natural life can be distinguished by the three main levels of biological hierarchy: genes, species and ecosystems (UNEP, 1995; WCMC, 1992; Wilson, 1992).

According to Magurran (1988), there are three reasons why biological diversity has become a central focus of ecology:

- The spatial and temporal variation in diversity which intrigued early biologists and naturalists still holds the fascination of the modern ecologist;
- measures of diversity have come to be viewed as indicators of the well-being of ecological systems;
- considerable debate continues to surround the measurement and definition of biological diversity, despite the extensive range of indices and models that have been developed for measuring diversity.

To some extent, current scientific debate over the meaning and relevance of various indices and models of biological diversity reflects the various concerns and uncertainty over what declining biodiversity might mean for ecosystems. For example, to ecologists the loss of biological diversity is not simply a problem of the extinction of a few charismatic species, such as African rhinos, the spotted owl or the panda. There is also a concern about depleting the pool of 'wild' genetic material available for scientific, medical and educational research, as well as concern over the impacts of the declining diversity of natural ecosystems on their ability to provide life support functions and essential resources and services.

On the other hand, emphasizing the important ecological role of diversity at the genetic, species and ecosystem levels has made it very difficult for the scientific community to develop a consensus definition of biological diversity that can be made operational for policy purposes. Even though ecologists may agree that conservation of biological diversity is a good thing, it is not always obvious what policy objective should be pursued to achieve this goal. For example, the paramount goal of biodiversity conservation has been characterized by some ecologists as ensuring sufficient variation in the genetic make-up of species.

Alternatively, conservation of biological diversity has also been interpreted to mean reducing threats to species extinction and richness. Finally, at the broadest level, biodiversity conservation has been equated with the conservation of natural ecosystems and their components in the face of conversion and modification from human activities. For recent discussion of the various interpretations by ecologists and conservationists of biological diversity, see Ehrlich and Ehrlich (1992), McNeely et al (1990), Reid et al (1993), UNEP (1995), WCMC (1992), Weissenger (1990) and Wilson (1992). For a history of biodiversity loss as a scientific and historic concern, see Barbier et al (1994) and Wilson (1992).

Thus despite the increased scientific attention paid to biological diversity as an important indicator of ecological well-being, defining a single comprehensive indicator of biological diversity for policy purposes has remained an elusive goal. To many ecologists, the concept of biodiversity 'is like an optical illusion. The more it is looked at, the less clearly defined it appears to be and viewing it from different angles can lead to different perceptions of what is involved' (Magurran, 1988). Indeed, some scientists go so far as to dismiss the term as a non-concept (Hurlbert, 1971).

However, some ecologists and conservationists have argued that developing a single indicator of biodiversity is the wrong approach, as no one indicator can possibly convey to policy makers information on diversity simultaneously at the genetic, species and ecosystem level. Instead, recent efforts to provide a framework for assessing conditions and trends in biodiversity status focus on developing an appropriate set of multiple indicators for guiding policy decisions. Rather than attempting to provide a universal indicator of biodiversity status and trends, such approaches acknowledge that the difficulty in capturing a complex concept such as biodiversity in a single index suggests that indicators must become more policy specific. That is, a different indicator should be used depending on the stated objective of conservation policy.

For example, Reid et al (1993) argue that, if the conservation objective is to minimize species extinction, then a useful indicator would be changes in the number of species over time. Alternatively, if the objective is to minimize the loss of species diversity, then such an indicator is misleading as it says little about the distinctiveness of each species. As shown in Table 5.1, the authors suggest a set of 22 alternative indicators of biodiversity based on three categories:

• Indicators used to measure the diversity of wild species and genetic diversity;
• indicators used to measure diversity at the community/habitat level;
• indicators used to assess domesticated species (the diversity of crops and livestock).

Table 5.1 A *Multiple Set of Indicators for* Biodiversity *Conservation*

Indicator	Biodiversity conservation concerns		
	Genetic diversity	Species diversity	Community diversity
Wild species and genetic diversity			
1 Species richness (number, number per unit area, number per habitat type)	X	X	
2 Species threatened with extinction (number or per cent)	X	X	
3 Species threatened with extirpation (number or per cent)	X	X	
4 Endemic species (number or per cent)	X	X	
5 Endemic species threatened with extinction (number or per cent)	X	X	
6 Species risk index	X	X	
7 Species with stable or increasing populations (number or per cent)	X	X	
8 Species with decreasing populations (number or per cent)	X	X	
9 Threatened species in protected areas (number or per cent)			
10 Endemic species in protected areas (number or per cent)			
11 Threatened species in *ex situ* collections (number or per cent)			
12 Threatened species with viable *ex situ* populations (number or per cent)			
13 Species used by local residents (number or per cent)			
Community diversity			
14 Percentage of area dominated by non-domesticated species		X	X
15 Rate of change from dominance of non-domesticated species to domesticated species		X	X
16 Percentages of area dominated by non-domesticated species occurring in patches greater than 1,000km^2		X	X
17 Percentage of area in strictly protected status		X	X
Domesticated species diversity			
18 Accessions of crops and livestock in *ex situ* storage (number or per cent)	X		
19 Accessions of crops regenerated in the past decade (per cent)	X		
20 Crops (livestock) grown as a percentage of number 30 years before	X		
21 Varieties of crops (livestock) grown as a percentage of number 30 years before	X		
22 Coefficient of kinship or parentage of crops	X		

Source: Reid et al, 1993

With a comprehensive set of multiple indicators at their disposal, it is then up to policy makers and planners to choose the right indicator to help set priorities for biodiversity conservation. Moreover, the choice of indicators should also depend on the scale of the decision making, whether it is at the local, national or global level, as well as on whether genetic, species or community diversity is being assessed (Reid et al, 1993).

Developing multiple indicators to represent different priorities for biodiversity conservation may be one practical solution to the problem of the lack of scientific agreement over a precise definition and measurement of biological diversity. It may also have some merit in that, through their choice of indicators, different decision makers (eg non-governmental organisations, scientists and politicians) will reveal their respective opinions on what mattersin biodiversity conservation. Once revealed, such objectives and views can then be open to public debate, and hopefully, resolution into agreed and clearly stated priorities for conservation.

However, there are several criticisms of this approach. The danger of developing different indicators of diversity is that ultimately they may confuse conservation priorities by being based on inherently incomparable and inconsistent measures of biological diversity. As argued by Weitzman (1992 and 1995), we need to come up with 'a more-or-less consistent and usable measure of the value of diversity' – a 'value-of-diversity objective function' – in order to resolve real-world conservation choices. What is needed, then, is some idea of the value of diversity as opposed to the value of biological resources. If a value of diversity function can be meaningfully postulated, then it can, at least in principle, be made commensurate with other benefits and costs, and society will therefore be able to determine how much diversity ought to be preserved at the expense of sacrificing other choices open to us. An illustration of the approach suggested by Weitzman is shown in Box 5.1.

Nevertheless, a major stumbling block to constructing a value of diversity function is that such a function still presumes that it is possible to come up with a single biodiversity indicator. Development of an indicator for measuring diversity in itself implies not only consensus on what we mean by diversity and how it should be measured but also that we agree on what it is about biological diversity that we value. Even if we are close to consensus on measuring the diversity of any given collection of biological entities, we are far from agreement on what constitute the ecological and economic implications of having more, as opposed to less, biological diversity. Once again, we are confronted by the problem that the term biological diversity is used as a catch-all for distinctly different phenomena – genetic, species and ecosystem diversity. As both ecologists and economists have pointed out, analysis of the ecological and economic implications of biodiversity loss in terms of

---

Box 5.1 *Weitzman's Value of Diversity Function*

The economist Martin Weitzman (1992 and 1995) has argued that, if any biodiversity indicator is to be truly useful for policy purposes, then at some point it must be translated into a value of diversity function. Ideally, this function would show the increased benefits, or value, to society of an expected increase in diversity, as measured by a suitable biodiversity indicator. However, as the benefits of biodiversity are so difficult to quantify, the value of diversity function could instead reflect qualitative choices, or rankings, of different biodiversity conservation options as to the increase in expected diversity (or the avoidance of an expected loss in diversity), compared to the amount of conservation expenditure required by each option. If such a value of diversity function could be constructed, then it could, at least in principle, be made commensurate with other benefits and costs, and society would therefore be able to determine how much diversity ought to be preserved at the expense of sacrificing other choices.

Weitzman illustrates the correct use of a diversity indicator with the example of the operational criteria for determining preservation site priorities of the US Nature Conservancy. Its mandate is to purchase land in order to preserve rare or endangered species or natural communities, which are ranked by how rare they are as well as the number of site occurrences. These criteria are used in turn to determine an overall biodiversity ranking of sites and to prioritize the acquisition of sites. The resulting biodiversity ranking system gives a site a higher value if it contains more endangered species and/or if the survival probability of those species is more greatly improved when the site is preserved. According to Weitzman, the Nature Conservancy's ranking system corresponds roughly to identifying sites whose preservation would cause a relatively large change in expected diversity. Thus the expected diversity loss per preservation dollar among species can be compared. A similar approach has been developed by Polasky et al (1993) to compare the relative option values of conserving species.

---

one of these levels of biological hierarchy does not necessarily yield the same results at another level (Perrings et al, 1995).

However, even if we are concerned with diversity at only one level of biological hierarchy – say, species diversity – and we agree on a common measurement of diversity – say, the genetic difference among species – determining a value of species diversity may still have to be modified depending on the problem under consideration. That is, the diversity as measured by the genetic differences between species may have a different value to us depending on what we perceive to be the economic and ecological implications of species diversity for human welfare. This is demonstrated in Box 5.2 with the example of wild and domesticated grasses in rangeland systems.

To summarize, the current scientific debate about biological diversity indicators appears to be moving in two directions. Although there is a diverse range of indicators, biodiversity is still generally equated with species diversity. Even the development of multiple indicators of biodi-

---

Box 5.2 *What Value Diversity? The Example of Domesticated and Wild Grasses in Rangeland Systems*

Perrings et al (1995) use the following example of wild and domesticated grasses in rangeland systems to argue how different considerations of the ecological and economic roles of these species can determine whether increased species diversity is necessarily a good thing.

The wild and domesticated grasses found in rangeland systems are genetically different, but depending on which of their uses we consider, they can be viewed as either substitutes or complements – on the one hand, both grasses can be alternatively used as fodder staples, and on the other, they both work together to maintain the ecological functioning of rangeland systems and their overall resilience (the ability of such systems to maintain their functioning in response to externally imposed stresses and shocks). Because both wild and domesticated species have similar value in consumption as fodder, there is very little lost in the substitution of domesticated for wild grasses. If we consider the use of grasses for fodder only, then there may be little additional value to be gained from maintaining the diversity of grasses in rangelands. In contrast, both types of grasses are necessary for the maintenance of rangeland ecosystem functioning and resilience. As a consequence, in terms of maintaining diversity a mix of both grasses, is important. Focusing exclusively on the fodder value and not the ecological role of wild grasses can lead to the conclusion that diversity of grasses is not necessary in the rangeland system. Taking into account the ecological role will lead to the opposite conclusion.

---

versity tends to be dominated by indices at the species level (see Table 5.1). Economists who are interested in developing a diversity value function more appropriate for policy use tend to rely mainly on conventional species diversity measures as the basic biodiversity indicator used in such functions (see Box 5.1). In the next section we take a closer look at indicators of species richness and extinction as key ecological measures for use in sustainable development policy.

However, there are other economists and ecologists – those associated mainly with the ecological economics school (see Chapter 10) – who are less happy with the current state of biodiversity indicators. According to this view, not only do current indicators and assessments of biodiversity status tend to focus predominantly on species diversity but they also tend to emphasize only certain characteristics of species, such as their genetic properties, their relative abundance across sites, their endangered or threatened status, or whether they are wild or domesticated (eg see Table 5.1). Such characteristics by themselves tell us very little about the ecological role of biological diversity, that is the role of living organisms in underpinning the functioning and resilience of ecosystems. It is this role, and its implications for human economic activity and welfare, that must be analysed more closely if we are to be able to set more appropriate biodiversity conservation priorities, and of course sustainable development policies more generally. We return to this point of view in Chapter 10, and later in this chapter we examine the use of different concepts of ecological resilience and stability as important indicators of sustainability.

Species Richness and Extinction

Species diversity is usually defined as species richness, or the number of species in a site or habitat (WCMC, 1992). Moreover, although the loss of biological diversity may take many forms, the extinction of species is usually taken to represent its most dramatic and irreversible manifestation.

Conservationists, in particular, have almost invariably translated biodiversity conservation in terms of conserving species richness. This is usually based on the rationale either that species have a right to exist or that they have an actual or potential economic benefit to humankind (IUCN et al,1980 and 1991). However, conservationists have also been quick to point out that declines in species and genetic diversity are clearly interrelated. Continuing loss of species diversity – and certainly species extinction – implies a reduction in the overall pool of global genetic material as well, with profound significance for both natural evolutionary change and artificial selective breeding. Moreover, conservationists argue, the loss of both genetic and species diversity is mainly due to human activities. It occurs both directly through over-exploitation of species and sub-species via hunting, collection and persecution, and indirectly through the loss or modification of habitats and ecosystems. Conversion and alteration of habitats and ecosystems are by far the most important factors; consequently, conservationists have increasingly called for the preservation of species-rich habitats and ecosystems as the basic strategy for biodiversity conservation (Ehrlich and Ehrlich, 1981 and 1992; McNeely et al, 1990; Myers, 1979; WWF, 1989).

Some economists, too, have stated the need for habitat preservation to conserve endangered species. For example, more than forty years ago, Ciriacy-Wantrup (1952) argued that, as a result of species extinction, future societies may discover that they have forgone significant benefits. In order to avoid species extinction and the corresponding loss in benefits, then society today ought to preserve a minimum viable population of the species and its required supporting habitat. This approach was called the safe minimum standard strategy for avoiding extinction in day-to-day resource management decisions. Exceptions would occur only when the costs of avoiding extinction are 'intolerably large' or that other social objectives must take precedence (see also Bishop, 1993). However, as will be discussed further in Chapter 10, in practice any attempt to adopt meaningful policies based on such a strategy has floundered precisely on the problem of defining 'intolerably large'. This is not an easy issue to resolve, and it is not surprising that the widespread implementation of a safe minimum standard approach to avoiding species loss has been generally avoided, over concern that the costs of such a strategy in terms of the well-being of current human populations may be extremely high.

The modern conservationist argument for preserving habitats as means to protecting threatened species and valuable genetic material contained within them – often referred to as *in situ* conservation – has challenged the notion that the use of zoos, botanical gardens, breeding programmes, germplasm laboratories, gene or seed banks and other methods of maintaining species and genetic stocks away from their natural habitats is sufficient for this purpose. Increasingly, scientists have come to the same conclusion. For example, Weissinger (1990) stresses the importance of conservation through germplasm technologies in maintaining genetic diversity, but he also acknowledges that such methods cannot conserve the whole range of an organism's diversity; rather they preserve a sample of it. Moreover, this sample is necessarily incomplete. It represents only a portion of the population at the moment of its extraction. Similarly, in reviewing similar recent developments in major conservation efforts over recent years, Wilson (1992) maintains that they may save a few species beyond hope, but the major source of biodiversity conservation must come from preservation of natural ecosystems and habitats.

Thus it is not surprising that most biodiversity indicators focus predominantly on species loss – partly because of the limitations on data, partly because biodiversity has been traditionally equated with species diversity, and partly because much attention has been focused on species extinction as a barometer of the health of global biodiversity.

A recent and comprehensive compilation of global biodiversity status and trends has been undertaken by the Wildlife Conservation Monitoring Centre (WCMC, 1992). Following established tradition, the study quantifies rates of species extinction to provide the most straightforward indicator of biodiversity status. Historical data on actual extinction rates are most readily available for birds, mammals and molluscs (see Table 5.2). Documented island extinctions began almost two centuries before continental extinctions. However, for all animals, extinctions increased rapidly from the early- or mid-19th century until the mid-20th century. The apparent decline in extinctions since 1960 is most likely attributable to the increase in conservation efforts.

Estimating rates of loss for habitat and ecosystems is much more difficult, as ecosystems are not easily delineated and habitat alteration

Table 5.2 Historical Trends in Animal Extinctions

Period	Molluscs	Birds	Mammals	Other	Total
1600–59	0	6	0	2	8
(% on islands)		100		100	100
1660–1719	0	14	0	2	16
(% on islands)		100		100	100
1720–79	0	14	1	0	15
(% on islands)		100	100		100
1780–1839	0	11	3	5	19
(% on islands)		91	0	100	79
1840–99	69	27	12	9	117
(% on islands)	100	93	42	78	91
1900–59	79	35	15	46	175
(% on islands)	61	83	33	52	61
1960–	13	7	5	19	44
(% on islands)	69	71	60	37	54
No date	30	1	22	37	90
(% on islands)	83	100	91	73	81
Totals	191	115	58	120	484
(% on islands)	79	90	59	62	63

Source: WCMC, 1992

hard to define. Usually, fairly simplistic measures of land use change are employed. For example, the global expansion of land under crops, mainly at the expense of forests and woodlands, between 1700 and 1980 is shown in Table 5.3a. As indicated in Table 5.3b, the most rapid land use change is currently the conversion of forests in tropical regions. Preliminary estimates from the United Nations Food and Agricultural Organization (FAO) suggest that the annual area of tropical deforestation during the 1980s was approximately 170,000 km^2, or a rate of around 0.9 per cent of the total lost each year (FAO, 1991).

Tropical deforestation is considered a significant factor in global biodiversity loss because the vast majority of terrestrial species occur in tropical moist forests. As a result, most predictions of global extinction rates – as opposed to historical rates – are usually projected on the basis of estimates of species richness in tropical forests combined with actual and projected deforestation trends. Table 5.4 summarizes some of these recent estimates. As methods of estimation have improved, it appears that predictions of species loss have been revised downwards somewhat. Nevertheless, even the most conservative calculations would suggest a rate of species loss of 1 to 5 per cent per decade.

As noted in Table 5.4, and explained further in Box 5.3, most projections of species extinction are made using simple species-area relationships. However, Lugo et al (1993) suggest that estimations of

Table 5.3 *Historical Trends in Land Use*

A   Global Land Use, 1700–1980

	Area (10⁴ km²)					Change 1700–1980	
	1700	1850	1920	1950	1980	Percentage	Area (10⁶ km²)
Vegetation types	1700	1850	1920	1950	1980		
Forests and woodlands	6215	5965	5678	5389	5053	–18.7	11.62
Grasslands and pasture	6860	6837	6748	6780	6788	–1.0	0.72
Croplands	265	537	913	1170	1501	+466.4	12.36

B   Tropical Forest Area (10³ km²), pre-1650–1990

Region	Pre-1650	1650–1749	1750–1849	1850–1978	1980–1990
Central America	12–18	30	40	200	135
Latin America	12–18	100	170	637	695
Asia	640–974	176–216	596–606	1220	360
Africa	96–226	24–80	16–42	469	503

Note: Table A original source Richards, 1990; table B original source FAO (1991) for 1980–90 and Williams (1990) for all other periods.
Source: WCMC, 1992

species loss based on projections of deforestation through simplified species-area relationships are misleading. In particular, such models fail to take account of land use after forest clearing; they essentially assume that such uses involve little or no species diversity. Although substantial species loss occurs due to forest clearing and degradation, certain land management practices, such as the establishment of plantations and secondary forest, can restore a significant amount of species diversity. Thus the development of better indicators of global species loss will require further research on the relationships between species diversity and forest clearance.

Resilience as a Measure of the Sustainability of Ecosystems

Although species extinction is the most fundamental and irreversible manifestation of biodiversity loss, many ecologists believe that the more profound implication of such loss is for ecological functioning and resilience. As noted in Chapter 2, by ecological functioning, ecologists usually mean those basic processes of ecosystems, such as nutrient cycling, biological productivity, hydrology, and sedimentation, as well as the ability of ecosystems to support life. In turn, by ecological resilience,

Table 5.4 *Estimated Rates of Extinction Based on Tropical Deforestation*

Estimate	Percentage global loss per decade	Method of estimation	Reference
One million species between 1975 and 2000	4	Extrapolation of past exponentially increasing trend	Myers (1979)
15–20% of species between 1980 and 2000	8–11	Estimated species-area curve; forest loss based on global 2000 projections	Lovejoy (1980)
12% of plant species in neotropics; 15% of bird species in Amazon Basin	NA	Species curve $(z = 0.25)$	Simberloff (1986)
25% of species between 1985 and 2015	9	Loss of half the species in area likely to be deforested by 2015	Raven (1988)
5–15% of forest species by 2020	2–5	Species-area curve $(0.15 < z < 0.35)$; forest loss assumed twice rate projected for 1980–85	Reid and Miller (1989)
0.2–0.3% per year	2–3	Species-area curve (low z value); 1.8% forest loss per year	Ehrlich and Wilson (1991)
2–8% loss between 1990 and 2015	1–5	Species-area curve $(0.15 < z < 0.35)$; range includes current rate of forest loss and 50% increase	Reid (1992)

Source: WCMC, 1992

ecologists usually mean the capacity of an ecosystem to recover from and thus absorb external shocks and stresses, whether they be natural (eg drought, fire, earthquakes) or human-induced (eg pollution, biomass removal).

Most ecologists now believe that some minimal level of biological diversity is necessary to maintain ecological functioning and resilience, which in turn are necessary for generating the biological resources (eg trees, fish, wildlife and crops) and ecological services (eg watershed protection, climate stabilization and erosion control) on which economic activity and human welfare depend. Unfortunately, it is difficult to determine exactly what level of biodiversity loss is tolerable before the impacts on human welfare become severe, as the precise impacts of the loss of biodiversity in ecosystems are difficult to predict. Nevertheless, many ecologists would argue that the most important indicator of the inherent sustainability of an ecosystem is not its loss of biodiversity per se, but its capacity for resilience in the face of externally imposed

Box 5.3 *Using Species-area Curves to Project Species Extinctions*

The basic ecological models used to evaluate the relationship between extinction of species and deforestation rely on islands biogeography theory (eg see Table 5.4). Estimations are generally derived from an assumed species-area relationship. The typical relationships used is depicted in the equation where S is the number of species, A is the area of habitat and C is a parameter that depends on the type of species, its population density and the biogeographic region:

$$S = CA^Z$$

The shape of the species-area curve is determined by the exponential parameter Z, which is often referred to as the Z *factor* of the region or habitat. The following figure shows how different values for Z will affect the estimates of species loss attributed to deforestation, if the equation is used.

As the above relationships show, the higher the Z factor, the more species are lost as a given area of habitat is converted or degraded. Most regions of the world are characterized by Z factors of between 0.16 and 0.39. Islands tend to have Z factors of about 0.35, whereas comparable continental areas have Z factors of about 0.20. Z factors tend to increase as the area under consideration becomes smaller. Unfortunately, our understanding of factors that affect the value of Z is still incomplete. Nevertheless, as the above figure shows, for low values of Z (< 0.20), the equation predicts that more than 50 per cent of the land area can be deforested before the slope of the extinction curve rises rapidly with increasing deforestation. Conversely, at high values, (> 0.60), extinction rates are almost proportional to deforestation rates. Thus most estimates of species extinction are highly sensitive to the assumed value of the parameter Z (see Table 5.4).

Critics of this approach of using the equation above to estimate global species loss maintain that this method grossly exaggerates the extent of such loss. For example, Lugo et al (1993) demonstrate that limited bird and plant data for the island of Puerto Rico indicate that the equation over-estimates extinction rates even when Z values are extremely low (< 0.15). In particular, this approach fails to take into account land use after deforestation, as it implicitly assumes that land is biotically sterile after forest clearance. Furthermore, habitat diversity is not accounted for in the species-area relationship, except in the crude assumption that larger areas have more habitats. Finally, the equation is based on the analysis of a single species, whilst it may be more useful to look at assemblages of species in biodiversity loss.

To illustrate their points, the authors examine a case study from Puerto Rico where plantations have been established on degraded lands when agricultural activity is no longer possible due to poor soil productivity. Management practices that facilitate natural successional processes and the development of species-rich understories have enabled greater levels of biological diversity to prevail and may serve as refuges for threatened species, although efforts to reestablish forest land use activities are unable to offset the full, and often irreversible, losses of species diversity resulting from the original forest conversion.

Source: Lugo et al, 1993

stresses and shocks. For example, preliminary field experiments involving prairie grasslands have shown that each additional species lost from these ecosystems has a progressively greater impact on drought resistance (Tilman and Downing, 1994; Tilman et al, 1996).

However, as in the case of biodiversity indicators, agreement on how to measure the resilience of ecosystems is not unanimous. In particular, the resilience of a system has been interpreted in two very different ways in the ecological literature. Each view has, in turn, different implications as to how resilience should be measured.

As indicated in Box 5.4, the more traditional view focuses on resilience in the context of the efficiency of function. From this perspective, resilience can be equated more with ecological stability, and can essentially be measured by some key ecological indicator that reflects the resistance of the entire system or of a particular function of that system to an external disturbance. Underlying this view is the assumption that the natural state of most well-functioning ecosystems is some long-run or climax steady-state, and any external stress or shock will effectively disturb the system from this equilibrium. Alternatively, for specific biological populations or ecological functions that are subject to long-term patterns of growth or cyclical flux, the capacity of these populations or functions to return to their normal growth or flux patterns after a disturbance would be an indication of their ecological stability. Thus, the resilience or stability of a particular ecological function, a biological population or even the whole ecosystem to an external disturbance can be determined by measuring both the resistance to the deflection caused by the disturbance as well as the speed of recovery to pre-disturbance conditions (Beeby, 1993; May, 1974; Pimm, 1984 and 1991).

However, as described in Box 5.5, other ecological perspectives focus on resilience in the context of existence of function; that is, the amount of disturbance that can be sustained and absorbed before a change in system control or structure occurs (Holling, 1973 and 1986; Holling et al, 1995; Kay, 1991). In contrast to the traditional view of defining resilience in terms of an ecological steady state, this alternative perspective emphasizes the tendency of external disturbances to affect the long-term cycle of successional phases of an ecosystem, causing instabilities that can quickly flip the system into another regime of behaviour (Holling et al, 1995). In particular, this view suggests that there is no permanent or equilibrium state of an ecosystem, but a dynamic flux or cycle of ecological processes that control the functioning and structure of natural ecosystems. Although natural or internal perturbations within the ecosystem aid these long-term processes, external disturbances can cause them to fluctuate wildly and destructively. Thus a resilient ecosystem will be able to return to its normal dynamic

Box 5.4 *Ecosystem Resilience as 'Efficiency of Function' or 'Stability'*

The notion of ecological resilience as stability has been the traditional view in ecology for some time (Beeby, 1993; May, 1974; Pimm, 1984 and 1991). Essentially, stability means the ability of some key ecological indicator to resist an external disturbance and return to its original state. As noted by Beeby (op cit), the same principle can be applied to an individual, population, a community, an ecological process or function, or even to the entire ecosystem. Stability can also be classified according to the nature of the original state:

- Homeostasis: the capacity to return to an original steady state after disturbance
- Homeorhesis: the capacity to return to an original trajectory or rate of change after a disturbance.

The following figure illustrates the concept of ecological resilience as adjustment stability:

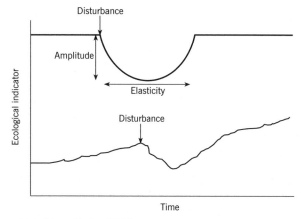

Source: adapted from Beeby, 1993

Resilience as Ecological Stability

The top half of the diagram shows how stability might apply to a key ecological indicator, such as a biological population, that is in a steady-state equilibrium over time. The fact that the population is constant may in turn be a reflection of the overall steady-state condition of the ecosystem The occurrence of an external event such as pollution disturbs the ecological equilibrium of the system, which causes the population to fall. After some time, the population may recover, thus indicating the ecosystem's return to its previous equilibrium state. As shown in the diagram, the resilience or adjustment stability of the system can be determined by measuring the maximum size or amplitude of the displacement to the ecological indicator caused by the disturbance, and by measuring the speed of recovery or elasticity of the indicator to its pre-disturbance equilibrium. The bottom half of the diagram shows that the same approach can be applied to an ecological indicator that is not in a steady state initially, but instead shows a normal, long-run pattern of fluctuation, cyclic behaviour, or in the example shown, growth.

processes of system control and functioning, but a fragile system will be unable to recover and thus be transformed permanently.

Some natural disturbances, such as events triggered by fire, wind and herbivores, are an inherent part of the internal dynamics of ecosystems and in many cases set the timing of successional cycles (Holling et al, 1995). Hence, these natural perturbations are part of ecosystem development and evolution, and seem to be crucial for ecosystem resilience and integrity (Costanza et al, 1993). If they are not allowed to enter the ecosystem, it will become even more vulnerable to external disturbances, and thereby even larger perturbations will be invited with the risk of massive and widespread destruction. For example, small fires in a forest ecosystem release nutrients stored in the trees and support a spurt of new growth without destroying all the old growth. Subsystems in the forest are affected but the forest remains. If small fires are blocked out from a forest ecosystem, forest biomass will build up to high levels and when the fire does come it will wipe out the whole forest. Such events may flip the system to a totally new system that will not generate the same level of ecological functions and services as before. This was the case in the recent management of the Yellowstone National Park in the US, which was severely destroyed by a fire that was allowed to burn naturally although the system had lost its own natural function of fire control.

Although intellectually appealing, it is very difficult to construct a policy-relevant indicator of ecological resilience based on the interpretation of the concept as put forward by Holling and others. Not surprisingly, this has led many ecologists to recommend a more traditional measure of resilience, such as the speed of recovery indicator suggested by Pimm, as a preferred indicator – even though the latter may be an oversimplification of what ecological resilience implies in terms of the sustainability of ecosystems. Still others suggest that, since there is a link between the biological diversity of an ecosystem and its resilience, then perhaps focusing on various biodiversity indicators remains the best way of measuring the overall health of an ecosystem, including its capacity to recover from external stresses and shocks.

Resilience and the Sustainability of Agro-ecosystems

Some ecologists have suggested that the concept of ecological resilience can be more usefully applied as an indicator of sustainability in the case of managed or human-modified ecosystems, such as agro-ecosystems. These latter systems are essentially ecosystems that have been deliberately modified or managed by humans in order to produce one or more outputs or products that have an economic value. Examples include agricultural systems, timber plantations and managed forestry systems,

Box 5.5 *Ecological Resilience as 'Existence of Function'*

Holling (1986) has described ecosystem behaviour as the dynamic sequential interaction between four system phases or sequences: exploitation, conservation, release and reorganisation. The first two phases are similar to ecological succession, which ecologists have traditionally defined as the development of ecosystems from colonization to mature or so-called climax stages (Odum, 1969). Exploitation is represented by those ecosystem processes that are responsible for rapid colonization of disturbed ecosystems during which the species capture easily accessible resources. Conservation occurs when the slow resource accumulation takes place in the ecosystem that builds and stores increasingly complex structures – the characteristic features of the climax stage of an ecosystem. Connectedness and stability in the ecosystem increase during the slow sequence from exploitation to conservation and a capital of nutrients and biomass is slowly accumulated. The next sequence is that of release or creative destruction. It takes place when the conservation phase has built elaborate and tightly bound structures that have become over-connected so that a rapid change can be triggered easily. The stored capital is then suddenly released and the tight organization is lost. The abrupt destruction is created

The Four Ecosystem Phases of the Natural Succession Cycle

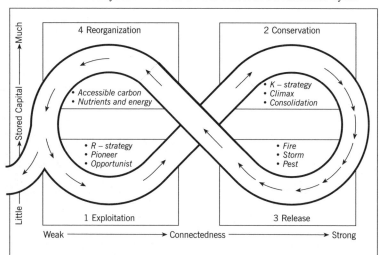

Notes: The arrows show the speed of flow in the ecosystem cycle, where arrows close to each other indicate a rapidly changing situation and arrows far from each other indicate a slowly changing situation. The cycle reflects changes in two attributes:
(i) the Y axis: the amount of accumulated biological capital' (nutrients, carbon) stored in the current system as it progresses through its phases and (ii) the X axis: the degree of connectedness among the various components of the biological capital
The exit from the cycle indicated at the left of the figure indicates the stage where, in response to an external disturbance, the system could flip into a different type of system, which could be more or less productive and organized than the previous one.

Source: Holling, 1986 and Holling et al, 1995

internally but caused by an external disturbance such as fire, disease, or grazing pressure. This process of change both destroys and releases opportunity for the fourth stage, reorganization, where released materials are mobilized to become available for the next exploitative phase.

The figure above, constructed by Holling, depicts the interrelationship between these four system phases, which describe the inherent succession cycle of a natural ecosystem. The stability and productivity of the system is determined by the slow exploitation and conservation sequence. Resilience, that is the system's capacity to recover after a perturbation (disturbance), is determined by the effectiveness of the last two system phases, which essentially should act as macro-regulatory functions in response to an external disturbance. Some natural disturbances, such as events triggered by fire, wind and herbivores, are an inherent part of the internal dynamics of ecosystems and may actually reinforce ecosystem resilience and integrity (Holling et al, 1995; Costanza et al, 1993). If they are not allowed to enter the ecosystem, it will become even more overconnected and thereby even larger perturbations will be invited with the risk of massive and widespread destruction. Human-induced disturbances, such as over-exploitation, degradation, pollution and habitat destruction, tend to undermine the resilience and integrity of an ecosystem, thus causing the system to flip or transform. This transformed system is likely to be less organized and productive, and hence less resilient, thus making it even more prone to de-stabilization in the face of further human-induced disturbances.

fish ponds and aquaculture, and livestock rangeland systems. As the structure and control processes of these systems have been deliberately modified to be productive in terms of an economically valued output or outputs, then the ability of these systems to recover from disturbances essentially amounts to their ability to sustain their levels of productivity in the face of such stresses and shocks.

This view of resilience, or sustainability, has been developed by Conway (1987) in examining the key properties of agricultural systems – or more appropriately agro-ecosystems. As noted, Conway suggests that the most valued feature or property of an agro-ecosystem is its productivity, or yield, the amount of valued output per unit of resource input. For example, productivity can be measured in purely physical terms, such as kilograms per hectare, or in monetary terms, such as gross or net crop income per hectare. Alternatively, both measures could be expressed in terms of an input other than land, such as kilograms of nitrogenous fertilizer or hours of employed labour.

The key to Conway's approach is the distinction between the sustainability of production in the agroecosystem and its stability.

Analogous to ecological resilience, sustainability is defined by Conway as the ability of an agro-ecosystem to maintain productivity when subject to an external stress or shock. Keeping in mind that agro-ecosystems function both as ecological systems influenced by natural processes, and as human-directed production systems influenced by economic and social processes, then agro-ecosystems may be subject to a range of possible stresses and shocks from ecological, economic and social sources. Thus, in this context, a stress could be defined as a regular, sometimes continuous but relatively small and predictable disturbance, and could include such diverse influences on an agro-ecosystem as the effect of salinity, toxicity, erosion, declining market demand or indebtedness. On the other hand, a shock would be an irregular, infrequent, relatively large and unpredictable disturbance, which could include a rare drought or flood, a new pest, or an unexpected rise in input prices (eg a doubling of labour costs due to a shortage of workers).

In contrast, Conway defines stability as the degree to which the productivity of an agro-ecosystem remains constant in the face of small, normal fluctuations and cycles in the surrounding environment. Such influences might include the expected changes in climatic or seasonal conditions, or fluctuations in the market demand for agricultural products.

Figure 5.1 illustrates the basic distinction between stability and sustainability. As both properties are defined in terms of impacts on the productivity of an agro-ecosystem over time, both are inherently measurable. For example, assume that productivity is measured in terms of kilograms of crop output per hectare. As shown in the figure, if an agro-ecosystem is highly sustainable, then after the initial impact of a long-term stress or short-term shock, the productivity of the system should recover fairly rapidly to its long-term trend over time. If the agro-ecosystem is unsustainable, then its productivity is unlikely to recover from a stress or shock, and thus yields will remain considerably lower than previously. In comparison, stability can be measured by the degree of short-term fluctuation in output per hectare in comparison to the long- run trend rate of productivity. Thus an agro-ecosystem with low stability will be prone to large fluctuations in short-term yields, whereas in a highly stable system short-term yields will hardly diverge from long-run productivity trends.

The final agro-ecosystem property of interest to Conway is equity, which he defines as the evenness of distribution of the product among the beneficiaries of an agro-ecosystem. Depending on the scale of the agro-ecosystem, the beneficiaries might be the farm household, village, or the whole population of a rural region or nation. Thus a high level of equity would suggest that the output of an agro-ecosystem is fairly evenly distributed among its beneficiaries, whereas in an inequitable system only a few beneficiaries gain from the output.

Conway has used these four properties to characterize different agro-ecosystems across the world. In particular, this approach has facilitated assessment of how agricultural and rural economic development

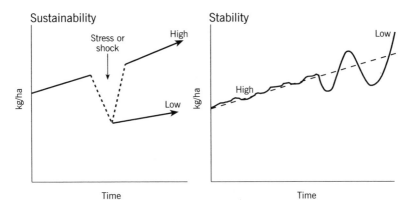

Source: Adapted from Conway, 1987; Conway and Barbier, 1990

Figure 5.1 *Conway's Distinction between Sustainability and Stability in an Agro-ecosystem*

may have affected the various trade-offs between, on the one hand, improved productivity of an agro-ecosystem, and on the other, declining stability, sustainability and equity. Such an assessment has been useful in explaining why the green revolution in developing countries may have been extremely successful in improving cereal yields on favourable agricultural lands and for farmers who are able to obtain the complementary input packages of high-yielding seed varieties, fertilizers and pesticides. It has been less successfully transferred onto marginal, rainfed lands which have poorer quality soils, erratic rainfall and often steeper slopes, and where poor farming households cannot afford the necessary inputs nor land improvement investments to improve their farming systems (Conway and Barbier, 1990; see also Box 5.6). As has been pointed out, the type of agricultural monoculture that results from green revolution technology is a highly vulnerable system with many similarities to a highly stressed natural ecosystem (Table 5.4).

Ecological Carrying Capacity

A long-standing concept in ecology has been the notion of carrying capacity, which can be generally defined as the maximum number (or density) of individuals of a species that an ecosystem will sustain (Beeby, 1993). The existence of a carrying capacity for every species suggests that no living population can grow forever. Competition between species for space, food and other resources imposes a natural limit on the number of individuals of a population that any ecosystem or habitat can support. Thus the availability of limited resources is dependent on the

Box 5.6 *The Four Agro-ecosystem Properties and Agricultural Development*

Conway has used his approach of characterizing agro-ecosystems into their four key properties of *productivity, sustainability, stability* and *equity* in order to compare and contrast the effects of green revolution intensive monoculture and other forms of agricultural development at the farming system level across developing regions, especially in Asia. In particular, Conway (1983) notes that it is possible to view agricultural development in Asia as a progression of changes in the relative values of these four agro-ecosystem properties. The table below is a summary of the four contrasting generic agro-ecosystems found in Asia.

Agricultural Development in Asia as a Function of
Agro-ecosystem Properties

	Productivity	Stability	Sustainability	Equity
Shifting cultivation	Low	Low	High	High
Traditional croppingsystem	Medium	Medium	High	Medium
Improved rice I (IR8)	High	Low	Low	Low
Improved rice II (IR36, IR42)	High	High	Low	Medium

Source: adapted from Conway, 1993

Shifting cultivation systems in Asia are characterized by low productivity and stability but generally display high sustainability and equity. Traditional sedentary cultivation systems such as the cultivation of a local rice variety followed by soybean tend to be more productive and stable and are still highly sustainable, although possibly less equitable. However, the introduction of rice monocultures in Asia has caused a major change in rice agro-ecosystems. The initial phase of the green revolution with the introduction of the first International Rice Research Institute high-yielding rice varieties, such as IR8 and similar hybrids, led to substantial improvements in productivity. However, yields fluctuated widely, and the sustainability of the monocultures have been affected by the growing problem of pest and disease attacks. Problems with equity of distribution were also severe. The more recent varieties such as IR36 and IR42 and similar hybrids combine high productivity with better stability, particularly in variable rainfall conditions, and thus more widespread distribution across rice farmers, but susceptibility to pest and disease remains a persistent problem (Conway and Barbier, 1990).

number or density of a biological population, and in turn, these density-dependent factors will restrict the population to the carrying capacity limit of its natural environment.

The concept of carrying capacity, or a maximum size of a population, is widely used to determine growth rates for individual populations and communities in ecological models of population dynamics and in economic models of biological-resource harvesting (May, 1981; Clark, 1976). These models in turn have led to a greater understanding of the ecological and economic conditions influencing the exploitation of biological populations, predator-prey relationships, habitat-resource interactions, and so forth. However, carrying capacity has also been used more directly by ecologists as a means to influence conservation policy objectives. These approaches range from employing carrying capacity in a more conventional way as a means to selecting key natural habitats and wild areas for preservation, or alternatively expanding the concept to look at the resource demands and total ecological impacts of human populations. We have already seen how the concept of species diversity can be translated into an indicator for environmental policy, for example by being used as the basis for selecting preservation sites (see Box 5.1). Carrying capacity has been used in a similar way to determine habitat conservation priorities.

If carrying capacity reflects the natural limit to a species, then it should also represent the minimum natural habitat required by a species in order to guarantee its survival. Thus, estimating the habitat requirements of an endangered or threatened species through some measure of carrying capacity may be an important indicator in deciding priorities for the establishment of nature reserves, preservation areas and other species conservation goals. This may be particularly useful where the threatened species or groups of species are associated with a unique and clearly identifiable natural habitat.

As noted by Beeby (1993), devising habitat indicators based on carrying capacity has had an instrumental role in influencing the choice of wetland preservation sites for bird species in North America and Europe. Prioritizing wetlands habitat through estimating carrying capacity of key wetland species is a prominent feature of the habitat evaluation procedure developed by the US Fish and Wildlife Service. The first step in the procedure is to group various species into guilds, which consists of those species with more or less the same resource requirements and roughly the same role in wider community. For example, one guild may include all nectar-feeding insects; however, nectar and fruit-feeding large birds would comprise a separate guild. For each guild, a representative or indicator species is chosen, and for that species, measures of habitat area are used in conjunction with a habitat suitability index to determine an estimate of the carrying capacity. The evaluation procedure not only facilitates the selection of critical wetland habitats for preservation, but can also be used as an indicator of the effect of various possible human impacts in terms of the likely reductions in carrying capacity, and thus key species habitats.

Perhaps the most ambitious attempt to develop the ecological concept of carrying capacity as a major policy indicator was the study by the FAO to determine the human population carrying capacity of land and food resources across 117 developing nations (FAO, 1984). The basic biophysical data for the study consisted of the detailed FAO soil maps, classifying the world by soil, terrain and bedrock formation, combined with agroclimatic data from the FAO Agroecological Zone Project, which classifies the world by rainfall, radiation, temperature, length of growing period and other critical agroclimatic data. Based on these maps, the study was able to determine the particular food crop that would provide the greatest amount of protein and calories for each land/climate unit, thus yielding a rough estimate of the maximum food producing capability of each developing country. The theoretical carrying capacity of each country was then calculated by dividing each nation's total potential calorie production by the FAO's minimum daily calorie requirement per capita, thus estimating the number of people that the country could hypothetically support. This potential population-supporting capacity was then divided by the actual 1975 population of each country and the projected population in 2000.

Although the overall results were encouraging – the developing world appears to be able to support twice its 1975 population even at low-input levels – the country-by-country results were less optimistic. At the 1975 low-input level, 55 countries were considered critical (ie showed a carrying capacity ratio of 1:1 or less), whereas 64 countries were projected to be critical by 2000, including the entire region of South-West Asia.

The FAO study has been followed in recent years by a variety of similar assessments of potential global food security that use further work and data from the Agroecological Zone Project combined with recent UN population and food demand projections (Penning de Vries et al, 1997; Sivakumar and Valentin, 1997). Although the term 'carrying capacity' is not explicitly used by these assessments, the basis of the methodology is essentially the same as before, which is to use available biophysical and agroecological data for different global zones to estimate the amount of plant biomass required to feed the future populations in major regions of the world, and to compare the results with the amount of food that could be produced sustainably from an agroecological and technical perspective. The results for developing countries are similar to those achieved by the previous FAO study. Although the food producing carrying capacity is still ample in Central and South America, Central Africa and Oceania, throughout much of Asia the ratio of potential food supply to projected food demand is likely to be critical (Penning de Vries, op cit).

Although carrying-capacity studies of these kinds provide potentially useful indicators for projecting global and regional food supply, such studies in themselves are not sufficient to predict global food prospects accurately, as they ignore the ability of various populations to import and export food and to adopt new technologies for crop improvements. A recent analysis of the global food situation conducted by the International Food Policy Research Institute (IFPRI) has concluded that, during the next 25 years, the world will produce enough food to meet the demand of people who can afford to buy it, and real food prices will continue to decline (Pinstrup-Andersen et al, 1997). In contrast to the carrying-capacity studies, the IFPRI projections suggest that food security within the rapidly growing Asian countries should not be a major problem, as these countries should have sufficient foreign currency reserves to finance their growing food gap – the difference between domestic production and demand for food. Instead the main concern is with many low-income countries, including sub-Saharan Africa, which may not be able to generate the necessary foreign exchange to purchase all their food needs on the world market. In addition, many poor people within these countries will not be able to afford food purchases to meet their subsistence needs.

Despite the obvious limitations of carrying-capacity concepts as a guide to policy making, they continue to be explored in the ecological literature. For example, some ecologists have argued that the true ecological carrying capacity required to support human populations is not simply the land and agroecological resources needed to meet food demand. Because human populations live in advanced economic systems that employ sophisticated technological means to generate a variety of production processes and commodities, and thus require abundant resources and produce substantial waste products, the total ecological impact of modern-day human livelihoods is substantial. Thus these ecologists maintain that actual human carrying capacity:

> '*must be interpreted as the maximum rate of resource consumption and waste discharge that can be sustained indefinitely without progressively impairing the functional integrity and productivity of relevant ecosystems* wherever the latter might be.' (*Rees and Wackernagel*, 1994)

Although directly measuring human carrying capacity is extremely difficult, recent efforts have focused on providing an approximate indicator by estimating the ecological footprint associated with major consumption activities (see Box 5.7). The basic approach is to determine the equivalent land area required to sustain the current consumption of key commodities by a population of a given region. As indicated in the Box, recent estimates of the ecological footprint of food, energy and forest

Box 5.7 *Total Ecological Impact and Ecological Footprint*

The concept of an ecological footprint is concerned with determining how much productive land and water area in various ecosystems is required to support a region's human population indefinitely at current consumption levels. This approach essentially inverts traditional carrying-capacity measures that are concerned with the maximum size of population that a given ecological region can sustain indefinitely.

Related to the ecological footprint concept is the notion of total ecological impact – the total human impact on ecosystems of the resource degradation and pollution caused by human production and consumption activities. Usually, ecologists have devised fairly straightforward measures of total ecological impact. For example, Hardin (1991) has suggested the following formula:

Total human impact on the ecosphere = (population) x (per-capita impact)

Similarly, it has been suggested that human ecological impact is the product of population, affluence (per-capita consumption levels) and population (Ehrlich and Holdren, 1971; Holdren and Ehrlich, 1974):

Total human impact on the ecosphere = (population) x (per-capita consumption) x (technology)

The problem with such formulae is that some of the key variables (eg per-capita impact and technology) are difficult to determine and are open to subjective interpretation, and the impacts associated with the resource demands and waste generation may vary across every type of human production and consumption activity.

The ecological footprint approach attempts to overcome this problem by determining the effective land requirements of several major types of commodities for a given human population, and then aggregating these land requirements to determine the total area required to maintain any given population. The major commodities that are generally investigated through this approach are food, energy, forest products and specific waste by-products. Typically, such ecological footprint calculations show that populations in developed regions of the world, plus urban populations more generally, consume much more land (and hence ecological resources) than that contained within the actual geographical area that the population inhabits.

For example, Rees (1992) and Rees and Wackernagel (1994) have calculated the total forested and arable land requirements for the current population of the Vancouver-Lower Fraser Valley region of British Columbia, Canada, in terms of consumption of domestic food, forest products and fossil energy. To support just their food and fossil fuel consumption, the authors estimate that the region's population of 1.7 million requires 8.7 million hectares of land. An additional 0.85 million hectares is required to sustain the population's forest product consumption. As the total area of the region is only about 400,000 hectares, the ecological footprint of the population living in this region is at least 22 times the actual area that they occupy. The authors report similar findings for other developed regions. For example, the Netherlands is estimated to have an ecological footprint that is 14 times its geographical area – approximately 11 million hectares for food and forestry products and 36 million hectares for fossil fuel.

product consumption of the population of the Vancouver–Lower Valley Region of British Columbia, Canada, suggest that the region effectively imports a productive carrying capacity for these products that is 22 times that of the actual area inhabited by the population. For the Netherlands, the ecological footprint for these same commodities is 14 times the size of the country (Rees, 1992; Rees and Wackernagel, 1994).

In general, most ecological footprint studies have reached similar conclusions, namely that populations in developed regions and urban-based populations consume much more land, and thus have a greater ecological impact, than the actual area that they inhabit. Effectively, this means that such populations import much more carrying capacity than they currently occupy, which suggests that the ecological impact of their production and consumption activities are substantial.

However, it is unclear what additional contribution the ecological footprint literature is making to our overall understanding of sustainable development. At most, the approaches advocated simply account for the amount of resource use occurring in a given location. If this leads to a policy recommendation that resource use per person is too high and therefore must be lowered, it is unclear what is new in such an approach. Unlike other ecological approaches, the ecological footprint literature appears to offer no insights into the key sustainability issues that we must resolve, such as the role of natural capital in sustaining economic and ecological systems and the degree to which such environmental goods and services can be substituted for by other economic assets, such as human and physical capital.

Conclusions

Ecologists have developed several important indicators to reflect the ability of natural and human modified ecosystems to sustain human activity. Given the important role that many ecologists ascribe to biodiversity in maintaining the functioning and integrity of ecological systems, it is not surprising that much work has focused recently on measures of species diversity and richness as key indicators of ecological health.

Another important contribution of ecology has been to improve our understanding of the ability of ecosystems to recover from external disturbances, especially human-induced impacts such as pollution, resource exploitation and environmental degradation. Thus the ecological notions of stability and resilience are probably the closest ecologists come to devising an ecological concept of sustainability. Despite some disagreement over these concepts in the ecological literature, some economists and ecologists have found the notion of ecological thresholds, stability and resilience to be extremely useful in analysing the ecological sustainability of various economic activities (see Chapter 10).

As noted in this chapter, this concept can be applied both to natural systems, such as pristine old-growth forests, and human-modified production systems, such as agricultural systems.

Finally, ecologists have also suggested different interpretations of the concept of carrying capacity as a means to determining the ecological sustainability of human population and activities. Indicators based on carrying capacity are routinely used as a guide for prioritizing habitat sites and natural areas for conservation. However, as discussed in this chapter, such approaches remain crude instruments for policy, as they routinely ignore the benefits and costs associated with conservation. Although it is claimed that the concept of carrying capacity can also been developed more directly into ecological sustainability indicators – such as total resource demands of human populations and their ecological footprints in terms of total land requirements to support current production and consumption activities – such indicators shed very little light on the actual value of ecosystem goods and services and thus have very limited relevance to practical policy making.

Ecological approaches concerned with biodiversity, ecological functioning and resilience, and carrying capacity in a general ecological sense will continue to have an important influence on sustainable development thinking. Overall, such approaches are concerned with assessing humankind's impact on ecological systems. To the extent that economic analysis of sustainable development is also concerned with such impacts, then it is important that economists are aware of the contribution of ecological approaches to sustainability. Some of these approaches may also help in resolving the issue, discussed in Chapter 2,

Table 5.5 *Similarities between Intensive Monocultures and Stressed Ecosystems*

High dependence on extra energy
Short residence time of energy
Increase in exported or unused primary production
Increase in nutrient turnover
Increase in nutrient loss
Decrease in resource-use efficiency
Increase in growth-species
Increase in parasitism, diseases and other negative interactions
Increase in horizontal one-way transport
Decrease in vertical cycling
Few, simple, rapid, open (leaky) cycles
Shortening of food-chains
Network with low average mutual information
Simple structures with few hierarchical levels
Low complexity, low diversity, low system efficiency
Throughput-based systems due to reduced internal cycling

Source: Odum, 1985; Folke and Kautsky, 1992

of whether some forms of natural capital are essential to overall ecosystem functioning and thus human livelihoods and well-being. Others may form the basis for new ecological economic approaches to complex environmental problems, such as assessing the welfare implications of biodiversity loss, which may require the combined analysis of economics, ecology and other disciplines. We happen to disagree with this latter view, but this is an important issue which we return to in Chapter 10.

6

The Causes of Environmental Degradation

Introduction

Much of the current literature concerned with global environmental degradation attributes the source of the problem to one or more principal causes: economic growth, population change and, in the case of developing countries, poverty. For example, it is claimed that economic growth contributes substantially to environmental loss because current patterns of global economic development are currently unsustainable – economies expand by excessively degrading and depleting the natural capital provided by the environment. This increased demand for the conversion and depletion of natural capital is further fuelled by rising populations; that is, the more people there are in the world the more pressures are put on the natural resource base to sustain them. Finally, widespread global poverty is also thought to be a major cause of environmental degradation because poor people are often caught in a cycle that forces them to deplete and degrade natural resources, because their subsistence livelihoods are dependent on such exploitation.

Although these popular perceptions of growth, population change and poverty as the main causes of global environmental degradation contain some elements of truth, in the following chapter we argue that such explanations are somewhat incomplete and simplistic. What is more, they can lead to equally simplistic – and potentially dangerous – policy prescriptions.

For example, proponents of the view that economic growth is the principal cause of environmental degradation often argue that the solution to this problem must be lower rates of global economic growth, and even zero growth. We addressed this debate in Chapter 2. Equally, if rising populations pose a threat to the global environment in the coming decades, then it is often suggested that very stringent population-control policies must be implemented immediately, especially in the poorest and populous countries of the world with rapidly expanding populations. Finally, if the poorest of the poor in developing economies are caught in a poverty-environment trap, then raising the income and wealth of these households must surely be the quickest way of both freeing them from such a trap and saving the remaining natural environments of the developing world.

In this chapter we take the view that this debate misses an important point: it fails to look beyond the apparent causes of environmental degradation to examine the true underlying or contributing factors behind many environmental problems.

In the previous chapters we have already discussed two of these key factors behind environmental degradation and unsustainable development: the failure to assess properly the true economic value of the many goods and services provided by natural capital, and equally, the failure to account properly for the economic consequences of natural-capital depletion and degradation. We now focus on a third underlying factor, namely the failure of institutions, markets and government policies to provide adequate incentives and investments for efficient and sustainable management of natural capital.

Market, Institutional and Government Failures

Market failure exists when markets fail to fully reflect environmental values. The presence of open access resource exploitation, public environmental goods, externalities, incomplete information and markets, and imperfect competition all contribute to market failure. Usually some form of corrective public or collective action, involving regulation, incentives or institutional measures, is required – provided that the costs of such measures do not exceed the potential benefits.

Institutional failure arises through the lack of appropriate social institutions, or where existing institutions are inadequate or ineffective. Often in environmental mismanagement, institutional and market failures will overlap. For example, the failure to establish and enforce clearly defined rights of access, tenure and control over productive resources is clearly related to the market failure of open access resource management. Institutional failures contributing to environmental damage can be wide-ranging, and include political failings such as a lack of participatory mechanisms and public accountability, or public servants seeking to exploit commercial opportunities for their own financial gain. Inefficient bureaucratic procedures and conflicting or mismatched responsibilities can also have important effects on the use of natural resources. A major structural failure in existing institutions is the definition of institutional authority along sectoral or geographic lines that do not correspond to the range and types of environmental problems. Many countries distribute responsibility for environmental affairs among a number of public agencies, creating serious problems of coordination. Examples may include a lack of policy coordination between agricultural and environmental departments over pesticides or fertilizer policy, or conflicting local government policies on the management of resources straddling administrative boundaries.

Government or policy failure occurs when the public policies required to correct for market and institutional failures over- or under-correct for the problem. They also occur when government decisions or policies – in areas where there are no market failures – are themselves responsible for excessive environmental degradation. For example, environmental damage may arise from policies designed to promote economic growth or to improve income distribution, due to inadequate attention to their impact on the environment. The potential for governmental failure is considerable, given the myriad ways in which policies can influence economic and political outcomes, which in turn have both intended and unintended environmental impacts. Figure 6.1 illustrates this by showing some examples of how a vast range of macroeconomic and sectoral policies can potentially affect environmental management.

Market, institutional and policy failures all lead to a distortion of economic incentives. That is, the private costs of activities which result in environmental degradation do not reflect the full social cost of that damage, in terms of environmental values forgone. The failure to take full account of these social costs may result in excessive levels of environmental degradation. To indicate how fundamental this is to many environmental management problems, we now turn to a number of key examples illustrating the links between non-environmental policies and impacts on the environment.

Economic Growth and the Environment: the EKC Debate Revisited

In Chapter 2 we suggested that the recent literature on the environmental Kuznets curve (EKC) produces very little evidence in support of the view that countries ought to be able to grow out of their major environmental

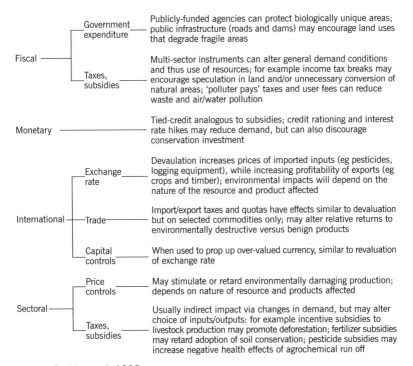

Source: Barbier et al, 1992

Figure 6.1 *Economic Policies and Environmental Management*

problems. For most indicators of environmental degradation, the turning point level of per-capita income at which the EKC peaks is well above the current level of per-capita income for most economies in the world. For example, as shown in Figure 2.2, the turning point in the EKC for sulphur dioxide is just under US$5000 per capita, which is much higher than the current average income per capita of the vast majority of developing economies, newly industrializing countries and economies in transition.

The implication of these findings is that for a variety of global environmental problems, degradation will continue to worsen as the world economy expands. As shown in Box 6.1, Stern et al (1996) take the EKC relationship for sulphur dioxide depicted in Figure 2.2 and use estimations of future economic and population growth across countries to project global levels of sulphur dioxide into the next century. This and similar projections for other environmental indicators suggest that environmental damage is likely to increase, rather than decline, as the world economies and population continue to grow.

However, one should be careful not to interpret such projections as providing support for the view that economic growth is inherently bad

---

Box **6.1** *Projecting Environmental Kuznets Curve Relationships*

The fact that turning-point levels of income estimated for most EKC curves are generally high, and that the current global distribution of income is far from normal, suggests that most countries have not yet reached levels of per-capita income for which environmental improvement is likely to occur (Barbier, 1997). The implications are a worsening global problem of environmental degradation as the world economy and populations expand, even for those environmental indicators that display EKC relationships.

Stern et al (1996) illustrate this with the sulphur dioxide–EKC relationship estimated by Panayotou (1995), based on aggregation of individual country projections of future economic and population growth. The resulting projections

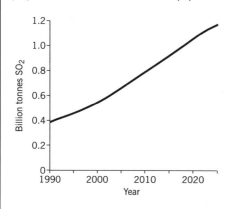

in the diagram below indicate that global levels of sulphur dioxide will continue to rise well into the next century. For example, global emissions of sulphur dioxide rise from 383 million tonnes in 1990 to 1,181 million tonnes in 2025, or from 73 to 142 kg per capita.

Stern et al (1996) also project deforestation rates based on a similar EKC estimate by Panayotou (1995) for this environmental indicator. The projection indicates that global forest cover declines from 40.4 million sq km in 1990 to a minimum of 37.2 million sq km in 2016, and then increases slightly to 37.6 million sq km in 2025; however, tropical forests decline from 18.4 to 9.7 million sq km over this period. Selden and Song (1994) conduct similar projections for the four air pollutants for which they estimate an EKC relationship: sulphur dioxide, solid particulate matter (SPM), nitrogen dioxides and carbon monoxide. Their results show world emissions increasing for all four pollutants through 2025, and for SPM and nitrogen dioxides, emissions rise through 2050.

---

for the environment. Recent evidence from the EKC literature suggests that relationships between various environmental indicators and the level of per-capita income are not fixed indefinitely but in fact are highly influenced by both structural economic conditions and policy interventions. Briefly, the findings of this literature are as follows.

The Role of Structural Economic Change

Several recent papers have sought to examine the structural economic factors that might underlie EKC relationships. For example, Komen et al

(1997) find that in 19 OECD countries over the 1980–94 period, for every 1 per cent increase in national income in these countries, public research and development funding for environmental protection also increased by around 1 per cent. This result indicates the key role of such public investments for environmental improvements in reducing environmental degradation as income levels rise, and could explain the strong EKC and even decreasing relationships found for some pollution indicators in OECD countries. In his breakdown of the EKC for sulphur dioxide emissions across countries, Panayotou (1997) examines the effect of shifts in the sectoral structure of the economy, as represented by industry's share of GDP. The income-induced sulphur dioxide abatement effect appears to be greater as the industrial share of GDP rises; however, with industry shares of around 20–30 per cent, sulphur dioxide emissions appear to rise to their highest levels. In comparison, de Bruyn (1997) finds that structural change is less important than technological innovation, represented by the change in the emission intensity across sectors, in explaining declining sulphur dioxide emissions in the Netherlands and West Germany. In interpreting these results, de Bruyn acknowledges that these two developed countries have fairly stable production structures, whereas in rapidly industrializing and developing countries the effects of structural change on emissions may be less obvious. Finally, Moomaw and Unruh (1997) demonstrate that the high correlation between CO_2 and income in most EKC analyses is largely attributable to structural economic transition, and only 16 countries – a subset of OECD member states – show a significant break in this positive CO_2–GDP correlation. Moreover, the N-shaped or cubic relationship between CO_2 and income for these countries is largely attributable to Canada, Luxembourg and the US, who appear to have undergone similar economic transitions.

Country-specific Effects

Stern et al (1996) conclude that 'a more fruitful approach to the analysis of the relationship between economic growth and environmental impact would be the examination of the historical experience of individual countries, using econometric and also qualitative historical analysis.' The diametrically opposite results for Malaysia and the US would support this view. For example, Carson et al (1997) suggest that, in their cross-sectional analysis of the US, the large differences in state-level per-capita emissions may be attributable to marked differences across states in allowing particular types of point sources to be built up in the first place, in enforcing federal pollution laws and, possibly most importantly, in employing outdated industrial technology. Vincent (1997) indicates that the increasing relationship between particulate matter and income in Malaysia may be due to the fact that low-income states are still sources of emissions because of land conversion through burning and replanting of tree crops, while at the same time high-income states are increasing emissions because of industrial processing and the burning of industrial and municipal wastes. Rapid urbanization and industrialization, which are correlated with rising income in Malaysia, are responsible for the increasing concentrations of ammoniacal nitrogen and acidity in water, as the expansion of municipal and industrial sewage treatment has lagged behind.

The Role of National and Local Policy

Virtually all EKC studies have concluded with the observation that any income-environmental degradation relationship is likely to be affected significantly by national and local polices. Several recent studies have attempted to estimate the influence of policy explicitly. Panayotou (1997) has found that improved policies and institutions in the form of more secure property rights, better enforcement of contracts and effective environmental regulations can help to flatten the EKC for sulphur dioxide across countries. In the case of the Netherlands and West Germany, the impact of technological change in reducing sulphur dioxide emissions is largely attributable to the instalment of better end-of-pipe abatement technology, which is in turn related to tougher environmental policy and regulation (de Bruyn, 1997). The implications of the findings by Komen et al (1997) are that increased public spending on environmental research and development as income levels rise may not only directly account for greater environmental improvement but also act as a catalyst for private spending on development of cleaner technologies. Carson et al (1997) have concluded that the absolute level of income of a US state appears significant in determining the 'zeal and effectiveness' of its air pollution regulatory structure, mainly because a richer state is likely to have more resources available to regulatory agencies, higher public preferences for improved air quality and a greater perceived danger from emissions.

The Role of Multilateral Policy

Cole et al (1997) analyse cross-country data both before and after the 1987 Montreal Protocol to provide evidence that a multilateral policy initiative may prove highly significant in influencing the relationship between per-capita income and an environmental problem with global effects, in this case emissions of chlorofluorocarbons (CFC) and halons. The authors find that CFC and halon emissions in 1986 appear to increase linearly with income, reflecting the fact that in 1986 countries may have been reluctant to reduce unilaterally their CFC and halon emissions.

However, the 1987 Montreal Protocol committed signatories to reduce the use of CFCs and halons substantially, and as a result, the estimate for emissions in 1990 shows an EKC-type relationship, with a turning point of US$12,600. However, the willingness of countries to agree stricter environmental targets through multilateral agreements may also be influenced, at least partly, by their levels of per-capita income. For example, de Bruyn (1997) shows that countries with higher per-capita income have agreed stricter environmental targets, although a dirtier environment (in terms of higher emissions per km^2) is a more important factor.

Overall then, the emerging EKC literature appears to support the view that improved policies for environmental management and sustainable use of natural capital appears to have the greatest influence on the pattern of economic development and growth, and thus its degree of impact on the environment (Arrow et al, 1995). Projecting future environmental damage by extrapolating impacts from population and economic change tells us only what is likely to happen if we continue to ignore pervasive market, institutional and policy failures that fail to correct for structural imbalances in our economy-environment relationships. As Panayotou (1997) has concluded, there is still a 'wide scope for active policy intervention to bring about more desirable (and in the presence of market failures) more efficient economic and environmental outcomes.'

International Trade and the Environment

Related to the view that global economic growth is a major cause of environmental losses is the view that international trade is bad for the environment. According to this argument, as trade is the principal engine driving the expansion of the world economy, and since this expansion cannot proceed without resource depletion and degradation, pollution and loss of natural habitats, then trade must be an important driving force behind global environmental degradation. The various examples often cited include the impact of the international trade in timber products on the destruction of the world's remaining old-growth tropical and temperate forests, the impact of the trade in wildlife and resource products on endangered species and the pollution and resource losses associated with major regional trade agreements, such as the North American Free Trade Agreement (NAFTA).

Although examples such as these can give the impression that international trade is the fundamental cause of many of the world's environmental problems, a closer examination of these problems often reveals that this perception is flawed. Instead, the most important factors are once again market, policy and institutional failures that work against the sustainable and efficient management of the environment. As discussed previously, such failures cause perverse incentives that lead to the unnecessary and excessive conversion of habitats, resource depletion and degradation and pollution. If these failures are not corrected, then international trade mechanisms simply reinforce these perverse incentives.

Hence, trade may give the appearance of being the fundamental cause of environmental degradation, but the actual role of trade is generally one of reinforcing the lack of appropriate market signals, effective policies, and institutional mechanisms that are the true underlying causes of many environmental problems. In fact, as we have demonstrated in studies of the role of trade in the management of African elephants and tropical forests, if perverse incentives are corrected and market distortions removed, then trade can actually enhance the incentives for more sustainable resource management (Barbier et al, 1990 and 1994).

Although international trade is not necessarily itself a major cause of global environmental problems, the role of trade in reinforcing market, policy and institutional failures that underlie environmental degradation can magnify the problem substantially. For example, Anderson (1992) has demonstrated theoretically how, in the absence of adequate environmental protection and management policies, trade liberalization that leads to greater use of environment resources can lead to undesirable impacts. Thus from the standpoint of the liberalizing country, the welfare gains from trade are somewhat diluted by the welfare losses arising from environmental degradation.

Moreover, sometimes the environmental losses that may be a byproduct of a major structural economic change such as trade liberalization are second-order effects that are not directly related to the initial implementation of liberalization policies. As Box 6.2 indicates, this may be the case for the possible impacts of NAFTA on deforestation in Mexico. However, as the Box also demonstrates, the appropriate policy response is not to limit the trade liberalization strategy of NAFTA but to introduce complementary policies and investments targeted to improving the productivity of existing rainfed agricultural land and livestock pastureland, thus reducing rural unemployment and migration to the forest frontier.

Poverty and Environment

Probably the most widely-cited linkages between poverty and the environment relate to deforestation and soil erosion. The 1990 global forest resource assessment indicated that the annual deforestation rate across tropical countries from 1981 to 1990 was approximately 0.8 per

Box 6.2 *NAFTA and Deforestation in Mexico*

Ratified in 1993, NAFTA is the first regional trade liberalization agreement that includes both developed and developing economies (Canada, the US and Mexico). Although much attention has been focused on the possible environmental and pollution impacts arising from rapid industrialization of the US-Mexico border, there is also concern that the agreement could accelerate widespread deforestation throughout Mexico.

Before the implementation of the Agreement, estimates of the annual rate of deforestation in Mexico ranged from 400,000 to 1.5 million hectares. However, virtually all estimates agree that 75 per cent of the deforestation is occurring in tropical areas, and the major cause is the rapid expansion of livestock production and rainfed agriculture (Masera et al, 1992).

A recent study by Barbier and Burgess (1996) estimated the key factors determining agricultural and livestock expansion, and thus deforestation, in Mexico during the pre-NAFTA period. The results indicated that maize and fertilizer prices appear to be the main influences on the expansion of planted area, whereas beef prices and credit disbursement influence cattle numbers. Population growth also affects the expansion of livestock and agricultural activities, and income per capita is positively correlated with cattle expansion. Based on coupling their estimations with economy-wide NAFTA simulation models, Barbier and Burgess concluded that liberalization of maize, fertilizer and beef prices, as well as removal of credit subsidies, may reduce the incentives for deforestation. However, these first-order effects may be countered and even outweighed by second-order effects of increased deforestation through employment and income impacts. Reducing these latter effects will require complementary policy reforms and investments targeted specifically to the agricultural and livestock sectors. These include:

- Removal of pricing and other policies that artificially subsidize the returns to conversion activities in frontier forest areas;
- Tightening land tenure, forestry and environmental laws to reduce the incentives for rent-seeking behaviour on the frontier or to improve the internalization of any environmental impacts associated with deforestation;
- Targeting specific investments for the agricultural and livestock sectors for improving productivity, infrastructure, research and extension, with the objective of bringing existing idle arable land into production as well as improving the productivity of rainfed land already under cultivation.

cent, or 15.4 million hectares (FAO, 1993). Although the highest rate of deforestation occurs in Asia (1.2 per cent), the area of tropical forests cleared on average each year in Latin America (7.4 million hectares), is almost as much as the total forest area cleared in Asia and Africa. The largest amount of deforestation is currently occurring in tropical South America (6.4 million hectares) followed by insular South-East Asia (1.9 million hectares), but the highest annual rates of deforestation are being experienced in continental South-East Asia (1.6 per cent) and Central America and Mexico (1.5 per cent).

A recent study of global trends in human-induced soil erosion for the period 1945 to 1990 indicates that over 20 per cent of the vegetated land in developing regions of the world is degraded, much of it suffering from moderate, severe or extreme degradation (Oldeman et al, 1990). Deforestation appears to be a major source of human-induced soil degradation in developing regions. In both Asia and South America, deforestation accounts for around 40 per cent of erosion, in Central America and Mexico 22 per cent and in Africa 14 per cent. Experiments on land clearing throughout the tropics have shown that deforestation leads directly to degradation of soil structure and changes the chemical and biological properties of the soil, decreases the porosity of the surface layer, increases soil compaction, and decreases infiltration rate (Lal, 1995).

Lastly, evidence suggests that the poorest 20 per cent of the rural population in developing countries are mainly concentrated on low-potential lands (Leonard et al, 1989). The latter are defined as resource-poor or marginal agricultural lands, where inadequate or unreliable rainfall, adverse soil conditions, fertility and topography limit agricultural productivity and increase the risk of chronic land degradation. Almost three quarters of the poorest 20 per cent of the rural population in Latin America, 57 per cent in Asia and 51 per cent in Africa can be found on low-potential lands.

As low-potential lands are considered to be prone to chronic land degradation, then clearly the problems of resource management by poor rural households and human-induced soil degradation are linked in developing countries. Moreover, given that many marginal and resource-poor lands are also likely to have been previously forested lands, then a strong rural poverty–deforestation link may also exist. Finally, the evidence that deforestation may itself be an important cause of human-induced soil degradation across developing regions raises the possibility of a cumulative causation link between rural poverty, deforestation and land degradation: poor rural households abandoning degraded land for frontier forested lands, deforestation and cropping of poor soils lead to further degradation, which in turn leads to land abandonment and additional forest land conversion, and so on.

Recent studies suggest that there are two overall aspects of poverty-environment linkages at the rural household level that are critical to the process of land degradation and resource conversion in developing countries, and which in turn feed back to affect the well-being of the poor (for a review see Barbier,1997).

First, poverty may not be a direct cause of environmental degradation but instead may operate as a constraining factor on the ability of poorer rural households to avoid land degradation or to invest in mitigating strategies. Empirical evidence suggests that poorer households in rural developing regions are more constrained in their access to credit, inputs and research and extension services necessary for investments in improved land and resource management. Poverty, imperfect capital markets and insecure land tenure may reinforce the tendency towards short-term production decisions, which may bias land use decisions against long-term management strategies. Consequently, a rational strategy for poor rural households with limited access to capital and alternative economic opportunities may be to extract short-term rents through resource conversion and land degradation, so long as there are sufficient additional land and resources available to exploit relatively cheaply. This process may be exacerbated if the smallholders are in debt (Barbier and López, 1999).

Second, poverty may severely constrain the ability of poor households to compete for resources, including high quality and productive land. In periods of commodity booms and land speculation, wealthier households generally take advantage of their superior political and market power to ensure initial access to better quality resources in order to capture a larger share of the resource rents. Poorer households are either confined to marginal land areas where resource rents are limited or only have access to higher quality resources once they are degraded and any rents dissipated. This relationship between poverty, resource access and land degradation is perhaps less well documented but may be highly significant, particularly in areas characterized by poorly defined property rights and competition between rich and poor for scarce environmental assets. As a result of these processes, the economic livelihoods of the poor become even more vulnerable to the risks posed by land degradation, and their ability and willingness to manage resources sustainably may become even more constrained. However, it is often overlooked that the initial catalyst behind the loss in environmental entitlement is the inability of poorer households to compete with the rich for higher quality land and resources (See Box 6.3).

These processes of poverty-environment linkages that drive land degradation and deforestation in developing countries appear fairly intractable. However, they are not necessarily insurmountable. The reason we observe a cumulative causation link between land degradation, forest conversion and rural poverty in developing countries is critically related to the role of economic incentives in influencing the behaviour of many poor rural households.

Yet economic incentives, even for poor rural households, are also determined by the markets and institutions in which these households operate. Markets and institutions are in turn affected by public policies and investments. Prevailing institutional arrangements, investments and policies may also favour wealthier households, who can take advantage of their superior political and market power to secure exclusive access to better quality resources.

Box 6.3 *Poverty, Entitlement Loss and Environmental Degradation*

The high concentration of the poorest rural groups in developing countries on ecologically 'fragile' land suggests that it is the welfare of the poorest that is at the greatest risk from continued land degradation. However, an important reason why so many poor households are concentrated in marginal areas in the first instance is due to their inability to compete with richer households for access to better resources, including high quality and productive land. Poorer households do not always end up in ecologically fragile areas out of choice, but because wealthier households generally take advantage of their superior political and market power to secure exclusive access to better quality resources. As a result poorer households find themselves confined to marginal land areas prone to degradation and with access only to poor quality resources.

As argued by Kates (1990), throughout the developing world the poor often suffer from three major processes of environmental entitlement loss:

- The poor are displaced from their traditional entitlement to common resources by development activities or by the appropriation of their resources by richer claimants;
- The remaining entitlements are divided and reduced by poor farmers having to share their resources with their children or to sell off bits and pieces to cope with extreme losses (crop failure, illness, death), social obligations (marriages, celebrations) or subsistence;
- The resources of the poor are degraded through excessive use and by failure to restore or to improve their productivity and regeneration – a process made worse by the concentration of the poor into environments unable to sustain requisite levels of resource use.

As a result of these processes, the economic livelihoods of the poor become even more vulnerable to the risks posed by land degradation, and their ability and willingness to manage resources sustainably may become even more constrained. However, it is often overlooked that the initial catalyst behind the loss in environmental entitlement is the inability of poorer households to compete with the rich for higher quality land and resources.

Thus if we are to discover ways to overcome the land degradation and deforestation problems faced by the rural poor, our starting point must be the analysis of the market, institutional and policy failures that have fostered such problems, as well as improving our understanding of why certain policy reforms and investments have succeeded where others have not. We are amassing a growing body of case-study evidence of such analysis from across the developing world. This literature points to several lessons that we need to learn – as well as many misperceptions that we must correct about poverty-environmental degradation linkages.

First, it is often assumed that the effectiveness of public policies and economic incentives in controlling environmental degradation in developing economies is limited by the existence of a poverty-environment trap. However, as noted above, poverty and environmental degradation may be positively correlated, but correlation does not imply causation. It is therefore erroneous to assume that poverty causes environmental degradation, or vice versa. If anything, recent evidence suggests that poverty-environmental linkages cannot be reduced to simple unidimensional cause-effect relationships. Hence, the term coined here – cumulative causation – is a more appropriate description of the complex linkages between poverty, land degradation and deforestation that are the crux of the problem in many rural areas of the developing world.

Second, there are numerous complex factors that influence the perceptions of poor peoples of the environment and their behaviour towards natural resource management. These range from the economic distortions arising from policy, institutional and market failures, to underlying labour and capital endowments and constraints (including pressures to increase family size) to access to alternative employment and income-earning opportunities, institutional and legal factors such as tenure or access security, property rights and delivery systems. Public policies and other factors often affect the incentive structures and redirect capital and labour flows between sectors and regions, with adverse consequences for the poor and their ability or willingness to manage resources sustainably. Box 6.4 illustrates this problem with the example of trade liberalization in Ghana and its counter-productive impacts on shifting cultivators in the western region.

As poor people have little or no access to capital and must rely on family or low-skilled labour for earning income, it would seem economically perverse that they would degrade any natural capital at their disposal. Poor people and communities are often acutely aware of the essential role of natural resources in sustaining their livelihoods, and equally, of the costs and impacts of environmental degradation. This would suggest that there exist tremendous incentives for the poor to manage and sustain the stock of natural capital at their disposal in order to maintain or enhance both their immediate and future livelihood options. Where they choose to degrade their environment – and there may be rational grounds for doing so under certain circumstances – it is because changing economic and social conditions have altered their incentive structures, including perhaps their control over or access to essential resources.

Thus from an economic perspective, simply observing that poor people are driven to degrade the environment – even when this appears to be the case – is not helpful. Designing appropriate policy responses to alleviate problems of poverty and environmental degradation therefore requires careful analysis of the determinants of individual behaviour.

Box 6.4 *Economy-wide Policies and Land Conversion:
Western Ghana*

Since 1983, Ghana has introduced major structural reforms to its economy,
including liberalizing its exchange rate, reducing public-sector spending,
decreasing industrial protectionism and removing distortions in the prices of
agricultural commodities, especially export crops such as cocoa. Despite these
reforms, further trade liberalization measures could still be implemented in
Ghana, including further decreases in protection to the import substitution
sector, particularly cereals, and additional reductions on the implicit export tax
to agricultural commodities.

These trade liberalization reforms would have an important impact not
only on the whole economy but also on the traditional agricultural sectors of
Ghana. One such sector is the shifting cultivation system of Western Ghana. In
such systems, land is cultivated for one or two years and then left idle for four
to ten years to restore its productive capacity. In the traditional bush-fallow
rotation, the biomass that is regenerated through fallowing the land serves as
natural fertilizer when it is burned and reabsorbed in the topsoil when the land
is next prepared for cultivation. Biomass is therefore an important input in
long-term agricultural production, and depletion of biomass through either
shortening of fallow periods or more extensive land cultivation is likely to cause
land degradation and loss of productivity. As naturally forested land is not
individually owned, too much conversion of this land can occur if there are
insufficient communal controls on over-exploitation. However, if communal
controls are adequate, then the community can gain through avoiding the costs
to all farmers of excessive loss of biomass, erosion and flooding in the communal area.

By modelling the agricultural production decisions of shifting cultivators in
Western Ghana, López (1997) has been able to estimate the key determinants
of both agricultural output and the demand for cultivated land by individual
farming households. First, it was estimated that biomass, measured in terms of
the proportion of land under forest cover, contributes 15–20 per cent of the
value of agricultural output in the bush-fallow systems. Second, several factors
appear to influence the total land area cultivated by farmers. The key variable
in particular appears to be the effect of the wage-price ratio on the demand for
land. A decrease in the wage rate or an increase in agricultural prices faced by
farmers in Western Ghana will lead to a significant increase in the area of land
that they will cultivate. In other words, if trade liberalization leads to rising
agricultural prices for farmers in the region, they are likely to respond by
increasing their cultivated area. Farmers will do this either by shortening their
fallow rotations, or by finding new forested land to convert. In both cases,
there is an overexploitation of biomass and loss of long-term productivity, since
the proportion of fallow to cultivated land will fall in the bush-fallow system.

Through a general equilibrium model, López (op cit) estimates that the
overall impacts of trade liberalization will on average cause a 2.5 to 4.4 per
cent decline in biomass in Western Ghana as a result of farmers increasing
cultivated area, mainly through affecting the wage-price ratio. Thus although
the result of reducing trade distortions is to increase income in the national
economy, these income gains may be more than offset by the loss in long-term
income from less sustainable and productive agricultural systems in Western
Ghana. The overall economy may gain, but poor smallholders dependent on
bush-fallow cropping systems could lose through greater land conversion and
degradation.

Such an analysis would clarify the factors leading individuals to degrade their environment, their responses to environmental degradation and the incentives required to induce conservation.

Where further analysis reveals that poverty is not the direct cause of environmental degradation, designing appropriate policy responses will nevertheless be affected by poverty's indirect role. The response of poor people and communities to incentives encouraging sustainable resource management may be affected by special factors influencing their behaviour, such as high rates of time preference induced by greater risk and uncertainty over livelihood security, labour and capital constraints, insecure tenure over and access to resources, imperfect information and access to marketed inputs and a variety of other conditions and constraints. For example, in a recent review of farmer adoption of agroforestry systems in Central America and the Caribbean, Current et al (1995) conclude that 'poorer farmers may find agroforestry profitable, but their rate and scale or adoption is often constrained by limited land, labor, and capital resources and their need to ensure food security and reduce risks.'

Moreover, the poor are not a homogeneous group. The work of Lipton (1988) highlights how the poor in developing countries all differ in terms of demographic, nutritional, labour-market and asset-holding characteristics. A study in Malawi illustrates how the poor face different incentives and constraints in combating declining soil fertility and erosion, which are serious problems afflicting smallholder agriculture (Barbier and Burgess, 1992).

In Malawi, female-headed households make up a large percentage (42 per cent) of the 'core-poor' households. They typically cultivate very small plots of land (< 0.5 hectares) often on the less fertile soils and steeper slopes. They are often unable to finance agricultural inputs such as fertilizer, to rotate annual crops, to use green-manure crops or to undertake soil conservation. As a result, these households generally face declining soil fertility and lower crop yields, further exacerbating their poverty and increasing their dependence upon the land. Thus policies to alleviate poverty and control land degradation must take into account the labour, land and cash constraints faced by such households, or they may not respond fully to policy measures and incentives that ignore such constraints on their land management decisions.

In fact, inappropriate policies are often at the heart of many poverty-environment linkages, which on a large scale create serious development problems. For example, in Colombia poor rural households are increasingly migrating to both marginal upland areas and equally fragile land in the forested Amazon-Orinoco basin (Heath and Binswanger, 1996). The result is continued unsustainable farming of both the Andean slopes and the Amazonian basin, followed by land abandonment as yields decline, and further expansion of farming on frontier and marginal lands. The problem is exacerbated less by failures in rural labour markets or policies than by the failure of agricultural and land policies to provide adequate rural labour absorption, efficient land use patterns, and most importantly, higher returns to existing smallholder agricultural land.

To summarize, the cumulative causation link between poverty and environmental degradation in developing countries does mean that the economic livelihoods and well-being of many poor rural households are at risk from continued land degradation and deforestation. In some cases, the processes that restrict poor households to fragile lands and poor quality resources stem initially from displacement by wealthier households. Although such environment-poverty linkages are pervasive, at the heart of the problem are economic incentives conditioned by market, policy and institutional failures, which are the key driving forces in these processes. It is these underlying causes that must be both fully analysed and eventually corrected if the twin goals of poverty alleviation and sustainable rural resource management in developing countries are to be realized.

Population Growth

Finally, we turn to population change and its impact on environmental degradation. Table 6.1 shows existing and projected population levels for the world and its main regions. As we write, the United Nations has estimated that the world's population has just passed six billion people. The official projections suggest that this could be 9.4 billion in just another 50 years, within the lifetimes of many who may read this book. Within 50 years, then, the world's environments will have to make way for more than 50 per cent more people. Nor can we avoid much of this growth: it is already built into the population we have and the projections already allow for expected early deaths from AIDS. There are two reasons why a probable 50 per cent increase in population cannot be avoided.

The first is that a considerable part of the growth comes about because of projected declines in mortality. People are simply living longer because of medical advances, the spread of primary health care and better nutrition. By the mid 21st century, global life expectancies may average over 82 years for males and 87 years for females.

The second is due to demographic momentum. Even if the number of current children per woman of child-bearing age falls to a level where new births just offset deaths (the fertility rate falls to what is known as the replacement level), population growth does not stop – population does not stabilize immediately. This is because the effects of past population change still have to work their way through the system. Past large cohorts of new births mean large increases in the number of young people and hence a high absolute number of births. Fertility rates (births per woman of age span 15–49) are anticipated by the UN to fall to 2.1, the replacement rate, in about 2040. If that is sustained for about 70 years, global population will stabilize at a little over 11 billion by 2100. Eleven billion is, of course, roughly twice the number of people currently alive.

Table 6.1 *World Population Growth (billion)*

	1998	2025	2050
World	**5.93**	**8.04**	**9.37**
Africa	0.78	1.45	2.05
Europe	0.73	0.70	0.64
N. America	0.30	0.37	0.38
C. America	0.13	0.19	0.23
S. America	0.33	0.45	0.52
Asia	3.59	4.78	5.44
Oceania	0.03	0.04	0.05
Developed	**1.18**	**1.22**	**1.16**
Developing	**4.75**	**6.82**	**8.20**

Note: All the projections shown here are subject to uncertainty, but the underlying messages are clear. The population of the currently developed world will stabilize at about 1.2 billion people. The population of the developing world will increase by over 70 per cent. More important than percentages are the absolute numbers. All of the extra 3.4 billion people expected to be alive in 2050 will reside in the current developing world.
Source: UN, 1997

World-wide fertility is declining. As real incomes grow, people choose to have smaller families, partly because they see the logic in terms of the costs and benefits of family size (remember, education tends to grow with income too), and partly because the need for children as labour and as a means of family care in old age declines. Those who call for more family planning are right, but family planning works best in contexts where it provides the means to fulfil the changed aspirations that come with changing incomes. It is important to note, therefore, that one of the surest means of lowering population growth rates is to raise income and education.

Short of major disasters, on a scale similar perhaps to AIDS, the world simply has to accommodate a substantial increase in the absolute number of people in the world. There are those who say that natural resources and food supplies are simply not enough to sustain this increase. Indeed, they would probably argue that population projections of the kind shown in Table 6.1 are unrealistic precisely because they ignore a modern form of Malthusianism – the increased population simply cannot survive. But whether natural resources are devastated in a rush for the survival of the fittest among this new 50 per cent of the world's population, or whether they are lost because that extra 50 per cent does survive, the implications for the world's environmental assets are formidable. There is a logic to the view considered at the beginning of this chapter – that, at the end of the day, rapid population growth does constitute a major threat to the world's environment. Against this, we have argued that addressing the many economic causes of environmental degradation will, at least, buy time on a scale to address the problems brought by a rising population. Whether enough time can be bought in this way is open to debate. But one thing is for sure – allowing population rise above its projected unavoidable level and neglecting to address the underlying economic causes of degradation is the surest recipe for disaster.

There are those who argue that rapidly rising populations are, in fact, a good thing (Simon, 1981). The arguments are that people are resources, so the more people we have the more resources we have. There will also be a higher number of entrepreneurs and geniuses, and a more efficient infrastructure provision for bigger populations. Of course, the more people there are, the more despots and genocidal maniacs we have too! A more sophisticated argument is that rapid population change is a spur to technological change (Boserup, 1965). As land extensification ceases because good land is exhausted, or as other factors prevent further development of new lands, intensification occurs – more technology is applied to the existing land. The resulting farmer-induced technological change is sufficient to support the new population level, the argument goes, although others doubt that farmer technology alone could support high rates of population growth. The result is a virtuous cycle between population, technology and growth. Some recent work has tended to give the Boserup hypothesis some support. The 'Machakos' study (English et al, 1994) is perhaps the most widely-cited modern study. Machakos in east central Kenya was regarded in the 1930s as a seriously degraded area. Inhabited by the Akamba people, the area today has five times as many people as then and a real per-capita agricultural output that is three times the 1930s level. Soil erosion still exists but is modest due to terracing of virtually all of the land, and repeated projections of fuelwood scarcity have not materialized because trees have been planted and are actively managed. The area cultivated has expanded by a factor of four to five. Livestock have increased, despite a decreasing social emphasis on their importance by the Akamba. New technology has expanded rapidly: the study found 45 technologies in place that were not there in the 1930s, including ox-drawn ploughs, early-maturing maize, use of crop residue for forage and animal manure for fertilizer, and monocropping in rows to facilitate weeding. Only some of the technologies owe their introduction to government support – the early-maturing crops being the main one. Most technologies have been introduced by the Akamba themselves without support. Nor has credit been used to achieve all this: profits from off-farm work have been reinvested in the technologies, as have profits from sales of cash crops. The nature of the crops grown has changed, from subsistence crops in the 1930s to cash crops today. The authors claim Machakos is a clear example of Boserupian forces at work.

Additionally, various reviews have suggested that reducing population growth cannot be demonstrated to have major impacts on economic growth. If there are impacts, they are modest, and hence the high profile given to population change as a cause of poor economic (and environmental) performance is not warranted (Kelley, 1988).

How sound are these arguments? In terms of the theory of economic development, population growth was thought to lower the ratio of capital to labour and hence lower the marginal product of labour, thus lowering wages. To keep pace capital must be widened and this may have deleterious effects elsewhere, for example in reducing funds available for infrastructure. Slow population growth permits a rising capital to labour ratio – capital deepening – and hence rising productivity and wages. This link between population growth and capital has tended to go out of fashion when capital is thought to be less important in growth. Given the reappearance of the role of capital in the theory of sustainable development (see Chapters 1–3) this view may be due for reappraisal.

A variation on the argument above is the burden-of-dependency argument. Rapid population growth leads to a higher proportion of young people in the population who are then dependent on the older working population. The latter have to divert resources to services such as care, food, housing and education. In poor countries dependence ratios imply one dependent per worker. In rich countries the ratio tends to be one dependent per two workers. In addition if the older population fails to divert resources, the young suffer ill-health and poor education. Growth worsens.

The household-effects model offers another perspective, by looking at the effects of large families on nutrition and education, for example. Here the arguments are that within families more children means spreading limited family resources widely but thinly: nutrition suffers. More children affect the health of mothers via rapid childbearing, and so on. In general, both parental and child well-being are thought to suffer in large families. Nonetheless, there are positive aspects: more children may be a straight parental choice. More children also mean more security in old age, and more labour in a comparatively short time. A more modern look at these issues stresses the outcome of endogenous growth theory – the role that education plays in generating positive externalities that stimulate growth (see Chapter 2). The argument here is that large families depress education, especially education of females, due to the resource spreading effect. Hence large families have a negative effect on economic growth overall.

Natural resource models also yield some insights. These are best discussed by resource type.

Land and Food

It is widely argued that until the Second World War food output increases were secured mainly by extensification. Since then they have been secured by intensification. More intensification as population expands leads to soil degradation which lowers the productivity of land relative to labour. More application of labour to land simply worsens the degradation. Degradation can only cease if labour out-migrates to the towns or if there is other off-farm employment, or if land-saving techniques are developed. One problem with these vicious-cycle-of-intensification models is that the evidence for declining food per capita is not there, despite heavily laden warnings from various commentators.

Fuelwood and Water

Here the argument is that population growth leads to rates of growth in demand that are greater than the regenerative capacity of trees and water, and a simultaneous ecological and economic crisis emerges. The kinds of indicators used to justify this pessimism are of the carrying-capacity kind – indicators suggesting the largest possible population that can be sustained usually at some subsistence level of resource consumption. Yet suspicion remains since it is not clear that the dire consequences of carrying-capacity arguments are borne out in practice. One possibility is that people adapt by investing in trees and in water efficiency and that we are not very good at detecting and measuring these changes. But the major effect of population on water is via food demand and hence irrigation. Seventy per cent of the world's fresh water is used for irrigation. Poorly managed and under-priced irrigation water also results in salinization of soils. Hence population growth threatens water supplies most by these indirect routes.

Returning to the Boserup theory we need to know how representative the Machakos example is of societal change in the face of natural resource scarcity. A number of commentators suggest that Machakos-style change is more an exception than the rule. First, it is argued that such situations arise mainly when there is strong external support for the new technologies, although the Machakos authors deny this was very relevant there. Second, if off-farm work does not exist, the chances are that other adaptations will take place, especially 'Ricardian' solutions in which internal conflicts marginalize the poorest of society on to marginal lands. Third, if all the policy signals are wrong, no amount of autonomous effort will prevent the vicious cycle occurring (Cleaver and Shreiber, 1993; Lele and Stone, 1989; Bilsbarrow and Geores, 1993).

The debate about the beneficial effects of population change will continue and it is highly likely that other examples of Machakos-style adaptations will be found. The question is whether we can expect that level of adaptation to pervade the three billion extra people anticipated to be on this earth in 50 years' time. Our central message remains. Gloomy as the prospect is for the world's environments in face of this increase in human numbers, the prospects are gloomier still if we fail to address the underlying economic causes of environmental degradation.

Subsidies

Substantial attention has been given in recent years to the role that financial subsidies play in environmnetal degradation. The argument is basically straightforward. Subsidies tend to encourage the activity that is subsidized, whether it is agricultural output, energy consumption or the use of water, for example. But if these activities have negative environmental impacts, then the subsidy itself exacerbates those harmful impacts. In practice, estimating the environmental impacts of subsidies is complex. To begin with, the definition of a subsidy is not straightfoward.

A subsidy is any form of intervention which lowers the cost of production of a producer, or raises the price received by the producer, compared to the cost and price that would prevail in an undistorted market. This definition allows us to distinguish subsidies from interventions which raise market prices but where the increase in price does not accrue to the producer, as for example all product taxes, such as sales taxes and value added tax. It also permits us to take account of the fact that, besides being aimed at lowering costs, subsidies often take the form of price guarantees, raising producer prices over the free market price, as is common with agricultural price support schemes. Finally, subsidies include all financial transfers to producers, regardless of whether they are targeted on products or simply take the form of cash sums payable to producers.

The problem with the definition is the meaning of an undistorted market. Few markets are genuinely competitive, and any element of monopoly will raise prices above their competitive level. So long as we keep the meaning of distorted to mean distorted by government intervention, then the definition is fairly safe.

The Producer Subsidy Equivalent

Probably the most accepted definition of a subsidy is the producer subsidy equivalent (PSE), a measure developed by the OECD. The formula is:

$$PSE = Q.[P_d - P_w] + DP - LV + OS$$

where Q is output (say tonnes of cereal); Pd is the domestic price to the producer (the price the farmer would receive); Pw is the world price, or border price (the price the cereal would get if it was sold on the world market); DP consists of any direct payments to the producer (from taxpayers to producers which do not raise the prices to consumer); LV consists of any levies on the producer (these must be deducted from the subsidy total since they are taxes on the producers); and OS which consists of other transfers, such as tax concessions, to the producer.

The first expression on the right-hand side reflects the fact that subsidy schemes often keep domestic prices above the world price (Pd > Pw). Essentially, the domestic market is protected. This gap accounts for the major part of OECD subsidies in agriculture (around 70–80 per cent of all subsidies to agriculture). DP and LV together give a net subsidy to producers if DP is greater than LV, which is certainly the case for the OECD countries. Many subsidies are quite subtle. For example, an industry may receive a tax break, being taxed at less than the normal rate, or being allowed to write off liabilities, or being eligible for low cost credit.

Producer subsidy equivalents are regularly calculated for agriculture and energy, with the estimates for agriculture being by far the most detailed. Information on subsidies in other sectors, such as water and fisheries, is patchy.

Table 6.2 records a best guess at the scale of world subsidies. The picture is a rapidly changing one and subsidies in the developing world are being reduced rapidly as those economies attempt to become more open in the context of world competition. Nonetheless, the estimates are instructive.

First, even allowing for the fact that only some subsidies have been identified (for example, subsidies to forestry and to fisheries are excluded), we see that world subsidies could amount to over US$600 billion per annum, and may be as much as $750 billion. To get some idea of the scale of these figures, the entire GNP of the world is about US$25 trillion (a trillion is 10^{12}, and a billion is 10^9), so the subsidies amount to 2.0–2.4 per cent of world GNP.

Second, total official development assistance (overseas aid) is about US$60 billion per year, so that world subsidies are at least ten times this figure.

Third, the subsidies are largest in the rich countries of the world: the OECD countries account for 75 per cent of the subsidies. It is interesting that advanced countries often criticize the poorer economies for bad management of their economies, when the rich countries persist in some of the worst forms of mismanagement through subsidization.

Fourth, agricultural subsidies in the rich world dominate the picture. These tend to take the form of price support – guaranteed prices to farmers. Of the US$335 billion agricultural subsidy, the European Union (EU) accounts for about one third, Japan for about a quarter, and the US for about a fifth.

Fifth, subsidies to nuclear power are quite important in the developed world and amount to US$9–15 billion annually.

Table 6.2 Estimates of World Subsidies (US$billion)

	OECD $bn	Non-OECD $bn	World $bn
Water			
irrigation	2	20	22
supply	na	28	28
sanitation	na	5	5
Energy			
coal			
oil/products			
gas	}10	62	72
electricity			
other			
nuclear	9–14	na	9–14
Agriculture			
transfers	335	<0	335
fertilizer	na	36	36
pesticide	na	>0	>0
Transport	55–174 (US) 52 (Jap, Ger, UK)		107–226
Totals	463–587	151	614–738

Why do Subsidies Matter?

Whatever the initial purpose of subsidies, they often tend to be environmentally damaging and hence do not contribute to sustainable development. The environmental effects of subsidies are of course only one aspect that is relevant to policy decisions concerning them. Some might be environmentally damaging but fair in terms of the degree of protection against high prices that is afforded to poorer groups in society, for example. Nonetheless, they need to be evaluated for their environmental impacts, not least because their reform is often feasible and the effects of reducing them tend to be immediate. Moreover, when the effects of subsidies are closely analysed it is often found that the poor are not the real gainers – subsidies tend to benefit middle-income groups most.

Harmful effects tend to come about because:

- The subsidy causes too much production of the subsidized product, and hence too many associated effects such as pollution;
- Governments have to find the money for subsidies and this will come from taxation or borrowing, causing macroeconomic problems, or, at the very least, diverting money from socially valuable uses such as health and education;
- Over-production has to be disposed of and this may result in dumping the excess, perhaps in developing countries, thus undermining their economies;
- Subsidies also divert resources away from higher-value uses to low-value uses. For example the Sacramento Valley in California has an arid climate, yet it grows rice based on heavily subsidized water and accounts for as much as 80 per cent of California's water consumption;
- Subsidies mean that true costs of supply are not recovered, so that the utilities supplying energy and water, for example, may not have enough revenues to secure surpluses that they can invest in new supplies. This is why public utilities in many developing countries are often locked into a vicious circle of poor supply and have little or no money for new investments;
- Subsidies create economic rents – money for doing nothing – and hence attract rent seekers. Those who benefit from the rents will organize themselves to prevent the source of the rent being removed. The popular picture is that subsidies are designed to benefit the poor, so if the poor object to the rents being removed or reduced, many people would be sympathetic to their cause. In practice, precisely because the subsidies create rents, the rents tend to be appropriated by the more powerful sectors of society. Far from the subsidies benefiting the poor, they often benefit the better off who are skilled at organizing lobbies to retain the subsidies. Those subsidies are the hardest to remove, yet are likely to be the ones where rent capture is most entrenched. Paradoxically, the easiest subsidies to remove are those that do benefit the poor since they are often powerless to resist the change in policy. Rent seeking – the search for opportunities where rents are created, often by legal restrictions such as bans or zoning of land use, but in this case by subsidies – is unproductive. It may keep lawyers and other lobbyists

in business but it does little or nothing to enhance social well-being. Much agricultural subsidization belongs in this category. For historical reasons, farmers tend to be quite powerful lobbyists. Taking their subsidies away therefore meets with strong resistance, whether in North America, Japan or Europe.

Not all subsidies are bad. It may well be that a subsidy can help lower-income groups, although, as noted above, they usually do not have this effect. The benefit to the poor may well be judged more important than any loss to the environment. There are also two contexts where subsidies can be good in terms of economic efficiency: subsidizing technological change, and paying for an environmental benefit.

The conventional recommendation when negative external costs are present is to impose a tax on the polluting source, say an energy source. This argument for eco-taxes was one of the main features of *Blueprint 1*. But, when polluting and less polluting fuels compete, one might equally well give a subsidy to the non-polluting source. However, there are several issues that need to be taken into account when comparing the merits of taxes and subsidies.

Subsidies have to be paid by someone. If paid directly by government to renewable/nuclear energy generators for example, government taxation or government borrowing has to be increased. If the source is taxation there are negative impacts on the well-being of taxpayers, and if the source is borrowing there is an increased borrowing requirement which may have detrimental macroeconomic impacts (for example on inflation and the crowding out of private investment). Second, subsidies have the effect of expanding the use of energy in general because they will lower the average price of energy.

The argument against subsidies therefore tends to rest on two issues:

- The extent to which the market expansion effect, due to a fall in the average price of energy, might result in pollution which offsets the pollution reduction arising from the substitution of the cleaner fuel for the dirty fuel;
- The problems of financing the subsidies.

A defence of subsidies is that society is paying for the avoidance of external costs from other sources. This is, for example, one of the arguments used to justify subsidies to public transport and activities like organic farming. Nonetheless, in real world political contexts, the term subsidy still tends to generate images of inefficiency, special pleading and handouts.

Further defences are possible. We know that new renewable and clean sources of energy are subject to learning curves – costs of production decline through time as the technology is refined and diffused – so the effect of expanding the supplies of renewable sources should be to further lower their costs. As noted, subsidies have market-expanding effects as well as substitution effects, so that subsidies to a declining-cost source of energy should encourage both effects even more. In line with the previous argument, this is likely to be beneficial on environmental grounds the bigger is the gap between the pollution intensity of renewables when compared with that of non-renewables.

Investing in new and clearn technologies is risky. Subsidy payments could greatly assist the reduction of those risks, stimulating further output of renewable/nuclear energy and further environmental benefits. Risk reduction requires investment. The only way in which greater assurance can be found with respect to costs is to undertake more clean technology investments. But investment decisions are very sensitive to expectations about the future and to the cost of the initial capital investment rather than to the costs of operation. This in turn suggests one vehicle for the subsidy payments, namely accelerated capital depreciation payments. These enable corporations to write off their investment costs against tax liabilities. They have the advantage of being 'up-front' payments that are not likely to be the subject of political whim about the taxation system. Thus, one argument against environmental taxes is that they can easily be highjacked by the need to raise or lower revenues, just like other taxes. Up-front payments provide a subsidy and also help give greater confidence of expectations about the future.

The discussion is enough to show that the tax-versus-subsidy debate is far more complex than initially appears to be the case. The very strong argument for environmental taxes remains, but the case for subsidies is also far stronger than might at first appear. But the conditions for subsidies to be beneficial need to be scrutinized very carefully. The overwhelming impression is that the subsidies estimated in Table 6.2 are not of the beneficial kind.

7

Solving Environmental Problems I: Property Rights, Markets & Macroeconomy

Introduction

Previous chapters have argued that efficient and sustainable management of environmental resources, or natural capital, is essential to the long-term development of economies and human welfare. We refer to this as environmentally sustainable development. Unfortunately, we find little evidence that sustainability is actually being achieved. Important environmental values are generally not reflected in markets, and despite much rhetoric to the contrary, are routinely ignored in policy decisions. Institutional failures, such as the lack of property rights, inefficient and corrupt governance, political instability and the absence of public authority or institutions, also compound this problem. The result is economic development that produces excessive environmental degradation and increasing ecological scarcity. As we have demonstrated, the economic and social costs associated with these impacts can be significant. However, possibly the greatest threat posed by unsustainable development may be the long-term, potentially serious impacts on the welfare of future generations.

In this chapter we focus on how current patterns of unsustainable development can be reversed. As noted in Chapter 6, the key task lies in tackling the market, policy and institutional failures that lie at the root of many current environmental problems. There are two critical aspects to this task. First, we must identify and correct those distortions in economic incentives that work against efficient and sustainable management of natural capital for economic development. Second, where policy interventions are required, we must target them at a level that is more appropriate and effective for correcting the environmental problem.

For example, if an environmental problem is truly global or transboundary, such as depletion of the ozone layer, global warming, regional acid-rain pollution, tropical deforestation and the decline in the world's biodiversity, then it will be essential to create global markets, institutions, and regional or international agreements as part of the solution. However, even if its impact is global or regional, an environmental problem may be predominantly caused by the distortion of the incentives faced by economic agents at the local level who more directly control and use environmental resources. As previous chapters have shown, there are numerous and diverse examples of this, such as the failure to control greenhouse gas emissions by major polluters, or the conversion and degradation of tropical forests and habitats for agriculture, livestock grazing and other land uses. This in turn suggests that, although it is necessary to implement international measures to control many of the more significant and complex global environmental problems facing the world, such an approach is unlikely to be sufficient. More successful solutions will require appropriate policy interventions at many levels: local, regional and global.

This chapter uses specific examples of key environmental degradation problems to illustrate how policies for sustainable development can best be designed and implemented. We demonstrate that, to be effective, such policies must be targeted at overcoming key market, policy and institutional failures that distort economic incentives, and to be appropriate, policies will have to be designed for different levels of interventions – global, national and local. We also show that the required policy interventions need to be innovative, and rely on a diverse range of approaches, such as the establishment of property rights, creating markets, employing market-based instruments, targeting investments and transfers of wealth and income, and overcoming government inefficiency and corruption. The rest of this chapter will explore briefly how some of these approaches can be used to tackle specific environmental problems. However, we begin by discussing more generally the task of reversing unsustainable development.

Towards Sustainable Development

Figure 7.1 illustrates the policy problem we face. At the core of the unsustainability problem is the vicious cycle whereby the failure of

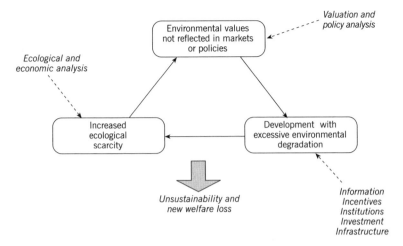

Figure 7.1 Reversing the Process of 'Unsustainable' Development

environmental values to be reflected in markets and government decisions leads to economic development with excessive environmental degradation, which in turn leads to increasing ecological scarcity. As discussed in Chapter 2, the rising scarcity of ecological resources and services will mean that they will increase in value relative to human-made goods and services produced in economic systems, and over the long term, could serve as an indicator of the increasing likelihood of ecological collapse and catastrophe on ever-widening scales. However, as Figure 7.1 shows, if environmental values are not reflected in market and public decisions, then any increasing ecological scarcity will also be ignored. The result is that the vicious cycle is reinforced, and the current pattern of economic development will continue along its unsustainable path.

Reversing this process of unsustainable development requires converting the vicious cycle into a virtuous one. Several important steps are involved (see Figure 7.1).

First, as we have emphasized both here and in *Blueprint 1*, an essential component in designing policies for sustainable development is improved environmental valuation and policy analysis to ensure that markets and policies incorporate the full costs and benefits of environmental impacts. Environmental valuation and accounting for natural capital depreciation must be fully integrated into economic development policy and strategy.

However, increasingly we are realizing the complexity of environmental impacts on the functioning, diversity and resilience of ecological systems and the goods and services they supply. The increasing ecological scarcity of these goods and services, and their potential long-term impacts on the health and stability of ecosystems, are difficult to quantify and value. In order to assess these impacts, economists will increasingly need to work with ecologists and other natural scientists to analyse such ecological effects. Thus an important second step in reversing unsustainable development will be more widespread interdisciplinary collaboration across the existing fields of economics, ecology and other social and natural sciences in order to analyse complex problems of environmental degradation (see Chapter 10).

Finally, the role of policy in controlling excessive environmental degradation requires implementation of effective and appropriate information, incentives, institutions, investments and infrastructure (the five I's). Better information on the state of the environment is essential for both private and public decision-making that determines the allocation of natural capital for economic development. The use of market-based instruments, the creation of markets, and where appropriate, regulatory measures all have a role to play in internalizing this information in everyday allocation decisions in the economy. Such instruments are also important in correcting the market and policy failures that distort the economic incentives for improved environmental management. However, overcoming institutional distortions and the lack of key institutions, such as property rights, is also critical. Providing an appropriate and effective infrastructure, including reducing government inefficiency, corruption and lack of accountability, also has an important role to play in reversing excessive environmental degradation.

The rest of the chapter discusses further the various policy approaches required in creating a more virtuous cycle towards sustainable economic development. We focus on four critical areas: property rights, market-based instruments and economic reforms, creating global markets and government efficiency. However, we begin with an overview of the various economic, regulatory and institutional policy approaches available for environmentally sustainable development

Policies for Sustainable Development: an Overview

There has been growing support around the world for the integration of environmental policy with economic development. Such an approach was strongly endorsed by the UN Conference on Environment and Development (UNCED) held in Rio de Janeiro, Brazil, in June 1992. For example, in its *Agenda* 21 pre-conference declaration, the UNCED Secretariat made the following statement:

'In the last two decades, there has been some progress through conventional economic policy applied in parallel with environmental policy. It is now clear that this is not enough, and that environment and development must be taken into account at each step of decision making and action in an integrated manner.' (UNCED, 1992)

The endorsement of the above approach at the conference has proved to be an important watershed. Since Rio, there have been a number of key innovations in economic, regulatory and institutional instruments for improved management of the environment, implemented not just in the developed OECD countries but also in low-income countries, newly industrializing countries, and economies in transition. A recent review by the World Bank (1997) of progress since Rio, groups these environmental policy innovations into four broad categories:

- Using markets;
- Creating markets;
- Implementing environmental regulations;
- Engaging the public.

For example, using markets involves both the removal of persistent market distortions and correcting failures that lead to excessive environmental degradation, as well as in some cases imposing additional taxes and subsidies to internalize harmful environmental externalities. Examples include subsidy reduction, environmental taxes and user fees, deposit-refund systems and targeted subsidies. In addition, a major source of many environmental problems is the lack of markets for natural resources and their services. Thus the key approach in tackling these problems lies in creating markets, for example, through establishing property rights, privatizing and decentralizing, implementing tradeable permits and rights, and initiating international offsets and other global markets. However, there is also a role in environmental management for more innovative forms of environmental regulation, in the form of standards, bans, permits and quotas. Finally, there is a more amorphous category of environmental policy instruments that the World Bank review calls engaging the public. These range from eco-labelling and other forms of information disclosure that assist consumers in making informed choices concerning environmentally friendly goods and services, to encouraging greater public participation in policy decisions that influence environmental management and sustainable development.

The review identified a vast range of such environmental policy innovations that have been implemented across the globe since Rio to improve resource management and control pollution. Tables 7.1 and 7.2

Table 7.1 Selected Examples of Policy Instruments for Resource Management

| Sector | Using markets | | | | |
	Subsidy reduction	Taxes	User fees	Bonds, refunds	Targeted subsidies
Water	Reduction in water subsidy: China, Hungary, Poland		Water taxes, pricing: Brazil, Germany, Chile, China, Colombia		
Fisheries				Oil spill bonds: US	
Land	Removal of land conversion subsidies: Brazil Removal of tax on undeveloped lands: France		Differential land use taxes: Germany Betterment charges: Korea, Mexico		Restoring natural cover: Canada
Forests	Reduction in conversion and livestock credit subsidies: Brazil, Central America	Forest product taxes: Brazil, Colombia, Venezuela	Stumpage fees: Brazil, Costa Rica, Honduras, Indonesia, Philippines, Malaysia Reforestation fees: Indonesia	Reforestation performance bonds: Costa Rica, Indonesia, Malaysia	Seedlings: India Reforestation credit: Costa Rica
Agriculture	Reduction in agricultural subsidies: various countries				
Biodiversity, Protected areas			Bio-prospecting fees: Costa Rica, Madagascar Watershed protection charges: Costa Rica, Indonesia Park entrance fees: Costa Rica, Indonesia, Nepal		
Minerals			Fees on mine wastes and tailings: Philippines		

Source: World Bank, 1997

Creating markets Property rights	Tradable permits/rights	Environmental regulations Standards, bans, quotas	Engaging the public Information disclosure, Public participation
Water rights: Chile, US Water supply management: Hungary	Water markets: Australia, Chile, India, New Zealand, US	Seasonal bans on certain uses: US Water use quotas: Israel, US	Water user associations: Argentina, Mexico, Turkey
Land title: Thailand	Tradeable quotas: New Zealand Transferable development rights: Puerto Rico, US	Land use standards/ zoning: Brazil, China, Guatemala, Korea, OECD, Pakistan	
	Tradeable reforestation credits: Costa Rica, Panama, Russia	Forest zoning: Brazil Logging/log export bans: Costa Rica Logging quotas: Malaysia	Eco-labelling: Nordic countries
Land ownership: Thailand Irrigation management: Argentina, India, Mexico, Philippines, Sri Lanka, Tunisia		Land zoning: Brazil Pesticides ban: Indonesia, Latin America	Eco-labelling: many OECD countries Community self-help groups: Kenya
Biodiversity prospecting rights and patents: Costa Rica, Madagascar	International tradeable conservation credits: Costa Rica, Mexico	Conservation zone: Brazil, China, Costa Rica	NGO involvement: Philippines
			Energy efficiency labelling: Australia

Table 7.2 Selected Examples of Policy Instruments for Pollution Control

Sector	Using markets Subsidy reduction	Taxes	User fees	Bonds, refunds	Targeted subsidies
Air	Reduction in energy subsidies: economies in transition, most developing countries	Emission taxes: Egypt, Korea, China, Eastern Europe, Kazakhstan, OECD Energy taxes: OECD Differentiated petrol prices: Egypt, Mexico, Philippines, Turkey Product taxes: Bangladesh, OECD		Sulphur tax refund system: Sweden	Industrial energy saving: Sweden
Water		Wastewater discharge fees: Brazil, China, Eastern Europe, Korea, Mexico, OECD, Philippines	Sewage charges: Brazil, Chile, China, Colombia, Indonesia, Malaysia, Mexico, Singapore, Thailand		Tax relief and subsidized credit for abatement: Brazil, Chile, China, Colombia, Ecuador, India, Korea, Mexico, Philippines
Solid waste		Waste disposal taxes: Canada, France, UK, US	Waste management fees: Ecuador, OECD, Thailand, Venezuela	Deposit-refund systems: Bangladesh, Brazil, Chile, Columbia, Ecuador, Finland, Jamaica, Japan, Mexico, Norway, Philippines, Sweden, Taiwan, US, Venezuela	
Hazardous waste	Reduction in agro-chemical subsidies: most developing countries	Disposal charges: China, OECD, Thailand Pesticide taxes: OECD Product taxes: Denmark			Subsidies for phasing out pesticides: Sweden

Source: World Bank, 1997

Creating markets Property rights	Tradable permits/rights	Environmental regulations Standards, bans, quotas	Engaging the public Information disclosure, Public participation
Private energy production: Philippines	Tradeable emission permits: Chile, Czech Republic, Poland, Kazakhstan, US Auctionable permits for ODS: Mexico, Singapore Carbon offsets: Latin America, Norway, Poland, Russia, US	Air quality and emission standards: Brazil, China, India, Korea, OECD, Philippines, Singapore, Turkey Ban on imports of ODS: China Emission quotas: OECD Area licensing for vehicles: Singapore	Public disclosure programme: Chile, Indonesia
		Wastewater discharge standards: China, India, Indonesia, Korea, Malaysia, OECD, Philippines, Singapore Industrial wastewater discharge quotas: Bahamas, China, Colombia, OECD	Public disclosure programme: Bangladesh, Indonesia, Philippines Community pressure: Korea
			Industrial waste exchange programme: Philippines
		Basel Convention: signatories Ban on some pesticides: Indonesia	

summarize some examples of the policies that have been applied, or are in the process of being instigated, across a variety of countries.

It is impossible to review the many types of policies indicated in Tables 7.1 and 7.2. We therefore focus on three key areas in which recent developments in environmental policy have been both dramatic and particularly innovative: the establishment and enforcement of property rights; the use of market-based instruments in conjunction with economic and environmental policy reforms; and the creation of global markets for international problems. However, designing improved environmental policies in these areas has not always been appropriate or effective. In the following review we therefore focus on the lessons learned from both the policy failures as well as the successes. Finally, the chapter discusses a further issue of importance in the implementation of environmental policy, which is the role of government and the efficiency of its intervention in markets.

Property Rights

The establishment and enforcement of property rights are often considered important steps in the creation of markets for environmental goods and services. Thus, an appropriate system of property rights is one of the key institutions determining the success of policies for sustainable and efficient management of natural capital.

Property rights are entitlements defining the owner's rights, privileges and limitations to use of a resource. Broadly, four types of property-rights regimes exist – although these rights tend to overlap, and there is also variation within each category:

- Private property – resource rights and ownership are conferred on an individual, group of individuals or a corporation, so that the owner has the right to exclude others from use of the resource and to regulate its use;
- State property – resource ownership is vested exclusively in the government, which determines and controls access and regulates use;
- Common property – resource ownership and management are in the hands of an identifiable community of individuals, who can exclude others and regulate use of the resource;
- Open access – access for resource use is effectively unrestricted; it is free and open to all.

A widespread misconception is that common property leads to over-exploitation by individuals – the 'tragedy of the commons' – and should be replaced by state or private ownership of resources. However, many common property regimes traditionally have involved the sustainable use of resources, but may break down due to overpopulation, policy failures, and the expropriation of resource ownership and rights. For example, in developing countries, this often occurs in the case of wildlife and natural habitats where community management of the wild resources consists mainly of important social rules and rituals governing traditional rights of access and harvesting. These rules and rituals are often informal and seldom legalized; consequently, they are easily undermined by external forces of change. Inequality of wealth among the various economic agents involved in common property management can also cause some problems. On the one hand, wealthier agents may appear to have a bigger stake in efficient and sustainable management of a natural resource because they may appear to gain more of the benefits (due to possessing a larger share of the boats, cattle or labour for example). On the other hand, richer agents are also likely to have more outside economic opportunities for investment, in which case they may choose to sacrifice conservation of the common property resource in order to invest the high rents earned from short-run over-exploitation in other economic opportunities. The latter effect is frequently observed in coastal and marine fisheries, whereby larger and more wealthy members of local fishing communities start acquiring more advanced fishing gear and boats, which in turn allows them to migrate to more distant fishing grounds once the local fishery is depleted. As a result the wealthier and more mobile fishermen are more interested in extracting rent from local fishing grounds, and often come into conflict with the small-scale, or artisanal, fishermen who are dependent on the local fisheries for their livelihoods (Balland and Platteau, 1996).

However, there are numerous cases where important natural resources are subject to open-access conditions. Open-access exploitation undeniably increases the risks of rapid resource degradation and depletion. As exclusion (or control of access) of users is problematic, each individual has the incentive to exploit the resource as quickly as possible. That is, the concern will be with maximizing returns from exploitation today – before they are lost to somebody else – rather than with the loss of future income due to resource depletion. Economists refer to this phenomenon as ignoring the user costs of resource exploitation. Perversely, the presence of surplus profit (excess economic rent), will also encourage over-exploitation – particularly under conditions of open access.

If large profits are available from resource exploitation but they accrue exclusively, say, to a single individual or the government, then the single resource owner can sustain the income earned indefinitely by limiting over-exploitation. However, if it is impossible to exclude others from exploiting the resource as well, then the existence of excess economic rents will be an incentive for many individuals to undertake this activity, or alternatively for the individuals already exploiting the resource to expand their activities. The result is that any profits will be quickly dissipated, as returns become rapidly dispersed over a growing number of individuals, none of whom will have any incentive to conserve the resource. Unfortunately, these conditions are characteristic of the exploitation of many of the world's remaining wild areas and resources, which are rich in biodiversity (Barbier, 1992). As highlighted in Chapter 6, government policies – fiscal incentives, pricing policies, regulations and land titling – often exacerbate these tendencies by reducing or distorting the direct costs of rapid resource exploitation and conversion. Once again, market, policy and institutional failures interact as the driving forces for unsustainable resource management.

Consequently, defining appropriate property rights to ensure the efficient and sustainable use of natural capital is an important instrument in designing policies for improved environmental management. The structure of property rights will strongly influence the success or failure of natural resource management, which will vary from one institutional design to another. The choice of a management regime itself could be anything from no action at all (laissez-faire) through market regulation and instruments, to communal, state or international governance.

How the design and implementation of an appropriate structure of property rights can affect natural resource conservation is illustrated for the case of biodiversity in Table 7.3. For example, under conditions of open access or ill-defined property rights, the establishment and enforcement of property rights may be essential steps in ensuring that local communities and the host country as a whole can capture some important benefits of biodiversity exploitation. However, there are also many examples of property rights being established, at least nominally, but they are either insecure, inappropriately defined or difficult for the owner to enforce locally. Examples include absentee ownership of land and resources in which the economic agents actually responsible for exploiting the resource are on short-term contracts or leases, poorly defined and short-term concession policies for timber extraction from publicly-owned forests, and the inability of owners to stop rent-seeking, squatting and encroachment on their property from other economic agents. In such instances, enforcement of property rights, monitoring of tenure arrangements, and defining appropriate terms of ownership and leasing can all improve the incentives of owners to manage and invest in the resource for maximum long-term profit and gains in efficiency. Finally, even if property rights are well defined and enforced within a country,

Table 7.3 *Property Rights and Incentive Effects for Biodiversity Conservation*

Original property rights regime	Property rights policy	Incentive effect
Open access and ill-defined or unenforced private, state or common property	Establishing/enforcing property rights, including intellectual property rights to genetic/taxonomic information	Allows local communities and host country to capture benefits of biodiversity exploitation, including bio-prospecting and ecotourism, through user fees and royalty deals
Private, state or common property, but insecure, inappropriately defined or difficult to enforce	Enforcement of property rights and guaranteeing security of tenure; define appropriate terms of ownership (including long-term lease or licensing agreements)	Allows private owner and state to manage the resource for long-term efficient management and profits, encouraging investments in activities with long-run paybacks, such as bio-prospecting, ecotourism, sustainable non-timber and timber harvesting
Private, state or common property, but no compensation for global benefits	Recognition of host country's right to sell global benefits in international markets, or to receive compensation for such benefits from the international community	Allows host country to receive compensation, either through globally created markets or through compensating funds via bilateral and multilateral mechanisms, eg the GEF, joint implementation deals, debt-for-nature swaps, tradable development rights, bilateral aid

Source: Adapted from Barbier et al, 1994 and Pearce et al, 1999

the global benefits associated with biodiversity conservation may not receive any compensation from the international community. Recognizing the host country's rights to market such global benefits internationally and receive appropriate compensation is an important part of the process of global market creation for biodiversity conservation. We will return to this key issue again later in this chapter.

Perhaps the most important benefit of establishing an appropriate system of property rights is that, if effective, it will lead to greater incentives to conserve natural resources at the local level. In some cases, direct ownership of the resource does not have to be transferred to, or conferred on, local communities. Instead, ownership of the resource will still be retained as state or private property, but local communities will have the right to share in the benefits arising from its exploitation. This can take the form of communities directly sharing in the profits earned from exploitation, or indirectly benefiting from a host of diverse activities associated with the resource-based development efforts, including building community-level conservation institutions, encouraging community involvement in both management and decision making about resource use, promoting ideas of sustainable agriculture and forestry, conserving and promoting traditional knowledge, providing education to local people, and generating development funds for infrastructure and other investment projects in local communities. Box 7.1 provides several examples of how these various measures have been used to ensure that local communities share in the benefits arising from protected area and wildlife conservation in Africa.

Finally, a note of caution. Table 7.3 indicates that the establishment of property rights may be an important solution to the problem of open-access over-exploitation of natural resources. However, unless the resulting property rights regime is effective and appropriate, it can reinforce rather than reduce the incentives for resource depletion and degradation. For example, as Box 7.2 illustrates, existing land titling regulations in many Latin American countries are most likely furthering the opening up of unoccupied forest lands and their conversion to agriculture.

Market-based Instruments and Economic Reform

Blueprint 1 drew attention to the benefits of using markets as the means both to correct environmentally damaging economic distortions and to internalize harmful environmental externalities. We noted that such an approach has had a long tradition in economics, dating from the original concept of market externalities in welfare economics originated by Pigou and Marshall in the early 20th century. In addition, the polluter-pays (or user-pays) principle as an important instrument in environmental policy had been endorsed since the early 1970s by the OECD.

However, just at the time we were writing *Blueprint 1*, the long-standing enthusiasm of economists for market-based instruments as environmental policy tools was tentatively being translated into implementation by policy makers, and grew quickly especially among OECD countries. This is reflected by two surveys commissioned at the time.

For example, a 1987 survey found a total of 37 charge systems in 14 OECD countries for environmental management – mainly pollution control – purposes (Opschoor and Vos, 1989). In addition, the survey also discovered that most of these were implemented in order to serve the financial objective of raising revenues rather than the incentive objective of reducing pollution. However, a follow-up review of market-based instruments across OECD countries just a few years later found that the number of charge systems adopted or under consideration had almost trebled, and their implementation had spread to around 21 countries (OECD, 1991). Moreover, more charges were being adopted or considered for

---

Box 7.1 *Sharing the Benefits of Conservation with Local Communities: Africa*

In Kasunga National Park in Malawi, local people have been given the right to harvest tree caterpillars and to establish bee hives in exchange for curbing other uses which are incompatible with the objectives of the Park. The gross income of these micro-enterprises is US$198 per hectare from tree caterpillars and US$230 from bee keeping. These earnings are higher than the income realized from subsistence farming of maize, beans and groundnuts, and could be used to increase agricultural productivity through purchasing scarce inputs.

In the Mount Kulal Biosphere Reserve in Kenya, several incentives have been designed in conjunction with the local people and which take into account their traditional pastoral tribal economy. They include: registering tribal range-lands to give them legal status; subsidies for the development of water resources; livestock marketing facilities; banking facilities to store wealth other than 'on-the-hoof'; providing security against raids from other tribes; conservation education in schools, wildlife extension in adult literacy classes, and information for government officials about the value of conservation; employment of local people in the system of protected areas; and income from tourism to the protected areas allocated to local developments.

In KaNgwane, South Africa, the site of the tourist lodge in the Mthethomusha Game Reserve is leased to the private sector, the lease being paid into a trust fund to be used for community projects selected by the tribal authority. In Richtersveld National Park, South Africa, the land on which the park lies is owned and occupied by the Nama community, which has leased it to the government but has retained rights to graze an agreed number of livestock and to the controlled harvest of natural products. The lease payments are deposited into a trust appointed by the community to manage the lands.

In Zimbabwe, to promote the conservation of the wildlife resources found on communal lands, private game reserves have been established where revenues from hunting are paid to local communities. Through this arrangement, about US$ 4.5 million has been paid out for development in remote parts of the communal lands over a period of seven years. Recreational hunting is now the most positive and widespread economic incentive for the conservation of large animals in Zimbabwe.

In Namibia, game populations have been conserved by giving ownership rights to ranchers, thereby giving them a financial incentive to protect game. In order to use huntable game commercially throughout the year, the property must be game-proof fenced and be larger than 1000 hectares. Hunting by people other than the owner is permitted only during the hunting season. The prospective hunter negotiates fees directly with the landowner, typical fees ranging from US$600 for kudu to US$100 for springbok. As a result, some protected species have now increased in numbers and breeding nuclei are sold to landowners at subsidized prices.

Source: McNeely, 1993

---

their incentive effects in reducing environmental damage and improved management rather than just for revenue-raising purposes. Market-based instruments were also being targeted for new areas of environmental control, such as CO_2 abatement and reducing fertilizer use.

Box 7.2 *Land Titling and Deforestation in Latin America*

The general open access conditions of unoccupied forest land is now recognized as a key condition underlying frontier agricultural expansion in developing countries (Pearce et al, 1990). In Latin America, this problem is further exacerbated by existing land ownership rules. In particular, land titling regulations which essentially acknowledge forest clearing as evidence of effective occupation and ownership for both agriculture and livestock raising have been documented as a major factor in frontier agricultural conversion in Costa Rica, Ecuador, Honduras, Panama and other Latin American countries (Kaimowitz, 1995; Peuker, 1992; Mahar and Schneider, 1994; Southgate et al, 1991; Sunderlin and Rodrígez, 1996). For example in Costa Rica, occupation of public lands has resulted in 60 per cent of farms lacking land title, and often competing claims for land (Peuker, 1992). This has provided an incentive to undertake activities on the land, such as clearing land of trees, which clearly demonstrate possession. Title to land can be obtained after ten years of possession, and a claimant can title up to 100 hectares of land if the property is devoted to agriculture and up to 300 hectares if it is devoted to cattle raising. The process has proved to be highly susceptible to fraud with respect to time of occupation, the area of the land to be titled, and the actual use of the land.

Land titling regulations can also affect the initial opening up of unoccupied frontier lands. It is often short-term extractive operations – such as timber concessions, mining concerns, large-scale commercial ranching and farming – that are more likely to be involved in initial frontier development. It is usually straightforward for governments to allocate large tracts of frontier land to commercial concerns and individual operators for extractive purposes, and often their activities receive subsidies or other fiscal incentives. Short-term land speculators may also be encouraged in this way. Generally, the objective of these extractive and speculative operations is to maximize short-term resource rents. Long-term investment in frontier economic development is not a major priority – particularly if it is difficult to acquire long-term property or use rights or to control illegal occupation. As a consequence, once sufficient rents are extracted, land abandonment and selling-off is common.

However, as noted above, once the frontier is opened by large-scale activities, the lack of secure property rights and general open access conditions prevailing on the frontier inevitably encourage rapid expansion of frontier agricultural activities by small-scale farming and landless households in search of new lands (Barbier, 1999; Schneider, 1994).

As discussed above and indicated in Tables 7.1 and 7.2, since the early 1990s the use of market-based instruments in environmental policy has spread even further. They are being implemented frequently for a variety of pollution control and resource management problems, and are being adopted not just in OECD countries but also more frequently by developing countries and economies in transition. What is more, they are being implemented as part of more general economy-wide and sector-specific reforms in these economies. This is an exciting prospect, as it suggests that they are being considered an important instrument in improving the link between economy and environment, thus helping to reverse the chain of unsustainable development (see Figure 7.1).

The growing attraction of market-based instruments as an environmental policy tool is that these instruments have the potential for being highly efficient through their reliance on using existing market mechanisms. As the name implies, they comprise those policy instruments that explicitly affect the private costs and benefits reflected in markets so that any unaccounted social costs (and benefits) of environmental degradation can be internalized to ensure the desired environmental improvement. Common types of such instruments are:

- Charges (taxes), fees or other additional prices to be paid for the social costs arising from environmental damages. Examples would include effluent charges on sulphur dioxide emissions, tax differentiation between leaded and unleaded petrol, user charges for public waste disposal, depletion taxes on mineral exploitation and stumpage fees for timber extraction;
- Subsidies to assist individuals in altering activities or conforming to environmental standards. Examples include subsidies for the development and adoption of clean technologies, tax allowances for energy conservation, soft loans for erosion control investments and price supports for paper recycling industries;
- Deposit/refund or fee/rebate systems, where a surcharge is levied on the price of a product leading to resource depletion or pollution which is then refunded if the product is recycled or if the depleted resource is restored. Examples include deposit/refund schemes for glass bottles, aluminium cans and other containers and reforestation rebates on timber stumpage fees;
- Tradeable or marketable permits, where rights to discharge pollution or exploit resources can be exchanged, either through a free or controlled permit market. Examples include tradeable permits for greenhouse gas emissions, marketable quotas for fish harvesting, tradeable depletion rights to mineral concessions and marketable discharge permits for water-borne effluents;
- Compensatory incentives, which are similar to subsidies in that market or financial inducements are created for certain individuals or groups who disproportionately bear either the risk or costs of environmental improvement or who possess unique environmental assets. Examples include compensatory financing of environmentally-friendly technology transfer to developing countries for compliance with international environmental agreements, debt-for-nature swaps and increased heating allowances for the poor and aged to compensate for energy or carbon taxes;
- Enforcement incentives for compliance with environmental regulations. Examples include performance bonds that are paid in advance

and refunded when compliance is assured, noncompliance fines that are levied when regulations are violated, and assigning legal liability for the costs of environmental degradation.

More recently, the definition of market-based instruments has been extended further to comprise the removal of subsidies and other public policy interventions that distort the private costs of resource use and pollution discharge (see Tables 7.1 and 7.2).

The potential cost-effectiveness of market-based instruments has meant that they are often considered to be superior to more traditional tools, such as regulations. However, as outlined in Box 7.3, there are many reasons why regulations may still be preferred, despite the greater efficiency gains that are likely to occur if market-based instruments are used. In fact, both have their role to play in improving environmental management. The key is making sure that the most appropriate and effective instrument is employed for each resource or pollution problem.

Many of the fears over the widespread use of market-based instruments are often misplaced. Although there is concern that, for example, in the energy sector the use of taxes and reductions in subsidies will negatively affect the performance of the overall economy, such claims are not substantiated by the evidence. Like all OECD countries, Germany and Japan have been taxing energy for many years. As shown in Table 7.4, this is reflected in the high rates of taxation on regular unleaded petrol in these countries. In contrast, China and Japan still subsidize energy consumption, yet their energy productivity (measured by GDP per kilogram of energy used) is around ten times lower than that of Japan and Germany. CO_2 intensity (emissions per dollar of GDP) is also much lower in Japan and Germany. In Germany from 1990 to 1994 while the economy grew by 1.1 per cent per annum, energy consumption fell by 1.5 per cent per annum.

In fact, since the mid-1980s China has been gradually reducing its energy subsidies, especially in the coal sector which supplies more than 70 per cent of the country's energy (World Bank, 1997). For example, subsidy rates for coal have fallen from 61 per cent in 1984 to 11 per cent in 1995. As a consequence, energy intensity has fallen almost 30 per cent since 1985. Energy consumption is 0.3 billion metric tonnes (in oil equivalents) less and CO_2 emissions 1.1 billion metric tonnes lower than they would be without the reforms. These reforms have contributed not only to energy conservation and environmental protection but also to reducing government spending significantly. As Table 7.4 shows, they may have also started to break the link between economic growth and energy consumption growth. From 1990 to 1994 China's GDP increased annually by 12.9 per cent, but its annual rate of growth in energy consumption was only 4 per cent.

Table 7.4 Cross-country Comparison of Energy Taxes and Subsidies

Country	Average tax (subsidy) rates (1995) (%) (a)	Per capita energy use (1994) (kg) (b)	GDP per kg of energy (1994) ($/kg)
China	(7)	647	0.7
Germany	78.4	4097	6.1
Japan	52.8	3825	9.6
Russia	(20)	4038	0.6
United States	33.3	7905	3.2

Country	Carbon dioxide emissions per dollar of GDP (1992) (mt/'000$)	Average annual energy growth rate (1990–94) (%)	Average annual growth rate GDP (1990–94) (%)
China	5.27	4.0	12.9
Germany	0.49	−1.5	1.1
Japan	0.30	2.3	1.2
Russia	5.43	−8.9	−10.6
United States	0.82	1.8	2.5

Notes: (a) For Germany, Japan and the US average tax rates on regular unleaded petrol; for China and Russia, average subsidy rates.
(b) Measured in oil equivalents.
Source: World Bank, 1997

Another attraction of market-based instruments is their flexibility. There is a wide range to choose from, and they can be easily adapted to meet local needs and requirements. This is illustrated in Box 7.4, which highlights the different policy approaches taken by the US and Singapore in order to meet their respective obligations to ozone-depleting substances under the Montreal Protocol. The US has chosen taxation, whereas Singapore has adopted tradeable permits. Both systems seem to be effective in achieving the desired objectives.

As noted above, the use of market-based instruments has also become more prevalent in both developing countries and in the economies of the former Soviet bloc and Eastern Europe that are undergoing major structural reform and transition. In the latter economies, the introduction of such instruments has often not been a simple matter of adjustment of markets, because for many resource-based sectors of the economy market mechanisms were either non-existent or highly marginalized and regulated. Instead, where they have been successfully introduced, they have had to become part of the overall transition to a market-based economy. As Box 7.5 shows, this was certainly the case for the water sector in Hungary, in which the reduction of subsidies and introduction of tariffs has been part of the overall market reforms instigated in the sector.

Many developing and newly industrializing countries have also been undergoing significant economic reforms as part of the overall economy-wide structural adjustment process. This has generally involved trade and market liberalization; the reduction of public sector involvement in the economy; and fiscal discipline and reform. As the overall objective has been to improve the market-orientation of the economy, the replacement of traditional command-and-control environmental regulations with market-based instruments has sometimes been part of the economy-wide policy package. This has particularly been the case in Latin America, where since the late 1980s many countries in the region have not only instigated major macroeconomic and sectoral reforms but also adopted a number of market-based instruments for environmental management purposes.

A recent study of the Latin American experience with such instruments in environmental policy has attempted to assess their overall effectiveness, including whether they have been helped or hindered by the market-oriented, economy-wide reforms being adopted across the region (Huber et al, 1998). The study confirmed that in recent years there has been substantial experimentation with market-based instruments in Latin America and the Caribbean. A full range of these instruments (for example charges, tradeable permits and compliance fees) is currently being applied in a variety of environmental management settings, including water supply and abstraction, water and air quality control, energy, forestry and agricultural sectors, solid and liquid waste management, reducing toxic substances, and noise abatement. A summary of some of the natural resource charges found in a selection of Latin American and Caribbean countries is depicted in Table 7.5.

The charges shown in Table 7.5 have met with varying degrees of success in achieving their environmental objectives (Huber et al, 1998). For example, forestry taxes have been set at very low levels, and suffer from weak enforcement particularly in frontier regions where monitoring is extremely difficult. In the case of charges in the energy and mineral sector, the taxation levels are generally too low to affect exploitation and use of the resource. However, the charges in Brazil, Colombia and Ecuador have been an important source of revenue for compensating local authorities in the affected regions and for environmental agencies. The most ambitious use of market-based instruments appears to be in the water sector in Brazil, Colombia, Mexico; that for Jamaica is under discussion. The proposed charge systems have the opportunity to improve water management while generating substantial revenue to overcome budgetary constraints. Unfortunately, the actual effectiveness of these systems has been severely limited, due to problems of lack of domestic capacity to administer them, enforcement difficulties, poor information, and lack of

Table 7.5 Natural Resource Charges in Latin America and the Caribbean

Country	Forestry taxation	Mineral and energy charges	Water use and pollution charges
Brazil	On forestry activities without adequate reforestation	On mineral and hydro-electricity production to compensate municipalities where exploitation takes place	Sewage tariffs based on pollution contents are in place in some states. Full water charges based on river basin authority are in place in some states and under discussion at federal level
Colombia	On forestry activities without adequate reforestation	On mineral and hydro-electricity production to compensate municipalities where exploitation takes place	Charges based on cost-recovery partially implemented, to be replaced by charges reflecting full environmental costs
Ecuador		On oil to finance environmental research and an institute for environmental management	
Jamaica			Under discussion
Mexico			Waste water charge at federal level partially implemented and under revision
Venezuela	On forestry activities without adequate reforestation		

Source: Huber et al, 1998

participation by stakeholders. In general, the overall experience of Latin American and Caribbean countries is that they are more of a complementary instrument rather than a substitute for more conventional environmental controls and regulation – their primary function is still mainly to raise revenue, and the main limitation on their effectiveness appears to be weak legislation, enforcement and institutions.

Although the simultaneous introduction of macroeconomic reforms in the region may have created the climate for the implementation of market-based instruments in environmental policy, some of the economy-wide reforms may have limited the effectiveness of such instruments. The main positive and negative environmental linkages are summarized in Table 7.6. The types of macroeconomic policy that appear to enhance their effectiveness and the attainment of environmental objectives generally are the removal of subsidies and other market distortions, thus allowing private costs to be more closely aligned with social costs (Huber et al, 1998). However, some reforms appear to be inconsistent with the implementation of market-based instruments, particularly in the case of public sector reforms that adversely affect or limit environmental legislation, regulations and institutions that are necessary for their operation.

To summarize, market-based instruments are a powerful, flexible and cost-effective policy tool for positively reinforcing economy–environment linkages that can guide an economy towards sustainable development. Their continuing widespread use and increasing adoption by a variety of countries at different stages of economic development, suggest that they will continue to have an influential role in policies for improved environmental management globally. In addition, the economy-wide reforms being introduced in some low-income economies, newly industrializing countries and economies in transition present an ideal opportunity to introduce them for environmental policy making. However, the effectiveness of their implementation will depend on the overall positive and negative environmental linkages of the general economic reform process. The fact that these instruments are often limited mainly to a revenue-raising role suggests that their full potential as an environmental policy instrument has yet to be tapped. Clearly, the next stage in their development is to exploit their full potential in furthering economy-environmental linkages for sustainable development.

Creating Global Markets

Improvements in the system of property rights, market mechanisms and government policies by a country to ensure that private benefit and costs reflect environmental values may still not conserve or protect the environment sufficiently from a global perspective. That is, unless a country receives compensation in some form for the management of its environment to provide values of global significance, such as conserving forests as carbon stores or as sources of biodiversity, then the country has little incentive to do so. In short, this is a problem of global market failure. A country may have an environmental asset that is, or may potentially be, producing benefits of global significance, but as there is no market in any other institution at the global level to enable the country to capture this value, it is unlikely to consider these global benefits in its decision whether to conserve, exploit or develop the asset.

Table 7.6 *Economy-wide Reforms and Environmental Linkages in Latin America and the Caribbean*

Policy	Positive linkages	Negative linkages
Macroeconomic stabilization		
Public price control	Induces efficiency into the management of resource-oriented public utilities	Creates barriers to including environmental costs in public tariffs to avoid inflationary consequences
Public deficit control	Induces removal of credit and fiscal subsidies in sectoral policies perverse to the environment; stimulates cost-recovery pricing in public tariffs	Reduces scope for improvement of public servant remuneration and budget allocation in the environmental management sector
Tight monetary policy (higher interest rates)	Induces recycling and conservation; offsets higher capital costs	Reduces financing capacity of firms to undertake pollution abatement, capital stock conversion and environmental expenditures generally
Privatization	Creates opportunities to introduce efficiency, eliminate subsidies and correct environmental liabilities in privatized state-owned economic activities, such as the provision of electricity, oil products, clean water, sanitation and solid waste collection	Reduces the scope, in the short run, to impose environmental costs on private firms
Trade liberalization		
Export promotion and globalization strategies	Induces dynamic export-oriented industrial and commercial companies to comply with international standards in environmental management, including eco-labelling	In the absence of appropriate regulations, monitoring and enforcement, induces more rapid depletion in resource-based sectors, such as mining, logging, fisheries and agriculture.
Import tariff reduction	Induces imports of capital goods with embodied clean technology	Creates opportunities for hazardous waste imports from developed countries
Fiscal reforms	Creates opportunities for the introduction of environmental criteria into conventional taxation and the elimination of harmful subsidies	Reduces the scope of specific environmental fiscal instruments that have earmarked revenue, if reforms aim to decouple revenue from expenditures

Source: Huber et al, 1998

Box 7.3 *Market versus Regulatory Instruments*

If they are appropriate, the potential cost-effectiveness of market-based instruments makes them attractive alternatives to regulatory controls. Regulatory instruments require the central authority to determine the best course of action, whereas economic instruments decentralize much of the decision-making to the single firm or household, which typically has better information for determining the appropriate individual response to given economic conditions. For example, studies routinely indicate that the costs of direct control of air pollution are two to over twenty times more costly than market-based instruments (Tietenberg 1990). In addition, such instruments provide cost incentives to adopt cleaner technologies and alternative resource inputs and processes, or to develop such improvements with time.

However, there are important qualifications to their inherent attractiveness:

• Important criteria other than cost-effectiveness may be used to evaluate and select environmental policy instruments (for example, the financial objective of raising revenues rather than the incentive objective of reducing pollution or exploitation);
• Under certain conditions (for example, the presence of uncertainty, threshold effects and pollution mixes) the cost savings from employing market instead of regulatory instruments may be minimal, or even negative;
• Market-based instruments are often used in conjunction with regulatory instruments, and in some instances, a mix of instruments may be the most cost-effective approach.

In addition, direct controls are still widely used as environmental policy instruments for several reasons.

Policymakers seem to prefer regulation because:

• A regulative tradition exists such that authorities are more familiar with the direct control approach, whereas switching to market-based instruments implies additional information requirements, higher initial administrative costs, bureaucratic opposition and more complex or at least unfamiliar processes;
• The effects of regulation are more certain, whereas the revenue and incentive effects of charges and other market-based instruments are seen as too uncertain;
• Charges and other market-based instruments are perceived as having undesirable impacts on inflation, income distribution and international competitiveness.

Firms and individuals seems to prefer regulation because:

• There is a fear that charges and other market-based instruments might be additional to compliance costs or that such instruments might be misused for financial rather than incentive purposes;
• They are also more familiar with the regulative tradition, and can influence this process better through negotiation;
• There is a risk aversion to instruments which have variable outcomes that may be difficult to predict or plan for, to the extent that even stricter, but more certain, direct controls are preferred.

Source: adapted from Barbier et al, 1994b

Box 7.4 *Applying Different Market-based Instruments to Reduce Ozone-depleting Substances: Singapore and the US*

Under the conditions of the Montreal Protocol, both Singapore and the United States have committed themselves to reducing ozone-depleting substances. Both countries have chosen to implement market-based instruments, but Singapore has opted for auctionable permits on consumption whereas the US has implemented an environmental tax on production.

In Singapore, each quarter the national quotas for ozone-depleting substances are allocated between importers and users, half on the basis of historic consumption and half through auction. The latter is conducted through a tender process conducted by sealed bid, in which each firm indicates the amount it would like to purchase and its offer price. Bids are then ordered by price, and the lowest winning bid (the one that clears the market) serves as the quota price for the full allotment, including the 50 per cent that was allocated on the basis of historic consumption. Initial operations of the auction process suggest that it is efficient. Once the quota price rose rapidly, firms started to make serious efforts at conservation and substitution. In addition, the auction allows the government to capture a large share of the quota rents, which are used to subsidize recycling services and encourage alternative technologies.

In the US, the tax on the production of ozone-depleting substances started at US$1.37 per pound in 1989 and increased to $5.35 in 1995. It is due to increase annually by $0.45. The tax was initially applied to eight chemicals but has been increased to twenty. To protect international competitiveness, border adjustments in the tax have been adopted. Not only has production of the most significant substances fallen to less than half of their pre-tax levels, overall production in the US of the five substances originally covered by the Montreal Protocol has never exceeded 65 per cent of the country's quota. In addition, the tax has generated substantial revenues for the federal government, starting at $360 million in 1990 and rising to over $1 billion in 1994.

Sources: IISD, 1994; Markandya and Shibli, 1995 and World Bank, 1997

As we have argued in Chapter 3, there are clearly a number of global environmental values that are not being captured by countries with abundant natural resources and unique ecosystems, due to the problem of global market failure with respect to these values. In recent years, and particularly since the 1992 Conference (UNCED), the international community has begun to explore various innovative ways to overcome this problem. The approach is generally referred to as creating global markets.

As the last row of Table 7.3 indicates, creating global markets essentially involves explicit recognition of a host country's right to sell global benefits and create the institutional means to do so. In some cases, this may lead to the actual creation of an international market for these benefits. In other cases, another form of global institution or mechanism will be established that allows the host country to receive compensation

---

Box 7.5 *Economic Reform of the Water Sector in Hungary*

In Hungary, subsidy reduction and the introduction of tariffs in the water sector have been part of the general economic reforms that have taken place since 1989. The reduction in water subsidies has been part of the process of cutting back on state intervention in the economy and curtailing budget deficits. For example, the subsidy for irrigation, which accounted for about 0.01 per cent of government expenditure was eliminated in 1990, generating an annual savings of US$2 million (1986 prices). The overall public water-supply subsidies have also been decreased from the pre-1989 rate of 100 per cent to 30 per cent. In addition, the share of central government investment in the water sector has fallen to less than one third, as ownership of existing water assets and water supply facilities has been legally decentralized to local authorities. Finally, water tariffs have been reformed and increased, based on a formula that includes the cost of inputs, depreciation, maintenance, and a markup of one to two per cent. The combined tariff for water and sewage now ranges from US$0.31 per cubic metre in Budapest to $1.42 in Siofok. The new tariff in Budapest represents a tenfold increase in the rate previously charged.

Source: World Bank, 1997

---

for such benefits from the international community. Although the creation of global markets for environmental goods and services has been a relatively new phenomenon, in recent years a number of wide-ranging international initiatives have been either discussed or actually launched.

Table 7.7 depicts and defines many of the key initiatives. Some, such as joint implementation, the Global Environment Facility (GEF) and environmental funds have been established quickly and have made important contributions to the conservation of some key global environmental benefits. Other initiatives, such as debt-for-nature swaps and bio-prospecting deals, have received substantial publicity, but their overall impact on global conservation may be overstated. Transferrable development rights and global overlays have yet to make an appreciable impact at the international level, but show potential. In comparison, regulation of resource-based trade and markets has generated significant controversy in recent years, especially with regard to the trade in elephant ivory and forest products. To illustrate both the promise and limitations of creating global markets for environmental benefits, we will discuss briefly joint implementation, the GEF and the regulation of resource-based trade.

Joint Implementation

Joint implementation, which is sometimes referred to as carbon offsets, has been specifically endorsed under the Framework Convention on

Table 7.7 *Creating Global Markets for Environmental Benefits –*
Selected Mechanisms

Type of mechanism	Compensating benefit to host country	Global environmental benefits
Global markets		
Intellectual property rights/bio-prospecting deals	Contracts and up-front payments to share any commercial returns from pharmaceutical and other products	Biodiversity, protected areas
Joint implementation/ carbon offsets	Foreign capital investment in energy and land use sectors (eg energy efficiency, fuel switching, renewables, forest conservation and restoration)	Reducing greenhouse gases, carbon store, biodiversity, protected areas
Debt-for-nature swaps	Purchase of secondary debt in exchange for establishing protected areas and conservation	Biodiversity, protected areas, carbon store
Market regulation/ trade agreements	Premium in importing markets for sustainable exploitation of resources	Biodiversity, wildlife, forests
Transferable development rights	Landowners/developers are compensated with alternative rights to develop areas with less environmental value	Biodiversity, protected areas, carbon store
International compensation		
Global Environment Facility	Payment of the incremental cost of conserving any global benefits	Biodiversity, protected areas, ecosystem services, carbon store, international waters, reducing greenhouse gases and ozone depleting substances
Global overlays	Modifying conventional cost-benefit appraisals of projects to account for any global benefits	Carbon store, biodiversity
Environmental funds	Long-term financing of environmental and community-based conservation projects	Biodiversity, protected areas, regional and trans-boundary benefits

Climate Change (FCCC). This approach allows a country to meet some of its carbon-emission reduction targets under the Convention by investing in emissions reduction in another country. The first country may gain, because it may be cheaper to invest in controlling emissions in another location than within its own borders. The recipient nation will also benefit from the additional investment in its country and from associated environmental benefits. The US has been particularly active in pursuing joint implementation. The projects are mainly concentrated in the energy and land use sectors, and cover diverse activities such as energy efficiency improvements, renewable energy investments, fuel switching, and forest conservation and reforestation.

Although joint implementation deals are primarily concerned with reducing greenhouse gas emissions, projects that lead to forest conservation and restoration also may produce global and local biodiversity benefits. Host countries are also likely to benefit from the improved efficiency and conservation, as well as reduced pollution, in their energy sectors. In addition, the 1997 Kyoto Protocol to the FCCC has stimulated further deals. It has been estimated that if only 10 per cent of the Annex I country obligations under the Kyoto Protocol were met from joint implementation, then the global market might amount to some US$1 billion by 2010 (Pearce et al, 1999).

However, to date, the overall number of joint implementation deals still remains fairly limited, although new deals are being concluded all the time. As Table 7.8 indicates, depending on the sector receiving the investment in the host country, there is also a great deal of variation in the price at which carbon is being traded. With the exception of afforestation and forest conservation schemes, the cost of carbon reduction ranges widely in each sector. In some sectors, the average cost of reducing carbon well exceeds prevailing estimates of the marginal damages likely to be caused by global warming (around US$30 per tonne of carbon). This suggests that some joint implementation schemes are highly inefficient, but this is most likely an indication that such an approach to global market creation is still in the very early stages of development and that some private companies may be investing in joint implementation purely for the public relations value.

The Global Environment Facility

The Global Environment Facility was established in 1990 and underwent a three-year pilot phase. Since 1994 the GEF has been restructured to become the permanent financing mechanism for the incremental costs in achieving agreed global environmental benefits through the FCCC, the Convention on Biological Diversity and the Montreal Protocol on ozone-

Table 7.8 *The Costs of Carbon Reduction through Joint Implementation*

Investment sector	Number of projects	Average cost ($/tC saved)	Highest cost ($/tC saved)	Lowest cost ($/tC saved)
Energy sector				
Renewables	36	71.5	861.9	19.7
Energy efficiency	24	148.0	653.3	2.3
Fugitive gas capture	2	180.0	384.6	0.04
Fuel switching	3	204.0	583.6	8.5
Land use sector				
Afforestation	2	1.2	3.0	0.1
Forest conservation	4	5.8	12.1	1.7
Forest restoration	2	39.2	242.4	5.4
Agriculture	1	na	na	na

Notes: $/tC = US dollar per tonne of carbon equivalent saved.
na = not available
Source: Pearce et al, 1999

depleting substances. The main thematic areas of the GEF are conserving biodiversity, mitigating pollution of international waters, protecting the ozone layer and reducing global warming. In addition, it has also provided support for a number of national and regional environmental funds. The principal beneficiaries are developing countries, who are perceived to bear the costs to modify development activities and land uses in order to conserve environmental values of benefit to the international community rather than themselves. However, the GEF has also financed environmental funds in central and east European countries.

Table 7.9 shows that since its inception the GEF has allocated more than US$767 million to global biodiversity conservation. The largest proportion of this funding has gone to forest conservation (40.4 per cent). The world's tropical forests are considered to be the major source of remaining biodiversity, yet they are threatened by development and conversion. Coastal, marine and freshwater systems are also highly diverse, as well as threatened with overexploitation and destruction. Around 16.8 per cent of GEF funds have been targeted to conserving the biodiversity of these systems. However, more than one fifth of the GEF financing for biodiversity conservation has been directed to short-term responses in developing countries. Although such funds have averted serious threats of biodiversity loss and provided immediate institutional assistance, this type of support does divert finance away from longer-term investments in ecosystem conservation and capacity building.

The GEF has demonstrated that the principle of international compensation for global environmental benefits can be implemented effectively in a remarkably short period of time. Moreover it can continue to operate as the principal funding mechanism for international environ-

Table 7.9 *Allocation of Global Environment Facility Funds for Biodiversity,* 1990–98 (US$ million)

Type of disbursement	Pilot phase (1990–93)	Restructured phase (1994–98)	Total ($ million)	(%)
Ecosystem specific				
Arid and semi-arid	29.6	51.8	81.4	5.1
Coastal, marine, freshwater	57.1	72.1	129.1	16.8
Forests	107.3	202.6	309.9	40.4
Mountain	18.3	29.9	48.2	6.3
General and institutional				
Enabling grants	14.0	25.2	39.2	5.1
Short-term response	107.9	51.3	159.2	20.8
Totals	**334.2**	**432.9**	**767.1**	**100**

Source: Pearce et al, 1999; GEF, 1998

mental agreements, thus eliminating the need to set up a proliferation of funds for each agreement. Its main limitation is the amount of funds at its disposal. For example, as Table 7.9 indicates, it is currently disbursing approximately US$90 to 100 million annually for global biodiversity conservation. Yet the total economic value of global biodiversity benefits – much of which are generated in developing countries – is roughly estimated to be of the order of a few billion dollars per year (Pearce et al, 1999). This suggests that the GEF is an important international compensating mechanism for capturing global biodiversity values, but its contribution is still small relative to the potential global benefits that remain to be conserved and captured by host countries.

Trade-related Agreements: Elephant Ivory

To operate as an effective incentive for increased conservation, any agreement on regulating trade in resource-based commodities or markets must aim to earn a global premium for host countries who have invested in the sustainable production of these commodities (Swanson, 1995). Such a premium provides compensation for those countries already investing in sustainable resource management, and it provides incentives for those not investing to do so. In addition, a market regulating scheme must be voluntary, non-discriminatory and be transparent to all producers and consumers involved in the resource trade that is affected. The overall objective should be a mutual agreement on the regulation of trade or markets in order to reinforce positive incentives for sustainable resource management and conservation, not to restrict trade or production per se.

Although in recent years many regimes for regulating trade and markets for resource-based commodities on environmental grounds have been proposed, and in some cases actually implemented, most have the aim of restricting rather than creating markets for these commodities as an incentive for sustainable production. Examples include the international ban on the trade in elephant ivory by the Convention on International Trade in Endangered Species (CITES), the use of CITES to ban the trade in selective endangered species of timber, and various proposals in Europe and North America to restrict the trade in unsustainably managed timber and other resource products from tropical countries. Yet, various economic studies have shown that these measures, at best, may succeed only in disrupting trade and increasing conservation in the short run (Barbier et al, 1990 and 1994a; Burgess, 1994; Swanson, 1995). In some instances, such shocks to badly managed trade and markets may be necessary, but they are rarely permanent solutions. Over the long run, trade bans and restrictions are difficult to enforce, they encourage huge profits from illegal trading and offer little incentive for host countries to invest in sustainable resource management. In most cases, a more long-term and effective approach is to develop an internationally agreed system of market regulation with inbuilt incentives for sustainable resource management by host countries.

The 1989 CITES ban on the ivory trade illustrates the problem. Although before the ban Africa's population of elephants had declined by half, numbers had actually increased in those (mainly southern) African countries that had used the proceeds from the ivory trade to invest in sustainable management and elephant conservation schemes, as well as anti-poaching activities, compensation to local populations for elephant damages and community-based wildlife schemes. In contrast, other African countries that had hardly invested in conservation of their elephants, including some that were earning substantial revenues from tourism, not only experienced rapidly declining elephant populations but also argued for the ban.

Unfortunately, the imposition of the ivory trade ban provided exactly the wrong incentives. Although the initial shock did disrupt the illegal trade and markets and cause prices to fall, the entire trade went underground and became difficult to monitor. More important, southern African countries who found themselves with drastically reduced funds to invest in their elephant conservation programmes have continually threatened to defy the ban, whereas other African countries that had previously under-invested in their elephants found themselves unjustifiably rewarded. Given these perverse incentives, it is not surprising that CITES has recently agreed a package of measures to allow Botswana, Namibia and Zimbabwe to resume a controlled trade in ivory, as well as to enable the 14 African countries with legally held and growing ivory stocks to make a one-off disposal in exchange for conservation funding. Thus it appears that CITES may be gradually moving to a system of regulated trade in ivory based on the sustainable management of elephant populations and conservation programmes, which has been proposed as a long-run market-based solution to the problem (Barbier et al, 1990).

Trade-related Agreements: Timber Certification

The idea that regulating or monitoring trade can lead to a green premium for exporters of a resource-based product, and thus encourage these exporters to invest in sustainable resource management, has been attempted recently with the trade in forest products (see Box 7.6). To reassure consumers that wood products are originating from sustainably managed sources, several international timber certification schemes have been implemented. Certification is also supposed to encourage many producers and exporters to invest in sustainable forest management, in order to capture the higher premiums for sustainably produced timber in importing markets. Overall, however, the results so far have not been too encouraging. Only a very small proportion of the world's forests and trade in timber products have been certified. Also, there is some doubt as to the green-premium effect of timber certification in importing markets. It is hoped that as the implementation of further timber certification schemes improves, and more markets, products and major producers are involved, then their impact on sustainable forest management and trade will be more marked.

In sum, creating global markets is still a relatively new instrument for tackling the huge problem of host countries failing to capture any of the global values associated with sustainable management of their environmental assets. Most mechanisms, including influential schemes such as joint implementation and the GEF, were initiated only in the 1990s. Thus the world is clearly still in the experimental phase of exploring the potential for creating markets for global environmental benefits. There have obviously been teething problems with some mechanisms, and some have been misguided in their application. Nonetheless, the whole approach could prove to be an innovative policy instrument for improving the linkages between economy and environment globally.

The Role of Government

In Chapter 6 we argued that the problem of government or policy failure is a major obstacle to the implementation of effective environmental policy. Correction of perverse government policies that damage the environment as well as taking appropriate and effective actions to overcome negative environmental externalities and other market failures is therefore extremely important to achieving more sustainable development. As we have shown so far in this chapter, there are now a number of policies, instruments and mechanisms available to governments to enact sound and sustainable environmental policies at the local, national and global level.

Clearly, there is a role for government in ensuring that the link between environment and economy is positively reinforced, and equally, there is popular concern around the world that governments should be actively involved in promoting more sustainable development. So why is more not being done to solve environmental problems today?

Perhaps ten years ago, when we first wrote *Blueprint for a Green Economy*, one could claim that policy makers and the general public alike were still ill informed of the importance of natural capital to overall economic welfare, and the need to develop an economic strategy for attaining sustainable development. That is, after all, why we wrote *Blueprint 1* in the first instance. However, ten years on, the world probably has a better appreciation than ever before of the role of the environment in sustaining economic development. Certainly, post-Rio, policy makers can no longer claim to be ignorant of sustainable development or be unaware of policy instruments for the environment. Moreover, as we have discussed throughout this book, we also have considerably more information than ever on the local, national and global values associated with key environmental assets.

When it comes to global environmental problems that require concerted and agreed international action by many, if not all, countries, then it is straightforward to see why it is difficult for governments to act collectively for the global good. This is particularly true with respect to forging international agreements on managing complex environmental management problems, which require cooperation by both developed and developing countries. Disincentives to cooperate explain why, for example, it has been extremely difficult to persuade all countries to sign the Convention on Biological Diversity or for the world community to negotiate an International Forest Agreement (Barrett, 1994; Sandler, 1993).

However, there are many other environmental problems that do not require collective international efforts, nor are very costly to solve through effective unilateral intervention by government at the local or even national level. Unfortunately, too often the failure of government to act in such instances has less to do with lack of resources, institutions or capacity and more to do with the protection of special interests, to the point of sometimes even collusion and corruption, and the subsequent persistence with misguided policies.

Box 7.6 *Timber Certification and Sustainable Management of Forests*

Timber certification is defined as a process which results in a certificate, attesting to the origin of wood raw material and its status and/or qualifications, often following validation by an independent third party (Baharuddin, 1995). Two steps are involved:

- Certification of the sustainability of forest management practices requires verification of the system in the country of origin, including the environmental and social impacts of forestry practices, against specified sustainable management criteria and standards;
- Certification of the product process involves inspection of the entire product processing chain of supply from the forest to final product, including any export markets.

Proponents of certification argue that it can promote sustainable forest management while simultaneously reassuring consumers. A properly designed, voluntary and independently accredited global certification scheme can hold producers accountable; it can provide a market-based incentive to improve forest management; it can meet consumer demands for wood from well-managed forests without creating trade discriminations; and it can be a mechanism for monitoring multiple factors involved in forest use (Dubois et al, 1995).

Others suggest that the evidence for considerable additional demand for certified wood products is unproven, and that any premium for certified timber exists only in small niche markets (Varangis et al, 1995). In fact, the additional costs of certification schemes might reduce the competitiveness of wood products in consumer markets. It is also argued that, although certification requires sustainable forest management as a necessary prerequisite, implementation of sustainable forest management does not require certification to take place (Kiekens, 1995). The promotion of certification globally should not either displace or divert resources from ongoing efforts in the major timber supplying countries to implement national forest policies, regulations and standards in accordance with international and national commitments to sustainable forest management. Finally, it is argued that the necessary but stringent conditions required for an accredited global certification scheme are bound to have only a limited impact on a small proportion of global timber production, and equally, on the sustainable management of a limited area of forests (Baharuddin and Simula, 1994; Kiekens, 1995).

Despite the proliferation of international timber certification schemes in recent years, the impacts on sustainable management of forests has been marginal. Total production amounts to around 3.5 million m^3 from about 5.1 million hectares of certified forests (Baharuddin and Simula, 1996). Certified production accounts for only 0.23 per cent of the world's industrial roundwood production. It is unlikely that the supply of certified timber and timber products will expand very fast, even under extremely optimistic projections.

Certification is thought to benefit timber exporters in:

- Gaining a green premium in importing markets; and
- Avoiding losses of market share and revenues due to any restrictions on these markets on unsustainably produced timber.

Varangis et al (1995) recently estimated the total gain from certification of tropical timber products to be US$428 million, or four per cent of current developing-country timber-product exports. These gains accrue largely from avoiding losses in markets and revenues in the absence of certification and not from the additional gains of any green premium – despite the generous assumption in the study that the latter might be as high as 10 per cent and with no substitution effects. It has been suggested that if both tropical and timber products were certified, more markets would certainly be affected, and as a result between 15 and 25 per cent of the total share of global forest trade could be influenced by certification (Baharuddin and Simula, 1996). However, a greater number of wood products and exporters certified may also mean less of a green-premium benefit.

The problem of government acting on behalf of special interest groups, for example in reinforcing the dominance of land markets in Latin America by wealthier households, is illustrated in Box 7.7. Not only do such policies perpetuate inequality and a skewed distribution of land resources but they also contribute to problems of land degradation, migration to the frontier and forest conversion by poorer households. Government protection of vested interests in the land market is therefore an important aspect of the deforestation problem facing Latin American countries.

However, government actions sometimes go beyond simply protecting the status quo and instead involve actual collusion with vested interests in environmentally damaging activities for short-term financial gain. One example of this is the growing problem of the illegal timber trade, which is particularly prevalent in tropical exporting countries (see Box 7.8). On the one hand, the incentives for this illicit trade are promoted by the policies of these countries in banning or heavily taxing exports of their own raw logs. This means that illegal harvesters and traders can earn substantial profits from their activities by smuggling logs into other markets. Corrupt officials in both importing and exporting countries also receive a financial reward for either failing to monitor and control the illegal trade, or from being actively involved in it themselves. The collusion is further compounded by governments wishing to hide the extent of the illegal trade, and the potential loss in forest revenues, by obscuring the statistics. Finally, not only are illegal harvesting activities usually destructive and damaging to forests but also the loss in export duties, timber royalties and income taxes to developing country governments means less revenues available to promote sustainable forest management and improve forest departments and institutions.

Another concern is the growing problem of governments developing misguided environmental policies. This problem occurs particularly in trade and environment issues, and is illustrated in Box 7.9 with some

---

Box 7.7 *Government Policy and the Inequality of Resource Access in Latin America*

In Latin America, inequalities in wealth between rural households have an important impact on land degradation and deforestation processes. Such problems are exacerbated by government policies that favour wealthier households in markets for key resources, such as land.

First, poorer households are often unable to compete with wealthier households in land markets for existing agricultural land. The result is two segmented land markets: the wealthier rural households dominate the markets for better quality arable land, whereas the poorer and landless households either trade in less productive land or migrate to marginal lands.

Second, although poorer households may be the initial occupiers of converted forest land they are rarely able to sustain their ownership. As the frontier develops economically and property rights are established, the increase in economic opportunities and potential rents makes ownership of the land more attractive to wealthier households. Because of their better access to capital markets, they can easily bid current owners off the land – who in turn may migrate to other frontier forested regions or marginal lands.

For example, in Colombia distortions in the land market prevent small farmers from attaining access to existing fertile land (Heath and Binswanger, 1996). That is, as the market value of farm land is only partly based on its agricultural production potential, the market price of arable land in Colombia generally exceeds the capitalized value of farm profits. As a result, poorer smallholders and of course landless workers cannot afford to purchase land out of farm profits, nor do they have the non-farm collateral to finance such purchases in the credit market. In contrast, large land holdings serve as a hedge against inflation for wealthier households, and land is a preferred form of collateral in credit markets. Hence the speculative and non-farming benefits of large land holdings further bid up the price of land, thus ensuring that only wealthier households can afford to purchase land, even though much may be unproductively farmed or even idle.

As in Colombia, tax and credit policies in Brazil generally reinforce the dominance of wealthier households in credit markets and the speculative investment in land as tax shelters (Mahar and Schneider, 1994). Because poorer households on the frontier do not benefit from such policies, their ability to compete in formal land markets is further diminished. This reinforces the sell-out effect of transferring frontier land ownership from poorer initial settlers to wealthier and typically urban-based arrivals, forcing the poorer households to drift further into the frontier (Schneider, 1994).

---

examples from the forest-products trade. In some cases, such as the US spotted-owl reservations, the policy was truly misguided, in the sense that the economic costs of the environmental policy were grossly underestimated, reflecting an ineffective and inappropriate conservation approach. However, of even more concern is the increasing use of environmental regulations as a form of disguised protectionism (a non-tariff barrier) to exclude foreign competitors from domestic markets. The policies are not simply misguided in their design; they are being deliber-

---

Box 7.8 *Government Collusion and the Illegal Timber Trade*

Illegal activities in the timber trade cover a number of widespread practices involving illegal logging, illicit trading (timber smuggling) and unauthorized pricing and classification of timber. For obvious reasons, assessing the extent of these activities is extremely difficult, and estimates can vary widely. For example, a recent review of studies by the Environmental Investigation Agency (EIA, 1996) cites World Bank estimates of illegal logging worldwide amounting to 5,000 km^2 each year during the early 1990s, an area nearly the size of the Indonesian island of Bali. However, a report by the World Wide Fund For Nature (WWF) claims that virtually all logging for export currently taking place in India, Laos, Cambodia, Thailand and the Philippines is illegal; and much logging in Malaysia and Indonesia could be classified as illegal. Although most of the recent concern has been with illegal activities in tropical countries, and the consequent loss and degradation of tropical forests, there is also evidence of significant illegal harvesting and other practices in temperate countries as well.

Although difficult to verify conclusively, there is some evidence that the scale of illegal trade in logs is continuing unabated and possibly even increasing. It is also evident that producer-country governments are colluding in at least hiding the scale of the activity, if not tacitly endorsing it. For example, the annual review of member countries' trade by the International Tropical Timber Organization (ITTO) has indicated a perpetual problem of under-reporting of log exports – the reported exports of logs from some countries are consistently and significantly below the corresponding levels reported by the importing countries. Trade statistics for some importing countries have indicated sizeable log imports from countries where a complete log export ban is supposed to be in force. Publicizing such discrepancies can have an impact. For example, as a result of the evidence of under-reporting in ITTO's annual review, Papua New Guinea has undertaken to tighten controls over its log exports.

To some extent, the growing illegal trade in logs is a consequence of many developing countries implementing export bans and restrictions, as well as prohibitively high tariffs, as a means of encouraging a shift in the composition of their exports away from logs to more highly valued processed timber products. The loss of export earnings and government revenue from any resulting increase in illegal log exports is yet another significant cost of such policies. Against this must be weighed the financial benefits that various corrupt officials are gaining from supporting and colluding with the illegal trade.

However, illegal logging and trade is also a serious setback for promoting sustainable forest management practices. By their very nature, such activities involve destructive and short-term practices that are damaging to forests. In addition, the loss in export duties, timber royalties and income taxes to developing country governments means there are less revenues available to promote sustainable forest management and improve forest departments and institutions.

---

ately perverted for non-environmental ends. Any environmental benefits are usually negligible at best, and of course the protectionism results in losses of economic efficiency in the affected markets. Persistent use of environmental regulations for such purposes can also foster distrust of environmental policy by the industry and the general public.

Box 7.9 *Misguided Environmental Policies in Developed Countries and the Forest Products Trade*

Developed countries are increasingly employing a variety of environmental regulations in their forest industries – both alone and in conjunction with export restrictions – that may have significant trade implications. Whether or not such regulations are being used intentionally for this purpose, they may lead to trade distortions and discrimination. For example, the combination of trade and environmental restrictions on logging in the Pacific Northwest of the US – such as the spotted owl reservations coupled with the state-level log bans – produced significant domestic and global trade impacts, including increases in global sawn log prices and regional shifts in production with related effects in major sawn wood and plywood markets (Flora and McGinnis, 1991; Perez-Garcia, 1991).

In many developed countries domestic policies to promote waste paper recovery and recycling have had important trade implications, particularly where they involve mandatory restrictions on the levels of virgin fibre and pulp use. For example, Bourke (1995) and Elliot (1994) discuss the trade implications for Canada – the world's largest producer and exporter of newsprint – of US state and federal recycled content laws for newsprint. In particular, the US recycled content laws may provide an unfair cost advantage to domestic producers because of the greater availability of used newsprint in the US than in Canada. Similar problems apply to packaging and reuse requirements, such as the recent EU packaging directive and Japan's regulations for recycling of paper, logging residues and dismantled houses. Such regulations all have the potential of being used as non-tariff barriers to competing paper product imports, particularly if there are requirements on suppliers to recover packaging or to impose deposit and refund schemes (Bourke, 1995; Weaver et al, 1995). Potential problems exist with other environmentally oriented regulations, such as the increasing restrictions on trade in wood panels using formaldehyde glue, regulations banning or controlling certain timber preservation processes and materials, and controls on processing materials, such as the use of chlorine in bleaching pulp.

Government has an important role to play in the design and implementation of policies for sustainable development. If government fails to act effectively and inappropriately to encourage sustainable and efficient management of economy–environment linkages, we must ask why this is the case. If the problem is tied to protection of special interests, collusion, corruption, or even simply a case of misguided policy, we must identify and correct this particular form of government failure. As indicated in Figure 7.1 and throughout this book, incentives are essential in determining whether economy–environment linkages will be sustainable or not. Households and firms require appropriate incentives in order to take into account the impacts their activities may have on environmental assets. Governments and public officials also respond to various incentives, and we need to ensure that the incentives are in place to allow governments to design effective environmental and sustainable development policies.

8

Solving Environmental Problems II: Choosing Policy Instruments

Introduction

After the advocacy of monetizing preferences for the environment, the most controversial issue in B*lueprint* 1 was the argument that environmental policy should be based more firmly on the use of market based instruments (MBI), such as environmental taxation and tradeable permits. Even though the polluter-pays principle was nearly twenty years old at the time B*lueprint* 1 was written, the idea that the polluter should pay a tax or charge for damage done, or pay to acquire permits to pollute, came as a surprise to many. Some ten years on, the language of polluter-pays, of environmental taxes (or, as they have sometimes been called, eco-taxes), and tradeable permits and quotas is commonplace. In this chapter we revisit the arguments in favour of the market-based approach and look at the experience of the last decade. We conclude that the arguments in favour of market based instruments have largely been accepted, that there remain concerns, and that not only the developed, but the developing world is moving, albeit slowly, towards a shift in the structure of environmental policy based on economic incentives. At the same time, some of the environmental incentive measures that have been introduced are a long way from the ideal design of such measures.

The Nature of Market-based Instruments

What are market-based instruments? While it is easy to think of examples, such as a tax on pollution, it is surprisingly difficult to produce a robust definition. They are usually taken to refer to two kinds of policy measure: an administered price or an administered market.

In each case, the free working of the price mechanism, in the sense of there being no interference by a regulatory authority, is not allowed. In the case of the administered price, market prices are charged for something that otherwise would not have a market price (for example, a tax is put on pollution emissions) or an existing price is modified through intervention (for example, a product price is modified through a charge on the product to reflect its impact on the environment). So, administered prices either create a price where there previously was none, or they modify an existing price to reflect environmental impacts.

In the case of the administered market, a market is created where there previously was no market. An example would be tradeable pollution permits which operate by permitting emissions and then allowing the permits to be bought and sold in a permit market. The permits can be bought and sold in the market. Since both instruments operate through the existing or created market, they have the name market-based instruments.

Most of the environmental economics literature tends to assume that any policy instrument that is not an administered price or administered market is command and control (CAC). Others define command and control as anything where some behaviour is mandated – 'do this but not that'. All standard setting would then become command and control. Some analysts (see, for example, Russell and Powell, 1996) prefer to divide up this broad residual category of command and control into sub-categories, reserving the term command and control for those instruments which do two things: direct the polluter what to do (for example, achieve a standard) and how to do it. Table 8.1 offers a template for making the distinction between market-based instruments and command and control.

Table 8.1 *Defining Market-based Instruments and Command and Control*

	Specifying what the polluter must achieve	*Not specifying what the polluter must achieve*
Specifying how to do it, that is how to comply	True command and control	Mixed system
Not specifying how to do it	Mixed system	True market-based instruments (tax) and others

Thus, a policy based on banning a product or technology is true command and control because it says what is to be achieved (zero output, or zero output by the banned technology) and it says how to achieve it. A fishery facing a limit on fish catch is being told what it must achieve. If it is also told that it must do this through fleet retirement or controls on mesh size, then it is also being told how to do it.

An emissions tax says the polluter must pay a tax, but does not give him a target pollution level (does not say what to achieve) and does not say how he is to modify behaviour in the light of the tax (how to do it), so it belongs in the bottom right hand corner of Table 8.1. A tradeable permit is a little less precise but does not fix a target for emissions for each polluter, since each polluter can emit whatever he likes as long as he has permits to do so. Nor does it say how his behaviour should be modified so as to get more permits. So, it too belongs in the bottom right hand corner.

A great deal of environmental policy does not set standards for emissions or ambient quality, but sets a standard for the technology that can be used. These technology-based standards, such as 'best available technology' or 'best available technology not entailing excessive cost' would belong in the top right hand corner of the matrix: they tell the polluter what to do but do not specify a pollution target. The target is, effectively, whatever comes about once the given technology is in place. They also lack the 'how to' flexibility of a market-based instrument.

While market-based instruments are often referred to as economic incentives, it is clear that all environmental policy is based on economic incentives. Even with command and control, if a polluter complies with the policy he has to spend money on abatement equipment – that is an economic incentive – and if he fails to comply with the policy then he risks financial fines and other forms of punishment. In what follows we use the terms market-based instruments and economic incentives inter-changeably, but in doing so we acknowledge that the terminology of economics-based environmental policy is not very precise.

Economic Instruments versus Command and Control

Blueprint 1 rehearsed many of the arguments for and against adopting market-based instruments. Since we wish to focus on the experience of their use we offer here a brief overview of the pros and cons.

Command and Control

The incentive system in command and control is financial and rests on the penalty for non-compliance. Such penalties derive only partly from the fine that a regulator may impose. It is more likely that the polluter will lose more from damaged public and consumer image if the pollution incident or situation is made public. This is especially true for major corporations claiming a green image, but may be just as important for a small firm with a local reputation.

Command and control regulations set standards which can be emissions based, ambient based, product based, or technology based.

An emissions-based standard sets out the regulation in the form of not emitting more than X tonnes of a pollutant, or, more likely, X units of pollution per unit of fuel (weight of SO_x per kilowatt hour for example), or per unit of time (weight of SO_x in a given 24-hour period for example), or per unit of output. In general, these measures are not cost-efficient because they tend to be applied uniformly across polluters. Efficiency requires that polluters who face the lowest cost of pollution control should abate more, whilst those with high costs of abatement should abate less. Making emission reduction targets the same across polluters is therefore inefficient: each polluter has to achieve a given level of emissions reduction regardless of the cost of achieving that reduction. To some extent, the problem of the cost of achieving the target is acknowledged in command and control regulation. The regulation may therefore say that emissions should be as low as reasonably achievable, or that a technology should be introduced provided it does not entail excessive cost.

Ambient standards set a given maximum concentration of pollution in the receiving environment. It is then up to polluters to ensure they do not exceed this standard. Since no one polluter will know what has to be done to achieve the standard, ambient standards are best thought of as overall targets. The actual control measure to achieve that target will have to be allocated between polluters and may consist of emissions limits or technology standards for example.

Technology based standards basically tell the polluter what technology they are permitted to use, usually the best available technology in the sense of the cleanest one. As noted above, the cleanest technology may be very expensive, so that best-available-technology regulations are often attenuated by clauses such as 'not entailing excessive cost'. This is an attempt not to over-regulate to the detriment of competitiveness and employment. Technology based standards leave no room for flexibility of response: a given technology has to be used. Hence they will also tend to be inefficient.

Command and control is typically regarded as being economically inefficient (overall compliance costs are not minimized) and dynamically inefficient (once the standard is achieved the polluter has no incentive to go further). But there is one case where it is clearly preferred, namely when the only option is to have zero emissions or ambient concentrations. Then the best policy is likely to be to ban the pollutant altogether, as has happened with certain pesticides.

Market-based Instruments

With market-based instruments the incentive is again financial: if the polluter chooses to pollute then he pays a price, that is he pays either the tax on pollution or the price of a permit to pollute. He will abate pollution if the cost of abatement is less than the price charged to pollute. Thus, while one sometimes still hears environmental tax solutions being criticized because they allow pollution, so long as it is paid for, the criticism is somewhat misconceived. No rational polluter is going to pay a price to pollute if it is cheaper to control the pollution.

Market-based incentives leave the polluter with the flexibility of how to respond – the choice of technology is not dictated. It is this flexibility that helps to minimize the costs of compliance. Why should we worry about minimizing the costs of compliance? After all, if pollution is wrong the polluter should simply pay and if it is expensive for this to happen so be it. This argument is heard less frequently than when we wrote *Blueprint 1*, but it is still prevalent in some circles. Making compliance expensive is, however, a serious mistake. First, it amounts to wasting money and money can always be used for other beneficial purposes, even if the benefits accrue to shareholders. Second, the more expensive compliance is, the more we build up resistance by polluters to further regulation. Polluters, it needs to be remembered, are firms and households, and both can be very effective lobbies against regulation. Third, the more expensive compliance is the greater the cost burden borne by the polluter. Rising costs can impair competitiveness between sectors, although the standard outcry of business against regulation on this basis is not always very persuasive. There is little evidence, for example, that regulation impairs competitiveness (and in a world where exchange rates tend to be free, higher costs should simply show up in exchange rate changes). Ignoring the cost of compliance is therefore a very short-sighted approach to environmental policy.

There are several problems with environmental taxes.

First, unless we know for sure how firms will react to taxes, we cannot be sure what their environmental impact will be. This is sometimes an issue of the elasticity of demand for the product in question. A tax adds to costs and this raises the price of the product. When prices rise, demand tends to fall, and the extent of the fall is measured by this elasticity – the percentage change in demand arising from a 1 per cent change in price. If we do not know the elasticity, we cannot say what effect the tax will have and this makes the tax an uncertain instrument of policy. As it happens, the issue is not quite so serious, since environmental taxes are meant to have their main effects through the adoption of abatement equipment. So, the issue is not so much the elasticity of response to the tax, as the relationship between the tax level and the

Box 8.1 *The Basic Analytics of Market-based Instruments*

In the diagram below we show money values (£) on the vertical axis and the quantity of pollution on the horizontal axis (*EP*). The simplest way to think about the diagram is to regard the pollution as coming from a single firm. Two curves are shown. The first is labelled *MDC* and shows the extra (marginal) damage to the environment that occurs as pollution increases. Note that we work with these incremental or marginal concepts because it helps pinpoint certain findings more clearly. Marginal damage, then, simply means the extra damage arising from an extra unit of pollution. We have shown the curve rising, but it could be horizontal (the extra damage is the same regardless of how much pollution there is) or even declining (a special case of some interest, but which we do not pursue here). The other curve is labelled *MAC* and this is the marginal abatement cost, that is the costs of reducing pollution by one extra unit. The shape of this curve is not so obvious and is best understood by reading it from right to left. At high levels of pollution it costs comparatively little to reduce a unit of pollution. As the firm gets cleaner and cleaner, however, the extra cost of removing the last units of pollution gets higher and higher. The two curves cross at a level of pollution equal to *EP** and a money price of *T**. The cross point is important. At this point, the extra costs of pollution damage (*MDC*) are just equal to the extra cost of avoiding or cleaning up that damage (*MAC*). It would not make sense to operate where *MAC>MDC* because it would cost more to avoid the pollution than the damage it does. Nor would it pay to operate where *MAC<MDC*, since we could improve the situation by reducing pollution more. So *MAC=MDC* is an optimum.

How do we achieve this optimum? The distance *OT** is in fact the tax that we should put on the pollution. To see this, look at the horizontal line emanating from point *OT**. A firm faced with this tax will avoid the tax by abating pollution – by incurring costs along *MAC*. But it will only abate as long as the costs of abating are less than the tax it would otherwise have to pay. We see this happens to the right of *EP**. To the left of *EP** the tax is less than the MAC so the firm will find it cheaper to pay the tax than to reduce pollution. In other words, by charging the tax *OT** we get to the optimum. The same argument applies if the firm had to pay a price *OT** for a permit to pollute.

Notice that the firm pays the tax *OT** on all its output of pollution; even though the pollution level *OEP** is in fact optimal pollution, it is an amount of pollution that is economically justified. It is this fact that causes some of the opposition to environmental taxes.

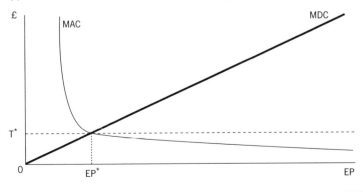

cost of abating pollution by one extra unit. We often know these abatement costs in much more detail, or, at least we do when the abatement takes place through the installation of off-the-shelf technology. We are less sure when the abatement measures occur through management changes, for example. This issue is discussed further below.

Second, environmental taxes are applied to all output. Suppose we wish to tax the output of pesticides, either at the point of production or at the point of use by farmers. We know that there is some optimal level of pesticide production and use. This is where it costs more to reduce pesticides than the environmental benefit society gets back (as illustrated in Box 8.1). But a tax is applied to all pesticide output (or input), regardless of whether the output is the optimal level or not. Apart from the fact that this seems somewhat unfair, it means that the polluter bears a tax burden that could be significant compared to command and control regulation. Indeed, it is widely thought that this tax burden argument explains a lot of the opposition to environmental taxes. What evidence we have suggests that, even with the excess imposition, environmental taxes remain cheaper in compliance terms than command and control.

Third, taxes raise revenues. This is both an advantage and a disadvantage. It is an advantage because the revenues can be used for beneficial purposes. Indeed, there is a growing move to couple such taxes with the recycling of revenues to industry or to environmental causes, or both. We illustrate this in Box 8.2 with reference to the landfill tax in the UK. If at least some of the tax revenue is recycled in this way industry's opposition to the tax is likely to be less. The tax effectively buys the polluter's cooperation. This feature of modern environmental taxes is sometimes known as the double dividend because the tax still has an effect on pollution, its stated aim, and also can be used to help solve other distortions in the economy, as for example by reducing labour taxes which act as a disincentive to work. The disadvantage of revenue raising is that governments might quickly lose sight of the main purpose of the charge, namely to help solve an environmental problem. Instead they may prefer to raise the tax in future for budgetary revenue-raising reasons. Again, this fear that environmental taxes will quickly become revenue-raising taxes explains some of the opposition to such taxes. But, provided the tax remains revenue neutral – the revenues are recycled in some way and do not count towards government income – then this problem should be minimized.

One problem that has arisen with environmental taxes is that some of them have been applied in practice without full understanding of the implications. A good example is the current proposal in the UK to tax aggregates – the extraction of minerals such as stone, sand and gravel.

Box 8.2 *The UK Landfill Tax*

Solid waste that is not recycled tends to be disposed of by landfill, which involves incineration, some composting and burial in the ground. Landfill sites can be the source of environmental problems. The disamenity of the sites is often significant with noisy lorries arriving regularly during the day to dispose of waste, with some litter blowing into neighbouring areas, associated with odour and vermin in some cases. Landfill sites also emit methane gas which is a greenhouse gas and carbon dioxide, although the extent to which the carbon dioxide gets locked in is debated. Quite a few developed economies have therefore introduced measures to improve landfill management. Much of this legislation involves standards of management and technical features to ensure that, for example, liquids from the site do not leach out to groundwater and river systems. But a number of countries have introduced landfill taxes. These tend to take the form of a tax per tonne of waste taken to the landfill site. As such, landfill taxes suffer from the deficiency noted in this chapter: the tax is on a tonne of waste rather than the externality itself. But if the aim is to divert waste to recycling this is acceptable. In the UK, the landfill tax was actually based on a detailed study of the money value of the externalities in question, although no detailed study then existed for site disamenity.

From 1996 to 1998 the tax rate for active waste was £7 per tonne and for inactive waste £2 per tonne. The current tax rate is £10 per tonne and this will rise by £1 per tonne per annum to reach a rate of £15 per tonne in 2004.

While the initial tax rate was based on measured money value of externalities, the proposed changes appear to have departed from this analytical foundation for the tax, having more to do with ensuring that behaviour does change. Put another way, the existing tax has not diverted much waste from landfill. Another risk with taxes of this kind is that they will divert waste to illegal outlets, so-called fly-tipping. But there is little evidence of such diversion. Most fly-tipped waste is household waste and households do not pay directly for the landfill of their waste, so have no incentive to fly-tip in order to avoid the tax. Oddly, the tax has been most effective in respect of inert waste – waste that does not decompose – with substantial reductions in flows of such waste going to landfill.

Mineral extraction imposes a number of environmental impacts: the noise and reduced amenity at the site, for example, and the emissions, noise and other effects of the lorries that transport the materials. Prima facie, then, a tax on aggregates should help to internalize the externality. Like many environmental taxes, the proposal is to tax the aggregates themselves, but a moment's reflection shows that the effect may not be very significant and that the only effect of such a tax would be to yield significant revenues to the government. This happens when two factors combine: first, the tax is levied on the output of the product rather than the externality; and when the demand for the product is inelastic, that is not very responsive to the tax charged. As it happens, the demand for aggregates appears to be inelastic, because the aggregates are used in infrastructure and property building, and the cost tends to be a small fraction of the overall cost of construction. So, significant price rises can occur without much change in demand. But if there is little change in demand, there will be little effect on the environment. What is happening here is that the tax is not having an effect via the output of aggregates. This suggests that we focus on the effect of such a tax on the introduction of management changes and abatement equipment in the industry. But a tax on output has no effect on such measures because however much the industry abates pollution it will still pay the tax. This is because the tax is levied on output and not on the externality.

It is always difficult to know if regulators understand the full logic of environmental taxation. If they do, then perhaps they are playing a game with the polluters. The game might be to threaten such a tax, knowing that it will cost the industry a lot of money, and wait for the industry to respond by offering a negotiated agreement of the kind discussed in Chapter 9. In other words, the tax is there mainly as a threat and in the expectation that the industry will institute abatement measures in return for the tax not being implemented. Indeed, there are many examples of such measures being introduced with the quite explicit understanding that industry should respond in this way: the game is completely open. A more cynical interoperation is that regulators know the tax will be environmentally ineffective, and that the tax is there mainly to raise revenues. Yet another view is that the regulators have not thought through the implications of such taxes, preferring to opt for the administrative ease of a per-tonne-of-product tax rather than the more textbook-justified tax on the externality itself.

Do tradeable permits have the same problems? Their growing popularity suggests that they are more readily accepted by industry. Why might this be? After all, the price of a permit acts just like a tax, so, in theory, there should be no difference from a polluter's point of view.

Industry prefers tradeable permits for a number of reasons. First, there is less risk that governments can abuse the system for other ends. A permit is a permit to pollute and it has a price in the market. Governments cannot raise revenues from them unless they auction them off to begin with, a solution that many economists would favour, but which is rarely practised. Second, the polluter pays only for those permits he needs. In terms of Box 8.1, the tax level 'T' can be thought of as the price of a permit to emit pollution. The analysis stays the same but the polluter pays only for the non-optimal emissions. Third, business feels more in control of a permit system.

Governments too may prefer permit systems, not least because the environmental standard may be more easily achieved. If for example the standard for nitrogen oxide emissions is set at 100 tonnes, then permits are issued for that amount and no one can emit without holding a permit.

In practice, permit trading systems are often complex to introduce and the usual problem they face is a geographical one. If A and B trade permits because A is a high-cost emitter and B is a low- cost emitter, then A will buy the permit and B will sell it. A does not then abate pollution but B does because his abatement costs are less than the price he gets for the permit. But their trade may affect C who is located downwind or downstream of A. C is the third party whose interests may be neglected in the trade between A and B. This problem is serious enough when all are firms, but is even more serious when they are states or countries. This third-party problem largely explains why we will see very little, if any, inter-country trading of sulphur and nitrogen dioxide permits in Europe, even though, in principle, such trades are allowed under the UN Economic Commission for Europe's Second Sulphur Protocol of 1994.

Probably the most exciting area for tradeable permits is in the context of global warming. Box 8.3 outlines some of the trading mechanisms allowed under the Kyoto Protocol of 1997.

The Experience with Economic Instruments

The OECD has reviewed the experience of economic instruments in OECD countries. By 1987 there were perhaps 100 economic instruments in these countries but few with any real incentive effect. By 1992, 169 instruments could be found in 23 countries, with product charges and deposit refund systems being the most common. (Product taxes tend to be on packaging, CFCs, fertilizers and oils.) The OECD's judgement is that economic instruments are not substituting but complementing other policies.

There is also a growing trend towards revenue neutrality, which may take several forms:

- Taxing polluters and using revenues for labour tax reductions. While this helps to buy cooperation, it still tends to leave many polluters opposing the tax if they are net losers;
- Taxing polluters and redistributing revenues to polluters in propor-tion to their output. This approach is used in Sweden and is thought to buy the cooperation of the industry, but if pollution is propor-tional to output this could offset the efficiency effects of the tax. The idea is to make the tax proportional to emissions but make the rebate proportional to output, so providing an incentive to cut emissions per unit output;
- Taxing polluters and using the revenues to subsidize disposal and recycling, for example, lubrication-oil taxes in Germany and the landfill tax in the UK (see Box 8.2).

Box 8.3 *Carbon Trading*

The Framework Convention on Climate Change of 1992 set out the outlines of an international agreement to curb greenhouse gas emissions. The targets set in 1992 applied only to developed economies and were voluntary – no international sanctions would apply if countries failed to comply. The basic idea was that developed countries should have carbon dioxide emissions in 2000 no higher than they were in 1990. In the event, not many countries will achieve this voluntary target. In 1997 the Kyoto Protocol, the first protocol to the FCCC, set out legally-binding targets for developed countries, roughly aimed at securing a five per cent reduction in emissions around 2010 compared to the 1990 emissions baseline. Countries accepted differential targets, with the EU having a separate burden-sharing agreement.

Significant features of the Protocol include the enablement of carbon trading mechanisms, the so-called 'Kyoto mechanisms'. Carbon trading involves *A* paying for carbon dioxide emission reduction in *B*, and counting the reductions as a credit against *A*'s emission target. *B* benefits from the transfer of technology, and *B* may also share some of the credits, holding them against future obligations when the second protocol is developed. The incentive for *A* to trade is that reductions in *B* are expected to be considerably cheaper than in *A*. Four kinds of trading are envisaged. First, there will be 'bubbles' over certain regions, notably the EU, so that, so long as the EU as a whole achieves its target, how countries in the EU choose to trade with each other is up to them. Second, there will be trading between Annex 1 countries and this could mean trades between rich countries or, more likely, trades between OECD countries and the economies in transition. This is joint implementation. Third, there can be trading between Annex 1 and non-Annex 1 countries, roughly speaking equivalent to trade between OECD and developing economies. This is known as the Clean Development Mechanism and trades will be subject to an additional test, namely that they contribute to sustainable development in the developing country. Finally, there is the potential for a fully fledged tradeable permit system whereby any signatory can trade with any other, but this cannot start before 2008.

How significant will trading be? The US is probably the most ardent advocate of trading because it fears that reducing emissions at home will be expensive and this will have adverse effects on competitiveness; and a corollary of this, it cannot force through the behavioural changes that the American people would have to make (such as higher gasoline prices). The US thus expects to make considerable use of trading mechanisms. While there is hostility to trading in some European countries – because of the moral feeling that cuts should be made at home – it also seems likely that Europe will be a significant trader as well. The main sellers will be the economies in transition and some developing countries.

While the idea of tradeable permits is not new (it dates back about 30 years) few would have guessed that the idea would take hold in such a significant way by the end of the 20th century. In *Blueprint 1* we advocated permits systems but on the basis of little comparative experience at that time. Now one of the world's foremost international environmental agreements is likely to rest for its success on the extent to which tradeable permits actually work.

Are these forms of earmarking efficient ? It is widely thought to be inefficient to earmark revenues since they flow to a given outlet regardless of whether the benefits from that use of the tax dollar are the best that can be made on cost-benefit criteria. But the social choice literature suggests it may not be inefficient, as voters can see where their tax dollar is going.

A widely reported concern is that some taxes are regressive, that is having a greater burden on the poor than on the rich in the sense that the tax is a greater proportion of income for the poor. This appears to be the case for carbon taxes, but other taxes such as those on gasoline may be progressive. Regressivity might be dealt with via lump-sum transfers to the poor, or reductions in other taxes, such as lifeline tariffs to poorer electricity consumers. Nonetheless, in political terms, regressivity of taxes is a sensitive issue. Oddly, the baseline is rarely discussed in this context. Few policy contexts take the form of 'either this tax, or no regulation at all'. Rather it is 'this tax or that command and control regulation'. Yet such regulations are almost certainly more expensive than taxes and must therefore raise prices more. If so, command and control regulation is likely to be more regressive than the tax. Yet most analyses of regressivity and environmental taxation do not ask what the alternative is, preferring to stop the analysis, somewhat misleadingly, at the point where the tax is expressed as a percentage of household income.

How Relevant are Market-based Instruments to Developing Countries?

The outline of experience above suggests that market-based instruments are making progress in OECD countries, though some would regard it as slow progress. How relevant then are they to developing countries?

The general problem is one of experience and know-how. Regulatory systems tend to be poorly defined and implemented in poorer countries but in rapidly growing economies such as Korea, Malaysia and Chile, for example, this is not so. In the poorer economies there is probably a genuine problem of asymmetric information – regulators know less than polluters. In the rapidly growing economies this is probably not true.

Market-based instruments stand less chance of introduction where there is regulatory capture. Regulatory capture exists when the regulators adopt a lenient attitude to the industry perhaps because of promises about future jobs with the industry, or even outright bribes. On the other hand market-based instruments may also threaten inefficiency that arises because of bureaucratic empire building. Regulators may actually oversupply regulation in some cases since regulation is the foundation of the empire of bureaucrats. So, such instruments may not stand a chance of being introduced if there is entrenched over-regulation.

But there are examples of market-based instruments in practice in the developing world and the economies in transition. In Korea and China, for example, there are charges for exceeding emission limits (non-compliance fees), but the incentives are generally weak due to the charge level being too low and with no real incentive for the polluter to adjust technologies or output. There are effluent charges in the palm-oil industry in Malaysia; tax differentials between leaded and unleaded gasoline in Thailand and Taiwan; environmental fees to finance environment (trust) funds in Poland and Korea; and deposit-refund schemes in Korea and Taiwan.

Tradeable Water Rights in Chile

Perhaps less widely known is that tradeable water rights exist on a significant scale in Chile. Water markets help to realize the full potential of water resources. They do this because they help to reallocate water away from uses where the water has low value to uses where it has high value. The market effectively gives a voice to all who demand water. Those with the highest willingness to pay will buy water and those with a low use value of water will be induced to sell water. Water markets involve the sale and purchase of rights to water. Water markets exist in various forms in many countries. In Chile, the Chilean Water Code 1981 separated rights to water from rights to land, so A can own the land but B can own the water on that land (or some of the water on that land). Water rights are private property and can be freely bought and sold. There are no priority uses for water rights, and the rights are allocated by the State. If there are two or more demands for the same water it is allocated to the highest bid.

Rights can be to consumptive uses and non-consumptive uses: the former involves no obligation to replenish the water, the latter does. Most non-consumptive use appears to be for hydro-electricity. Rights may be permanent or eventual: the former means the water can be used without restriction, the latter means that water can only be used once permanent rights have been satisfied. Continuous rights imply continuous use. Discontinuous rights imply use during specified periods, and alternate rights means two or more different users get alternative uses of the water.

The number of trades has been limited, perhaps amounting to 0.6 to 3 per cent of total water flow in the various regions. These are irrigation transactions and relate to trades that are separate from land (do not cover transactions where water and land are sold together).

Most transactions took place between farmers, on a scale sufficient to irrigate about 0.6 per cent of the relevant land area. Trades between farmers and water companies were also significant. One urban water company bought water from farmers, enough to supply 10,000 people.

While the trades appear small in number they are important because they show that a tradeable rights system can exist in countries where the institutional set-up is not very different to many developing countries. They also show that some clear examples of efficient trading emerge, for example the water company that preferred to buy rights rather than invest in a new dam.

Conclusions

Probably the most important finding of this chapter is that the language of economic instruments has now been widely disseminated and that the arguments in principle in favour of market-based instruments have generally been won. The remaining message is that the grafting of such instruments on to existing legislative contexts is very difficult. This perhaps explains why their potential is probably highest in those countries where detailed environmental legislation either does not already exist or where major legislative change is more likely – the developing world and the economies in transition. One message which we reserve for Chapter 9 is perhaps the least expected: some economic instruments are emerging from the corporate sector, sometimes in the context of achieving legislative compliance but also in the context of green corporate image.

9

Business and the Environment

Introduction

One issue that Blueprint 1 barely addressed was the role that corporations play in improving the environment. Ultimately, however, if corporations do not come on board in terms of cooperating with government initiatives and responding to citizens' demands for a better environment, little will happen. More than this, if business could take the lead in environmental initiatives, then there is a good chance that environmental improvement will go beyond compliance, and will set ambient standards and codes of practice stricter than those mandated by government and regulators. In fact there are strong signs that exactly this is happening. Some corporations have taken the lead, for all kinds of motives. But it is difficult to explain their activities fully without there being a strong commitment on the part of some of the business sector to improve the environment simply because it is a good thing to do.

Economics textbooks tend to emphasize the role that profit maximization plays as a corporation's main goal. But modern industrial organization theory stresses that firms may have not just different goals to profit maximization but a number of different (and sometimes conflicting) goals at the same time (Milgrom and Roberts, 1992). Firms may therefore seek to maximize or achieve various goals, and managers may have quite distinct views about those goals. For example, it may be that, regardless of the legal ownership of the firm, the interests of employees are ranked higher than those of shareholders. If so, maximizing profits may well involve giving precedence to benefits as seen from the standpoint of the employee, although ultimately no firm can ignore the wishes of its shareholders. Even then, shareholder interests may not be characterized simply as making maximum profits. The phenomenon of the ethical investor has also to be taken into account – see below. Exactly what the goals of the firm are will affect the firm's behaviour towards the environment.

While it is possible that firms will deliberately seek to achieve their goals, whatever they are, with higher resource costs than necessary, a reasonable corollary of the maximizing hypothesis is that they seek to minimize those costs. That is, whatever the goal, firms have an interest in not wasting resources in order to achieve those goals. Resource costs here include labour, capital, raw materials and land. The rationale for minimizing these costs is that the resulting surplus of revenues over costs per unit of output is available for distribution to meet the various goals of the firm – cost minimization becomes one of the mechanisms for achieving the goals. Note that minimizing costs is not the same as maximizing profits: a firm may decide on some profit level (to keep shareholders happy) which is not the maximum feasible profit level. It will still seek to minimize the costs of achieving that profit level.

What firms maximize need not coincide with what is best for society as a whole. If firms did maximize net social benefits, as opposed to net private benefits (the benefits to the firm) then there would be little rationale for regulation. Some advocates of deregulation and free markets would indeed argue that firms come at least close to maximizing net social benefits in the sense that the costs to them of achieving some social goal, such as a further improvement in environmental quality, exceed the benefits to society as a whole. If that is the case, then they should not go further than they do in pursuing social goals. For the US, Hahn (1996) suggests that in only 21 out of 61 cases of environmental regulation promulgated by the US Environmental Protection Agency between 1990 and 1995 did social benefits exceed costs. Pearce (1998a) suggests that, within the EU, several directives on bathing water and drinking water quality would not pass a social benefit-cost test. But there is no study for the European context similar to that of Hahn for the US. Other studies do tend to suggest that there are still areas of environmental degradation where substantial damages are being incurred (see Chapter 3). The essential role of environmental regulation, then, is to close any gap between the degree of environmental control exercised by firms and the degree that would be warranted by social benefit-cost analysis.

In the absence of regulation, how much investment in environmental improvement will the firm undertake? The answer is given by a point at which the extra benefits of improvement to the firm are just equal to the extra costs of environmental control. Note also that nothing is said about the ultimate beneficiaries: the benefits in question may be reflecting benefits to shareholders, managers, employees or other stakeholders. All that is necessary is that the decision makers within the firm reflect these concerns in their decision making. What then underlies the concept of the benefits to the firm from environmental control? To answer that, we need to consider the motives that firms have for undertaking environmental controls.

Why Firms Invest in the Environment

The different goals of the firm reflect the interests of the different stakeholders in the outcome of the firm's decisions. Shareholders will primarily be concerned with profits, but some shareholders may be members of ethical investment trusts in which case a green image or health and safety record may be more important than profits. Employees will also have an interest in profits because of job security, but may be just as influenced by green image or ethical stance because of the status effects of working for firms with good or bad images. Certain pressure groups may also be stakeholders, in that failure to meet some of their concerns could damage longer-term demand prospects through campaigns against the company. Management is likely to be concerned with profits for job security reasons, and because of profit sharing and bonuses, but they may also have some commitment to ethical image and doing what is right. However, whatever the management objectives, cost minimization will be pursued. As such, management should be concerned to invest in some environmental activities which result in cost savings. This motivation will apply even without profit maximization but it is obvious that the profit maximization motive would substantially reinforce the idea of cost minimization.

Protecting the Environment through Cost Minimization

Simply minimizing the costs of meeting a firm's objectives, whatever they are, will generally help the environment.

The first form is cost minimization through efficiency. It is efficient to invest in energy conservation, materials recycling, economies in the management of transport fleets, and waste minimization (the reduction of waste at source by for example, simply using less packaging material). The cost reduction motive is well established (Cairncross, 1991 and 1995). Some companies have formalized the cost-cutting role of environmental investment in acronyms: 3M's 'pollution prevention pays' (PPP); Chevron's 'save money and reduce toxics' (SMART); Texaco's 'wipe out waste' (WOW). 3M's programme is supposed to have saved the company

$500 million since 1975. The most pertinent question is why companies had to wait for an environmental revolution to appreciate that unit costs could be reduced by paying attention to raw materials, energy, transport and waste disposal. One answer is likely to be that these items tend not to be major portions of cost in most industries, compared, say, to labour costs. As such, they may have been neglected until the rise of environmentalism forced attention on to these cost items. Another likely explanation is simply lack of managerial expertise in the management and control of materials and energy. This is reflected in the fact that company accounts often do not enable anyone to determine just how much was spent on energy, raw materials, transport and waste management. Given the scale of some of the cost savings, however, there must be some doubts as to whether some businesses can always be regarded as being good cost-minimizers – they may simply be inefficient.

The second form of cost minimization is more subtle and arises out of the fact that many businesses have to deal, directly or indirectly, with environmental pressure groups. The costs of dealing with such groups can often be high because, ultimately, the pressure may show up in loss of market share if the firm fails to defend itself adequately. Costs may be reduced by avoidance of costly encounters with such groups. The philosophy of 'engage, not enrage' can, if there is an element of truth in the pressure group's arguments, be less expensive than confrontation, although it also seems fair to say that a number of corporations have all too willingly listened to, and accommodated, pressure group arguments. Striking a balance of judgement is difficult, but essential.

The third form of cost minimization focuses on the interests of employees. It is well known that employees have strong views on the status of the firm for which they work, and those views may not always be consistent with profit maximization. Notable among such employee concerns is the environmental profile of the company. Equally, management has a strong interest in meeting employee concerns for both profit and non-profit reasons: avoiding costly work disruption episodes, maintaining longer term continuity of staff, especially skilled staff, avoiding the transactions costs of labour turnover (searching for, selecting, and monitoring new staff), avoidance of a bad external image. Thus a complex of motives produces a positive attitude to environmental investments.

A number of surveys of industrial workers show that employees may be a potent force for ensuring that industries take on environmental commitments. In the OECD countries this phenomenon may arise because the environmentalists of the 1970s are now the middle and upper management of industry, instilling an environmental ethos into management generally.

Market Share: the Green Consumer

Just as employees may be green, so consumers may demand that products be environmentally friendly (a misnomer, to be sure, for any product other than one designed specifically to enhance environmental quality or save resources). The green consumer phenomenon is well documented, and meeting the interests of green consumers is consistent both with profit maximization and with customer loyalty, that is the retention of an established customer base, something that is not necessarily synonymous with profit maximization (Arora and Gangopadhyay, 1995).

Consumer perceptions of products can be manipulated of course and this has been the unintentional result of many cradle to grave analyses of products. Cradle to grave analysis is better known as life cycle analysis, the main constituent of which is a life cycle inventory of all the environmental impacts of a product going back to the extraction of raw materials and forwards to the disposal of the product as waste. Apart from the technical difficulty of many such analyses, which makes them less than transparent to the uninitiated, one result has been confusion in the mind of the consumer, who does not know which expert to believe. While it appears to be a scientific procedure, a life cycle analysis is in fact open to serious abuse and confusion on the part of the analysts themselves. Notable among these is the inclusion of scarcity measures for raw materials and energy, so that products using scarce resources are penalized more in the life cycle analysis than those using less scarce resources. But these resources have prices in the market place and, unless the market is very imperfect, those prices already reflect future scarcity. Accounting for it again in the life cycle analysis is at least double counting. Even where resources markets are imperfect it can often be shown that the prices charged for resources are too high compared to those that would prevail in a free market which still accounts for resource scarcity. Hence markets sometimes more than account for future scarcity. Oddly, some analyses go to the opposite extreme and include abundant resources, such as oxygen, in the life cycle impacts! Life cycle analysis is, unfortunately, only a pseudo-science and the result of pseudo-science is consumer confusion. But, for good or ill, it is established and many firms have felt obliged to make the case for the greenness of their products by employing one or more analyses, sometimes with catastrophic results. The consumer green image advantages of investing in the environment have perhaps been exaggerated. Green consumerism has been shown to have some stable and sustained elements and some highly volatile elements. Cairncross (1995) is of the view that: 'green consumerism will never be the main driving force behind corporate environmentalism. For one thing, it simply does not penetrate far enough.'

Box 9.1 *Green Consumerism: Certifying Forest Products*

Forestry is one of the world's industries that has attracted substantial critical attention from environmentalists. Current rates of tropical deforestation are estimated to be about 0.8 per cent per annum, as fast as some 30 years ago. While logging companies bear only partial responsibility for wasteful deforestation, they have been especially targeted by environmental groups. From initial responses which denied there was a problem, the industry gradually sought credibility by certification schemes. At first they themselves certified that their operations were sustainable but this was not regarded as credible by the pressure groups. Today, numerous certification schemes exist whereby independent auditors certify that the forest operation is sustainable and award what is effectively an eco-label. Perhaps the best known scheme is the Forest Stewardship Council (FSC) set up in 1993 on a non-profit basis. FSC accredits certification bodies which, in turn, apply certificates based on generally agreed criteria. Costs of certification range from about only US$0.2 to US$1.7 per hectare of forest. To date, some 10 million hectares of forest have been certificated. Major retailers and supermarkets are gradually entering into agreements to supply only certified timber. The certification movement reflects green consumer pressure but all the motives for acting sustainably are relevant.

Nonetheless, there are some important niche markets for environmentally sound products and production methods. The growth of eco-labelling for internationally traded products could be important here. The example of timber is relevant. Some developed economy companies have introduced schemes to ensure the import of sustainably managed timber only. Again, the coverage of such schemes is not likely to be very large since they again rely on the persistence of green consumerism and certifying what is sustainably managed timber is not straightforward. Nonetheless, such certification schemes are growing (see Box 9.1).

Financing the Corporation: the Green Investor

Corporate management faces demands from potentially green consumers, from green employees, from environmental pressures, and also from green investors. While the typical perception of an investor (a shareholder) is of someone who is concerned with profits, share prices and dividends, there is a growing movement towards socially responsible or ethical investment. While individuals may choose to act ethically with respect to their investment decisions, major players in the investment market may actually change the market by taking the lead. Notable players include pension funds: those agencies that are responsible for investing sums paid into pension funds by employees and employers. Such funds run to billions of pounds sterling in the UK alone.

Ethical investors can influence corporate behaviour in two ways:

- By simply not investing in, or withdrawing shares from, corporations which have poor environmental or social records;
- By investing in such companies and then actively seeking to persuade the companies to change their ways, for example through pressure at annual general meetings.

According to Lewis and Mackenzie (1998), the second, more active, involvement is more common in the US than in Europe where the passive role is still favoured. Nonetheless, instances of activism have grown in Europe and the issues that ethical investors may raise vary from the corporation's role in the arms trade, in developing-world debt, fairness to consumers, and environmental damage. Lewis and Mackenzie surveyed ethically minded investors in the UK to elicit their motives, finding that almost the whole sample wanted to avoid companies doing harm (even though such a possibility is in fact not feasible). Nearly all also wanted to invest in companies making some contribution to society. Over 80 per cent wanted their investments to be ethically clean but a lower percentage, around 60 per cent, wanted their money used to campaign actively for change in companies, but even this percentage was for campaigns conducted at a distance. Only 16 per cent wanted their money invested in bad companies with the object of changing their behaviour. How far the UK, and other European countries, will follow the more active model of intervention in the US remains to be seen.

Often overlooked are the origins of major investment funds. Some, for example, originate from church or other religious organizations. In other cases funds emanate from charities who need to be mindful of inconsistency between their own stated objectives and investing in companies which have doubtful ethical profiles. Specialist companies have emerged to advise on the meaning of ethical investment and on the environmental and social profiles of companies which funds may want to invest in.

Environmental Commitment

Commitment occurs when self interest cannot explain the decision to invest in environmental goods or assets. Commitment reflects a concern for the environment, a concern that may actually be inconsistent with the cost minimizing or profit maximizing goals of the firm. How far commitment explains environmental activity by corporations is doubted by some. As Cairncross puts it:

'Companies are not individuals, with a moral obligation to be good environmental citizens, even in situations where that is not in their commercial interest. They are owned by shareholders; and their overriding duty is to do what is in the long term commercial interest of their owners.' (Cairncross, 1995)

But as we note above, there are signs that the ethical investment movement is growing. How far it develops to contradict Cairncross's assertion remains to be seen. Some indirect evidence for commitment comes from an analysis of how firms respond to regulation. In principle, if they simply meet regulatory standards there is a presumption that they are not committed. This issue is discussed below.

Regulation and the Firm

The most common motive for environmental investment within the firm is compliance with regulations. Regulators may, in principle, set regulations which produce a level of environmental investment below or above that which is brought about by the unregulated goal-maximizing behaviour of the firm. This may seem counterintuitive since standard setting below what the firm achieves implies over-compliance on the part of the firm. But in principle there is no binding reason why the regulatory solution should improve on what firms do for themselves. Several factors explain why. First, as we have seen, firms have quite powerful incentives to adopt environmental controls based on various stakeholder interests. Second, what firms do for themselves may be counterfactual, that is the regulation occurs first and what firms would have done if left alone is never known because regulators are not in possession of that information (so-called, asymmetric information). Third, of course, regulators may simply under-regulate.

A firm with a voluntary optimum (environmental investment levels without regulation) less than the regulation is, of course, under-complying and that situation would not prevail for long in a regulatory regime where there is adequate monitoring and enforcement of environmental law. The explanation for under-compliance would simply be one of profit maximization: the firm judges that the expected value of a fine for non-compliance (the probability of being found out multiplied by the money value of the fine) is less than the cost of installing control measures to meet the standard. As argued above, however, non-compliance can be very expensive where the prevailing industrial culture is one of trading off stakeholder interests. This explains why environmental awareness programmes and education campaigns are important: they effectively make it more expensive for polluters not to comply with regulations, as well as providing further driving forces for high levels of voluntary environmental expenditures.

There are two contexts for over-compliance: where over-compliance results in lost profits for the firm and where it does not. The basic difference between these cases turns on the potential to extract a green premium in market prices. It is well known that consumers may be willing to pay a premium on prevailing market prices if they can secure assurance that the product is environmentally friendly (see Box 9.2). If so, firms may charge this premium and adopt cleaner technologies and/or cleaner products than required by a regulation, the revenues from the premium sales offsetting (and perhaps more than offsetting) the costs of the higher environmental standards. The situation in which profits are lost because of over-compliance is more complex. Here, management may be looking to green image to secure a longer-term profit at the expense of short-term profits; or they may be anticipating future regulation which they feel they can avoid by putting their own house in order now; or there may be a situation of genuine commitment – management may actually have as one of its goals the improvement of the environment – all motives that are discussed above.

Detecting commitment is extremely difficult, so much so that some commentators doubt its existence at all. It requires that voluntary optima exceed the regulatory standard, and that the over-compliance be for reasons other than profit maximization. The former is comparatively easy to measure; the latter is extremely difficult. The extent to which firms over-comply in order to avoid the threat of future regulation is also complex. Delayed expenditures will be less costly due to the effects of interest rates: the discounted value of the expenditure is less the further it occurs in the future. On this basis one would expect anticipatory compliance to be minimal (Baumol and Oates, 1988). But there are good reasons for supposing that anticipatory compliance is a fairly strong phenomenon. The regulatory process is one in which regulator and the regulated interact. Regulatory capture, whereby firms actually influence the nature and extent of regulation, is extensive. Hence firms can quite legitimately expect to influence future legislation by over-compliance now. A European example would be the industrial lobby against the introduction of environmental liability laws in the EU. It is well known that industry considers the introduction of such legislation (already present in the US) to be extremely expensive and it is perhaps not a matter of chance that voluntary environmental agreements have begun to proliferate in Europe at this time. Yet another reason for over-compliance arises from the lumpiness of pollution control investments, particularly where best available technology is the basis of the regulation. Such technology may well produce reductions in emissions and effluent over and above

Box 9.2 *Green Consumers and Green Tariffs*

Green tariffs (or green prices) provide a way for green consumers and industry to come together in a partnership aimed at environmental improvement. The essential idea is simple. A corporation sells its product at a market price, say £X. But the consumer is presented with two prices, £X and £X+5 per cent. The consumer must pay £X, but paying the extra five per cent is voluntary. The five per cent goes into a fund, usually matched in equal amounts by the corporation, so that the fund secures 10 per cent of X for every customer making the voluntary payment. In turn the fund can be used for any environmental purpose. Typically, however, such green tariffs are earmarked for securing reductions in greenhouse gases, usually CO_2.

Sophisticated schemes first estimate the CO_2 emissions from the corporation's activities. Suppose these come to Y tonnes and that this tonnage of emissions can be offset by growing trees (which absorb CO_2 from the atmosphere). The trees cost £Z per tonne of carbon sequestered from the atmosphere. Then, for the corporation to become carbon neutral – to absorb as much carbon as it emits – the fund must total £Z.Y, and, if the policy of pound for pound is pursued, half of this, that is £Z.Y/2, must come from consumers

Clearly, only some consumers will voluntarily pay the green premium. To date, those corporations experimenting with the approach have simply guessed at the likely response. A more sophisticated approach would use the technique of contingent valuation set out in Chapter 3.

Green tariffs are just one of many corporate ventures into marketing the environment. Others include setting self-determined targets from emissions reductions and then introducing schemes, including tradeable permit schemes, internal to the corporation. Yet others have adopted imaginative schemes of ranking raw material suppliers in terms of their emissions (usually CO_2) and then dropping the lowest ranked unless they improve their environmental performance.

regulatory requirements. Other motives for over-compliance have been suggested. One that assumes a high degree of sophistication and possible risk on the part of industry is that over-compliance is designed to force regulators to raise regulatory standards which in turn raises barriers to entry for new firms (Barrett, 1991; Salop and Scheffman, 1983). A variation on this theme – the Porter hypothesis – is considered later.

All this suggests that over-compliance will have its foundations in:

- Anticipatory compliance – attempting to capture the regulatory process so as to avoid future regulations;
- Preventing new firms from entering the market;
- Indivisibilities in pollution abatement technology, especially best available technology; and
- A pure commitment motive.

Voluntary Agreements

Over-compliance has been detected in the US where voluntary environmental agreements are a growing force in overall environmental regulation. A voluntary agreement is simply an agreement between the regulator and the firm to meet a given environmental objective, but without that objective being enforceable by the regulator, or, at least, not immediately enforceable. Of course, over-compliance can exist even without any form of agreement with the regulator, but the motivations to over-comply with the law are almost certainly the same whether a voluntary agreement exists or not. The United States Environmental Protection Agency runs a number of voluntary environmental agreements such as the 33/5 Program (on toxic chemicals) and the Green Lights Program (on energy efficient lighting). The US Government also relies on voluntary agreements to meet the US Year 2000 greenhouse gas target under the Framework Convention on Climate Change. There is also strong interest in Europe in voluntary agreements, but motivations appear to vary for firms to enter them. The success of the agreements also seems to vary significantly between industries and between countries and most are backed up by at least the threat of legislation (Box 9.3).

Arora and Cason (1995a and b) analyse the US EPA's 33/50 Program which was aimed at reducing emissions of 17 highly toxic chemicals between 1988 and 1995. The Program is voluntary and some of the motives for participation fit the cost-minimizing hypothesis above, since some of the chemicals can be replaced by substitutes which have a lower cost. In other cases the chemicals would have been reduced anyway to comply with the Montreal Protocol on ozone-depleting substances. Arora and Cason (1995b) test the proposition that firms' participation in the programme is due to longer-term expected profit increases, even though short-term profits may suffer. Factors thought likely to determine participation were:

1   Closeness to consumers: the closer the industry to the consumer the more public recognition and green image it gets;
2   Levels of research and development expenditures which make it easier to afford over-compliance;
3   The degree of concentration in the industry: the more concentrated, the more firms are able to pass on over-compliance costs to consumers;
4   The opposite of 3, that low concentration firms need to differentiate their products by establishing a green competitive edge;
5   That participating firms would have made the reductions anyway;
6   That firms with poor compliance records will join the programme to mask their failure to comply otherwise;

Box 9.3 *Voluntary Agreements in the Waste Sector*

Voluntary agreements have proved to be very popular in recent years in the context of waste generation, and especially so in packaging. A voluntary agreement is an agreement between government (or regulator) and industry to the effect that the industry will put its own house in order in return for the regulator not introducing environmental legislation. The idea is to achieve the environmental target of the regulator, but without the heavy hand of government and its associated costs for industry. Typical agreements in the waste sector have the following features:

- Obligations on either packers and fillers, or on the packaging chain as a whole, to take back packaging waste and to recycle or re-use it;
- Those with the obligation pay fees to recovery organisations;
- Coverage varies from domestic packaging waste only to domestic, commercial, some industrial and transit waste;
- Targets set for recovery and recycling, the former being higher than the latter. Some targets are material-specific.

The UK scheme is known as producer responsibility and involves a shared responsibility on industry for recovery and recycling of packaging waste. Raw material producers have six per cent of the target, packaging manufacturers 11 per cent, fillers 36 per cent and product sellers (those who finally discard the waste) 47 per cent. The scheme has met a number of obstacles and targets have proved difficult to achieve. Whereas other national schemes have involved single (or a few) authorities taking on the task of securing the recovery and recycling targets, the scheme operates with a number of competitive agencies, each charging different fees to member corporations. Anyone with an obligation pays a fee to one of the organizations set up to take over legal responsibility for that obligation (unless they arrange for the targets to be met themselves).

The scheme operates via packaging recovery notes, which certify that a particular recovery and recycling target has been met. These are tradeable, so that someone holding a recovery note showing that they have recovered/recycled more than the target, can sell the excess amount. Reprocessors (recyclers) issue the recovery notes to obligated corporations, or, more usually, the packaging compliance organization, who pay for them in cash. Their market price thus reflects their scarcity or abundance: they will be abundant if the capacity to recover and recycle is large, and they will be scarce if not. The price of packaging recovery notes is revenue to the reprocessors and it is from this revenue that investment in reprocessing capacity will come.

Some of the problems with the scheme are familiar in the context of any tradeable permit scheme. There are suspicions that reprocessors are hoarding packaging recovery notes to keep their price high. Reprocessors may also favour selling to compliance schemes rather than to retailers directly, so that the latter are thwarted in their efforts to claim recovery notes from their own actions. It has been unclear whether materials discarded by some retailers but collected by local authorities count towards the retailers' targets. Reprocessors have had no obligation to issue recovery notes for waste delivered by waste management companies who, in turn, have formed their own compliance schemes. Yet, with such recovery notes, waste companies would have an incentive to invest in separation and recovery schemes. Another issue concerns recovery notes for incineration. A set proportion of mixed waste has been declared to be combustible and hence allowable against the recovery and recycling targets. Incineration operators can therefore issue recovery notes for this amount. But, as they would have burned the waste anyway, the effect is to generate windfall profits for incineration companies without any of the revenue necessarily going into further recovery or incineration capacity.

The problems with the system appear to have arisen from a failure to design the system correctly.

7   That firms with good compliance records will join the programme so as not to sully their compliance record; and

8   That those who participate in one voluntary agreement are more likely to join another such agreement.

Econometric analysis of participation in the programme served to refute hypotheses 5 and 6, whilst hypothesis 1 receives most support. Over-compliance, then, would appear to be due to the market loyalty and market size arguments linked to the existence of green consumers.

In Europe, voluntary agreements are also known as producer-responsibility agreements. There is less evidence that these agreements involve over-compliance. Indeed, their origin in several countries is one of legislative threat: either the industry enters a voluntary agreement or there will be regulation. In this sense, many European voluntary agreements fit the model of anticipatory compliance above, that is a preference for self-regulation over regulation by diktat. In Germany, the packaging ordinance, for example, enables the packaging industry to set up its own recycling and recovery schemes to meet national targets, but failure to do so carries the explicit threat of the enforcement of legislation which would force the targets to be met by other means. Similarly, in the UK producer-responsibility agreements have made the most advance in the packaging waste sector, but the obligations in question assume a legal status, so that the voluntariness of the agreement lies more in the process of setting up the environmental objectives than in carrying them out, although a good deal of self-reporting is involved in the latter.

In the UK, producer-responsibility agreements are legally enabled under the 1995 Environment Act. Draft regulations were formulated in 1996 to achieve recycling of specific tonnages of packaging waste. The agreements apply to those who convert the raw material to actual packaging (the converters), those who pack or fill packages with produce, and those who sell the packaged product. Firms within this packaging chain may then meet the targets themselves, or join a compliance scheme which would take over the responsibility to meet the targets. Whichever is chosen, firms must be registered with the Department of the Environment. The major compliance scheme is known as VALPAK, and consists of a consortium of firms within the packaging chain. Individual targets have been set for raw material manufacturers, convert-ers, packers/fillers, sellers and importers of transit packaging. Along this chain, obligations to recover range from 6 per cent (raw materials) to 47 per cent (sellers) and 100 per cent for transit-packaging importers. The targets are then legal obligations: the issue of over-compliance can only arise in this case if individual firms choose to go beyond the obligations.

While the obligations are legal, procedures for monitoring them and securing accreditation are largely voluntary.

Other producer-responsibility agreements in the UK relate to tyres, vehicles, batteries, electronic goods and newspaper but, interestingly, these have developed without the legal obligations built into the packaging agreement. The reason for this is that the packaging industry felt it could not self-regulate without there being free riders – individual firms and even industries that would take little action – leaving the obligation to be met by others. A legal requirement was necessary to ensure that the industry would set up the necessary schemes (Department of the Environment, 1996). The Europe-wide legislative context for packaging is also more well defined, there being a Packaging Waste Directive which sets targets for recovery and recycling of packaging waste throughout the EU.

Is Environmental Protection Good for Competition? The Porter Hypothesis

One of the arguments explaining over-compliance was based on the idea that it would encourage regulators to set even higher environmental standards which in turn would act as a deterrent to new entrants to the regulated industry. This is an anti-competitive motive for over-compliance: limits on entry act as a protective barrier which keeps profits high. Much the same argument has been advanced in the context of international trade. High environmental standards in one country can be used to discriminate against imports which fail to meet those standards. If this is correct, we should expect to find industry being in favour of tougher environmental standards, rather than opposing them on the grounds that they raise costs and impair competitiveness. This view has achieved some prominence because of the work of Michael Porter, although his argument rests on very different grounds to the protectionist view (Porter, 1990 and 1991).

The Porter hypothesis says that firms can secure a competitive advantage by embracing higher environmental standards which have the effect of inducing cost reductions and innovation. The win–win nature of the hypothesis is obviously attractive: it implies that industry can expand, economic growth can be stimulated, and the environment can be conserved all through one mechanism:

> 'The resurgence of concern for the environment…should not be viewed with alarm but as an important step in regaining America's pre-eminence in environmental technology.' (Porter, 1991)

But not just any form of environmental regulation will bring about the gains to competitiveness. Porter is a little vague about what the right forms of regulation are. They appear not to embrace command-and-control measures such as standard setting based on best available technology, but they do embrace market-based instruments such as environmental taxes and tradeable pollution permits. They involve pollution prevention but not clean-up schemes. As Oates et al (1994) note, this last distinction is curious since clean-up is big business in the US and will become so as liability laws extend through Europe and elsewhere; that is, there are competitive gains to be had from the growth of this market (see later on the size of the compliance market).

The Porter hypothesis is not wholly persuasive. First, the prevailing forms of regulation, even in the US, still favour command-and-control type regulations, although major advances have been made in the introduction of tradeable pollution permit schemes for sulphur dioxide controls in recent years. Hence the hypothesis would only have validity in terms of current practice if industry was successful in persuading regulators to adopt more market-based approaches and less command and control. The relevance of market-based approaches to the Porter hypothesis arises because cleaner technology avoids the tax or cost of a pollution permit, so that adopting cleaner technology has a cost which may be offset by the reduction in tax or permit cost.

Second, meeting tougher regulations assumes that the abatement technology to achieve those new standards is feasible. If it is feasible, then firms must be able either to buy that cleaner technology off the shelf or to invest in research and development to secure the new technology. Either way, if they choose not to pursue the new technology it must be because they see profits (or any other objective) staying where they are. If they choose to pursue the new technology it must be because they see higher profits in so doing. In the latter case, it is unclear why they require regulators to legislate to achieve the new cleaner technology. The obvious exception to this conclusion would be if firms were unaware of the potential gain in profits from adopting the cleaner technology, and that the tougher regulations make them realize this potential is there. While this potential for surprise seems inconsistent with the assumption of the rational, objective-maximizing firm, the business and environment literature is replete with examples of firms that secured cost reductions by environmental action on energy consumption and waste management. If these examples are credible, it must mean that firms have not been cost-minimizing in the past: they have costs above what they could be. This situation is in fact quite realistic and is known as 'X-inefficiency' (Leibenstein, 1966). There do appear to be unexploited cost-saving measures that firms can adopt.

Conventional explanations stress problems of communication with the firm and lack of expertise in, say, energy efficiency as explanations for X-inefficiency. We return to one source of this information problem later, namely environmental accounting.

Third, the Porter hypothesis requires that tougher regulation is the means whereby the cost savings and innovations are secured. This suggests a somewhat odd strategy on the part of firms, for it argues that firms encourage the tougher regulations to secure cost reductions. But this in turn implies that they know the cost reductions are available, in which case why do they engage in the risky strategy of effectively inviting tougher regulations to achieve something that could be achieved anyway? It seems more likely that Porter sees the regulatory process as being independent of firms' behaviour – regulators regulate and firms respond, only to find that the tougher regulations are to their advantage.

Finally, is there any empirical evidence to support the Porter hypothesis? His own evidence is casual but in accord with the perception of many: Germany and Japan, for example, have strict environmental regulations and are competitively very successful. But while this is a popular perception, it may also have limited validity since Germany and Japan spend less of their GNP on environmental expenditure than the US (Oates et al, 1994), although there has to be some question about the efficiency of these expenditures. Market-based instruments are also less prominent in Germany and Japan than they are in the US, so in all cases we are looking at the wrong kind of environmental regulation, the kind Porter finds constraining of innovation and cost cutting. What limited statistical evidence there is suggests that environmental regulations probably have a modest and negative effect on competitiveness, contrary to the spirit of the Porter hypothesis (although not conclusively a refutation since, again, the regulations in question are generally command and control) (Jaffe et al, 1994).

Overall, the Porter hypothesis is attractive in many respects but seems difficult to justify.

The Environmental Compliance Market

One feature of regulatory compliance is often neglected. Compliance usually involves adopting some form of clean technology or management practice which, in turn, has to be supplied by someone. Hence there exists a compliance industry. The compliance market is the market for environmental technologies and services needed to meet environmental standards. This market has the potential to be supplied by environmental supply industries anywhere in the world, and, clearly, some world regions have developed a comparative advantage in the supply of specialised pollution abatement equipment. The compliance market extends across a whole range of activities. A European Commission definition of this compliance market is that it is covered by 'eco-industries' which:

> '*may be described as including firms producing goods and services capable of measuring, preventing, limiting or correcting environmental damage such as the pollution of water, air, soil, as well as waste and noise-related problems...(and) clean technologies where pollution and raw material use is being minimised.*' (*European Commission*, 1994)

The EC definition excludes renewable energy, biotechnology and green consumer products. Its inclusion of clean technology is problematic for measurement since it is not easy to see how expenditures on clean technologies can be calculated. Clearly, the extent to which any individual region gains from compliance depends in part on whether the industries supplying this compliance demand are indigenous to the region or not. A region's overall sustainable-development gains will be larger if the demands are met from indigenous supply.

Estimates of the size of the global compliance market are fairly consistent, but there are wide differences of view as to the composition of this market. Table 9.1 reports the available evidence. The important features of the table are:

* About now, the global compliance market will be of the order of US$500 billion per annum, or around 2 per cent of entire world GDP. This is in line with other estimates: that the market will be around US$300 billion by 2000 (OECD, 1996), and, using a broader definition for the industry, about US$600 billion by 2000 (IFC, 1992). It is worth noting that 2 per cent of GDP approximates to levels found for environmental expenditures in the rich world;
* While the rich OECD countries account for the bulk of the current market (around 67 per cent of the entire market), the Asia-Pacific region accounts for 10 to 18 per cent of the current global market, but could increase in importance to some 24 per cent of the market in 2000. Latin America accounts for perhaps a modest 2 per cent of the world market currently, and this might increase to around 3 per cent in 2010;
* While the regional estimates for Europe and North America are consistent across the different studies, there is a substantial difference between the estimates on the future size of the compliance market in the Asia-Pacific region. Japan may account for some 40

per cent of the Asia-Pacific market in 2000 and Taiwan for a little
over 20 per cent.

Table 9.1 *The Global Environmental Compliance Market* 1990–2010
(US$ *billion*)

Region	ETDC		EBI		ECOTEC		
	1990	2000	1992	1998	1992	2000	2010
North America	125	217	145	199	100	147	240
Latin America	–	–	6	10	2	4	15
Europe	78	213	108	159	65	98	167
Asia–Pacific	46	138	30	49	–	–	–
Rest of world	6	12	6	9	–	–	–
Total	255	580	295	426	210	320	570

Source: OECD, 1996
ETDC: Environmental Technologies Development Corporation (Canada)
EBI: Environment Business International (US)
ECOTEC: Ecotec Research and Consulting (UK)

While these data are undoubtedly crude given the varying definitions of
the environmental-compliance market, the estimates are sufficient to
establish that there will be a substantial global compliance market.
Moreover, the rate of growth of expenditure on environmental compliance is likely to be faster than the rate of growth of GNP.

What role will the markets in developing countries play? While the
data are poor, ECOTEC's forecasts suggest a developing-country share
of perhaps 3 per cent now rising to 9 per cent in 2010. If Eastern Europe
is included comparable figures are 5 per cent rising to 13 per cent. Thus,
while the bulk of the compliance market remains in the OECD countries,
a rapidly growing proportion of it will be in developing countries.

Accounting For Sustainable Development

Many businesses now issue environmental reports and statements, as
well as the environmental impact assessments that may be required of
them for development projects. However, few attempts have been made
to incorporate environmental impacts into company accounts, partly
because methodologies have not been agreed. But where suggestions
have been made on accounting reform, none of them appears to be
based on a rigorous approach to the meaning and measurement of
sustainable development as analysed in Chapters 2, 4 and 5.

Gray (1993) has summarized recent surveys of environmental reporting. His results suggest that environmental disclosure is on the increase
and that it is still confined to large corporations.

Gray also suggests that the quality of environmental reporting is low and that there is little by way of sound quantification. Even where there is quantification we may wish to add that it is often unenlightening. Endless streams of impact figures in different units – biochemical oxygen demand, tonnes of nitrogen and tonnes of sulphur dioxide for example – prevent an overall picture being obtained. This suggests that the business sector might try to emulate economics by securing socially quantified environmental accounts for companies (a suitable acronym would be SQUEACs).

A few examples of such accounts exist. Bebbington (1993) draws attention to the accounts of a Dutch company (BSO/Origin) specialising in information technology and consultancy (BSO/Origin, 1990). Those accounts show company value added gross and net of monetized environmental impact. The basic equation is:

$$gVA = VA - (D - E)$$

where gVA is green value added (or net value added in the accounts), VA is conventional value added, D is the monetary value of environmental damage, and E is company expenditure on pollution abatement. BSO/Origin refer to D–E as value lost. They value D as the sum of clean-up and abatement costs borne by others (Co) and the costs of reducing residual damages (Cr) left over after the company's own abatement costs (E). The use of abatement costs, which are measured by what it costs to achieve given environmental standards, rather than the economist's approach which would be based on willingness to pay to avoid damages, is likely to understate D–E if the standard is less than the optimal level of environmental quality, and overstate it if the standard is above the optimum. The resulting equation is then:

$$gVA = VA - (Co + Cr - E)$$

For 1990,

VA	=	255.6 mDfl
– (Co+Cr)	=	2.2
+ E	=	0.2
		253.6 mDfl

Environmental accounting makes little difference to BSO/Origin's accounts presented in this way. The adjustment is less than 1 per cent. There are two reasons for this. The first is that the company itself is hardly a major polluter. The second, however, is that this way of presenting adjusted company accounts is never likely to result in significant adjustments. Making use of the savings rule introduced in Chapter 4, makes a difference.

Recall that no business is sustainable if it lives off its capital. Companies need to put aside revenues as savings to offset the depreciation on their capital. This gives a very simple rule for sustainability in the form of a savings rule:

$$S > |dKm + dKn|$$

where S is savings, d is depreciation and Km and Kn are conventional and natural capital respectively (see Chapter 4).

Company savings are best thought of as being measured by undistributed profits, although, of course, distributed profits might also be turned into savings by shareholders. But, from the standpoint of company sustainability and environmental impact, what shareholders do with their dividends should not be relevant. The value of dKm can be read from company accounts. In BSO/Origin's case, for example, it is 10.4 mDfl. Total depreciation is therefore $dKm + dKn = 10.4 + 2.0 = 12.4$ mDfl. Company savings are more complex in this particular case due to various acquisitions during the financial year. However, if one takes recorded net income, the figure is 21.0 mDfl net of dKm or 31.5 mDfl gross of dKm. Dividends were 8.3 mDfl. This suggests that the comparison should be between gross profit (π) minus dividends (V) and the sum of the two depreciation elements. Sustainability requires:

$$(\pi - V) > (dKm + dKn)$$

which is met in the BSO/Origin case since

$$(31.5 - 8.3) > (12.4)$$

But now the picture looks far less trivial than it does if the adjustments are made to value added. Moreover, the figure for dKn may be too low in the BSO/Origin accounts for the reasons stated.

We conclude that company accounts can be modified for environmental impacts and that the most appealing approach is to monetize the impacts at least as far as is possible, and to place those impacts in a savings-rule context. In this way the company sector may be due for as many surprises as the application of the savings rule has so far produced for nations.

Conclusions

The vast literature on business and the environment is informative but frequently lacks an analytical structure. This chapter has suggested a way of imposing structure on the information by placing environmental investment decisions into a benefit-cost framework, but without assuming that profit maximization is the only goal of the firm. Such a framework enables a better understanding of the phenomenon of over-compliance and regulatory capture. It also casts some light on the Porter hypothesis that firms should deliberately embrace higher environmental standards in order to improve competitiveness, a hypothesis that tends not to be strongly supported by experience or by an analysis of motivations in the firm. Finally, we show how the literature on the economics of sustainable development can be brought to bear on the problem of environmental accounting reform for business. Adoption of a savings rule offers potential insights into the sustainability of company activities which have so far been missing in the literature on environmental accounting.

10

Ecological Economics: a New Paradigm?

Introduction

In Chapter 2 we discussed briefly the emergence of ecological economics and its contribution to our understanding of complex economic-environmental interactions as well as to the whole sustainability debate. Throughout this book we have illustrated how this type of interdisciplinary analysis is important to the design and implementation of policies for managing effectively complex environmental problems. In this chapter we look more closely at interdisciplinary ecological-economic approaches and ask the critical question: do these approaches signal the beginning of a new scientific paradigm? We explore this issue first by examining the nature of scientific thinking that is currently called ecological economics, and ask whether it is merely interdisciplinary or whether a new approach transcending conventional scientific disciplines is beginning to emerge. Our conclusion is that the latter claim is at best premature. However, this does not necessarily imply that ecological-economic approaches and interdisciplinary analyses of environmental problems do not have an important role to play in sustainable development. Using the problem of biodiversity loss as a general example, we illustrate how such approaches can assist policy analysis of the problem. Finally, we cite specific examples where economic analysis of environmental problems has benefited from interdisciplinary collaboration and thinking.

Ecological Economics: Interdisciplinary or Transdisciplinary?

The popularity of the term 'ecological economics' has increased considerably since the establishment of the International Society for Ecological Economics (ISEE) in the late 1980s. In the first issue of the ISEE journal, the President and Editor wrote:

> 'We have chosen the name Ecological Economics for this area of study because it implies a broad, ecological, interdisciplinary, and holistic view of the problem of studying and managing our world...it is intended to be a new approach to both ecology and economics that recognises the need to make economics more cognisant of ecological impacts and dependencies; the need to make ecology more sensitive to economic forces, incentives and constraints; and the need to treat integrated economic-ecological systems with a common (but diverse) set of conceptual and analytical tools.' (Costanza, 1989)

Such a grand vision of ecological economics explains its appeal to a broad spectrum. On the one hand, there are many researchers, including ourselves, who have long recognized the need for interdisciplinary collaboration across economics, ecology and other social and natural sciences in order to evaluate and find solutions for complex environmental problems. However, there are others who, disenchanted with the inability of a single discipline to solve such problems, are seeking in ecological economics the birth of a new discipline that essentially transcends conventional science and methodology. The latter view clearly has many adherents, and in recent years has been endorsed by the ISEE. For example, Costanza et al (1991) have suggested an additional interpretation of ecological economics that goes beyond interdisciplinary collaboration by economists, ecologists and other scientists:

> 'Ecological economics is a new transdisciplinary field of study that addresses the relationships between ecosystems and economic systems in the broadest sense. These relationships are central to many of humanity's current problems and to building a sustainable future but are not well covered by any existing scientific discipline...By transdisciplinary we mean that ecological economics goes beyond our normal conceptions of scientific disciplines and tries to integrate and synthesise many different disciplinary perspectives. One way it does this is by focusing more directly on the problems, rather than the particular intellectual tools and models used to solve them, and by ignoring arbitrary intellectual turf boundaries. No discipline has

intellectual precedence in an endeavour as important as achieving sustainability. While the intellectual tools we use in this quest are important, they are secondary to the goal of solving the critical problems of managing our use of the planet. We must transcend the focus on tools and techniques so that we avoid being a "person with a hammer to whom everything looks like a nail". Rather we should consider the task, evaluate existing tools' abilities to handle the job, and design new ones if the existing tools are ineffective. Ecological economics will use the tools of conventional economics and ecology as appropriate. The need for new intellectual tools and models may emerge where the coupling of economics and ecology is not possible with the existing tools.'

In short, adherents to this view appear to be indicating that ecological economics is the basis of a new paradigm for scientific approaches to the environment.

We disagree with this perspective on ecological economics on several grounds. First, as we have emphasized throughout this book, economics has an important contribution to make on its own to our understanding of many environmental problems, including assisting in the development of effective policy responses and solutions. The fact that problems of unsustainability still persist does not mean many techniques and tools in economics are wrong or inappropriate. Rather, it is an indication of the degree to which economic approaches have been underused so far in the analysis of environmental issues. But this is in turn a reflection of the fact that society has up to now underestimated the importance of environmental goods and services to the overall sustainable development of economic systems and human welfare. Nevertheless, as we have tried to demonstrate, standard economic tools and methods can be usefully applied to environmental problems, as well as to the overall concern of how to make economic development more sustainable. The real issue is whether society is prepared to look at the current and future welfare implications of today's environmental allocation decisions and consider them to be a serious economic problem worth addressing.

We do agree that there are many complex environmental problems which will require the collaboration of ecologists, economists and scientists from other disciplines. In addition, there is a considerable amount that economists and other social scientists can learn from ecologists, hydrologists, soil scientists and other scientists about the biophysical and natural workings of the environment that can improve the economic analysis of environmental problems. Although such collaboration and learning across scientific disciplines is increasingly occurring, our experience with interdisciplinary approaches to solving environmental problems is still fairly limited. It is therefore rather premature to suggest that the concepts and methods of our existing social and natural sciences are out-moded or inappropriate for the task. Developing new methods of scientific enquiry through interdisciplinary collaboration and learning cannot occur overnight. What we need are more efforts of such collaboration applied to complex economic-environmental interactions.

At the same time, the highly specialized analytical techniques and approaches that ecologists, economists and other scientists are currently using and developing further are extremely important tools for this task. Although each discipline may discover some of its tools to be more appropriate than others, progress on solving complex environmental problems through collaboration also requires each discipline contributing through its own specialized skill. Advances cannot be made if scientists show up with an empty tool kit. In short, a single-discipline approach may not be sufficient for tackling some of the more difficult and complex environmental problems we face, but the specialized skills of each discipline are necessary for scientific progress to be made through interdisciplinary collaboration.

Whether such interdisciplinary collaboration eventually leads to a new paradigm is rather a moot point at this stage. Rather, what is required urgently today is that ecology, economics and other disciplines begin applying their specialized knowledge and analytical methods collectively to extend beyond the current frontiers of their respective disciplines so that we can be sure of the appropriate interdisciplinary analysis of multi-faceted environmental problems. Thus, we would argue that:

> '*ecological economics is not a new discipline as such, but a new category of analysis or synthesis of approaches for tackling problems of economic-environmental interaction where a single-discipline approach will not suffice.*' (Barbier et al, 1994b)

Thus, this type of interdisciplinary perspective and analysis – or ecological economics for short – may change the emphasis we give to certain environmental issues in economics, but it does not as yet represent a new paradigm for scientific inquiry into such issues (Pearce, 1999).

Relevance to Policy Analysis

If ecological economics is to offer a new perspective on complex environmental issues, then it must be policy relevant. That is, interdisciplinary research and collaboration involving ecology, economics and

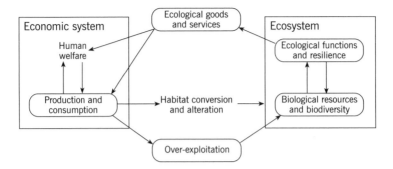

Source: Barbier et al, 1994

Figure 10.1 *The Economic–Environmental System and Biodiversity Loss*

possibly other disciplines should be able not only to improve our understanding of an environmental problem and but also to help design strategies for tackling it. In Figures 10.1 and 10.2 we illustrate how this might work with the problem of biodiversity loss and its possible ecological and economic consequences.

Figure 10.1 summarizes why the biodiversity problem may call for interdisciplinary analysis by economists and ecologists. As discussed in Chapter 5, biodiversity and biological resources are fundamental to the functioning and resilience of ecosystems, which in turn supply essential ecological services and resources to support the production and consumption activities of the economic system, and ultimately, human welfare and existence. However, the economic activities of production and consumption also lead to biodiversity loss, directly, through over-exploitation of biological resources, and indirectly, through habitat modification and destruction. Consequently, as shown in Figure 10.1, through these interrelationships the economic and ecological systems are not separate but fundamentally interconnected. The two are essentially subsystems integrated into a complete economic-environmental system. Many key insights into the welfare implications of biodiversity loss may only be understood in full through analysing these ecological-economic interrelationships, which in turn requires that economists and ecologists work jointly and cooperatively to provide this analysis.

However, ecological economics, and interdisciplinary research more generally, has no relevance if it is simply arcane research for research's sake. At the end of the day, the justification for pursuing interdisciplinary collaboration must be its policy relevance – it must pass a reality test that requires us to say what we would do that we do not already do or know about (Pearce, 1999). Figure 10.2 illustrates what would be the ideal framework for such policy analysis, if the ecological economics of

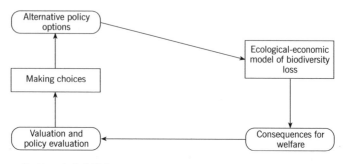

Source: Barbier et al, 1994

Figure 10.2 *Policy Analysis of Biodiversity Loss*

biodiversity loss is truly relevant to policy decisions concerning the exploitation of ecosystems and biodiversity. That is, if any new emerging ecological-economic models of biodiversity loss are valid, they must be able to inform policy makers of the full implications of the various alternative policy and management options available to them, and in particular, to indicate the costs and benefits of the different policy options relative to existing policy (the status quo).

For each policy option, the ideal ecological economic model should be able to trace through the various economic-environmental linkages, as shown in Figure 10.1, to determine the consequences for human welfare associated with that option. The evaluation of the different policy options may in turn depend, where possible, on valuation; that is the quantification of the specific welfare impacts – or costs and benefits – of each policy option to facilitate comparison by decision makers. Hence, the various economic valuation methods discussed in Chapter 3 are very much relevant for this welfare analysis. Where quantification of welfare impacts is not possible, then policy evaluation may be qualitative, which in itself presents no problem as long as the overall objective is the same: employing the results of ecological-economic analysis to inform policy makers of the various welfare consequences of alternative policy options to control biodiversity loss.

Finally, evaluation of the available policy options relative to the status quo will inform decision-makers about the choices available, and consideration of these alternatives may lead to adjustment in priorities and even the development of new policy and management options. These in turn should be evaluated, and the new questions for policy analysis may require further development of ecological-economic models for this purpose. Thus the process outlined in Figure 10.2 is never static but dynamic, leading both to improvements in our methods of ecological economic policy analysis, and hopefully, the policies to control biodiversity loss. It is also our reality test of ensuring the policy relevance of any ecological economics or other scientific approach that claims to offer new insights into a complex environmental problem, such as biodiversity loss.

Ecological and Economic Externalities

One important benefit to environmental economists of collaborating with ecologists and natural scientists is that the collaboration can yield important insights into certain key ecological issues that have been previously overlooked. For example, one such result of recent interdisciplinary collaboration through ecological economics is the growing acceptance by economists of the welfare implications of environmental regulatory functions of ecosystems.

Ecologists define ecosystems as biological communities that interact with their non-living or abiotic environment (Beeby, 1993). However, ecologists also recognize that ecosystems are not isolated but frequently interact with each other. In particular, the ecological functioning of one ecosystem may affect the functioning of an adjacent system. As a result, the overall productivity and stability of an ecosystem may be critically dependent on the maintenance of a few key external support functions provided by a neighbouring ecosystem. Examples include the role of coastal marshland and mangrove systems as breeding grounds and nurseries for off-shore fisheries; flood and sedimentation control provided by upper watershed and montane forest systems; sediment and nutrient retention by riverine wetlands; and semi-arid and arid brush forests protecting against desertification of rangelands. In effect, those external ecological support functions that appear to originate from one ecosystem but essentially support and protect the functioning and productivity of another system could be interpreted as ecological externalities (Barbier, 1999).

Of particular interest to environmental economists in recent years has been the class of ecological externalities that also contribute to important economic values, albeit somewhat indirectly, through supporting and protecting ecosystems that are in turn exploited through human economic activity (see Box 10.1). For instance, off-shore fisheries supported by mangrove breeding habitats may be harvested commercially, recreationally and for subsistence consumption; flood and sedimentation control by upland forests may protect lowland residential areas, industries and agricultural production; the waste treatment function of wetlands may reduce human health risks; and rangelands protected from desertification may provide grazing for livestock herds. Increasingly, economists are referring to such external ecological support and protection functions as good examples of indirect use value, or the value of the environment as a productive input (Barbier, 1994a; Freeman, 1993; Mäler, 1991). That is, these ecological functions may have an economic value that arises through their support of economic production and human welfare, or through protection of valuable assets and property. However, as this contribution is non-marketed, goes financially unrewarded and is only indirectly related to economic activities, the indirect use values of external ecological support functions are often extremely difficult to value.

Nevertheless, assessment of the indirect use value of many external ecological support functions may be critical because:

- The lack of markets for these functions means that those individuals benefiting from economic activities supported by the ecological supply of these functions have no automatic influence over the quantity and quality of this supply, even though this supply affects their well-being;
- The supply of these functions is in fact determined by the resource allocation decisions of another set of individuals, whose activities impact on the ecosystems where these ecological support functions originate, but who have no incentive to take into account the effects of these ecological externalities on the well-being of individuals elsewhere.

For example, fish farmers who convert mangroves to shrimp ponds do not take into account the economic implications for commercial fisheries of the loss of breeding habitat; loggers contributing to upland deforestation do not incur the costs of dredging downstream reservoirs or any resulting increase in sedimentation; and those who cut brush and trees for fuelwood do not necessarily face the economic consequences of increased wind erosion on grazing rangelands. Such situations describe the classic market-failure symptom that economists refer to as an economic externality (Cornes and Sandler, 1986). Thus, under certain conditions, the existence of ecological externalities also gives rise to economic externalities. As indicated in Box 10.1, this is clearly the case with habitat-fishery linkages.

Threshold Effects

In addition to being concerned by ecological externalities, economists have also increasingly been interested in the importance of maintaining the overall health and stability of ecosystem functioning which may be threatened by overexploitation and conversion threats (see Figure 10.1).

Box 10.1 *Valuing Habitat–Fishery Linkages*

An extensive literature in ecology has emphasized the role of coastal habitats in supporting neighbouring marine fisheries. The ecological function of particular interest is the role of mangrove or coastal estuarine wetland systems in serving as a breeding ground or nursery for off-shore fisheries. The main concern expressed by ecologists is that, as coastal wetlands around the world become increasingly degraded, converted or over-exploited, the resulting loss in fish nurseries and breeding grounds will have a significant impact on marine fisheries (WCMC, 1992).

There have been a number of recent studies that estimate the economic benefits of coastal wetland–fishery linkages. Much of this literature owes its development to the approach of Lynne et al (1981), who suggested that the support provided by the marshlands of southern Florida for the Gulf Coast fisheries could be modelled by assuming that marshland area supports biological growth of the fishery. For the blue crab fishery in western Florida salt marshes, the authors estimated that each acre of marshland increased productivity of the fishery by 2.3 pounds per year. Others have applied the Lynne et al approach to additional Gulf Coast fisheries in western Florida (Bell, 1989 and 1997; Farber and Costanza, 1987). Using data from the Lynne et al (1981) case study, Ellis and Fisher (1987) indicate the impacts of changes in the Florida Gulf Coast marshlands on the supply and demand relationships of the commercial blue crab fishery. They demonstrate that an increase in wetland area increases the abundance of crabs and thus lowers the cost of the catch. The value of the wetlands' support for the fishery – which in this case is equivalent to the value of increments to wetland area – can then be imputed. An important extension to Ellis and Fisher's approach has been made by Freeman (1991), who has shown how the values imputed to the wetlands are influenced by the market conditions and regulatory policies that affect harvesting decisions in the fishery.

More dynamic, or long-run, approaches to analysing habitat–fishery linkages have also been developed (eg see Barbier and Strand, 1998; Kahn and Kemp, 1985; McConnell and Strand, 1989). For example, in their case study of valuing mangrove–shrimp fishery linkages in the coastal regions of Campeche, Mexico, Barbier and Strand (1998) analyse the effects of a change in mangrove area in terms influencing the long-run equilibrium of an open-access fishery, ie a fishery in which there are no restrictions on additional fishermen entering to harvest the resource. Their results indicate that the economic losses associated with mangrove deforestation appear to vary with long-run management of the open-access fishery. During the first two years of the simulation (ie 1980–1981), which were characterized by much lower levels of fishing effort and higher harvests, a 1 km^2 decline in mangrove area was estimated to reduce annual shrimp harvests by around 18.6 tons, or a loss of about US\$153,300 per year. In contrast, during the last two years of the analysis (ie 1989–1990), which saw much higher levels of effort and lower harvests in the fishery, a marginal decline in mangrove area resulted in annual harvest losses of 8.4 tons, or US\$86,345 each year.

Source: Barbier et al, 1994

The main source of uncertainty is our ignorance of the functions and structure of ecosystems. For example, Chapter 5 discussed how the functioning and resilience of ecosystems is affected by biodiversity loss, and that our understanding of these relationships is basic at best.

The potential welfare implications of the enormous uncertainty surrounding ecological disruptions may be substantial, particularly if there are discontinuities or threshold effects in ecosystems (Perrings and Pearce, 1994). Such thresholds are usually defined by critical values for either populations of organisms or biogeochemical cycles. At these levels, the ecosystem begins losing resilience and functional integrity. For example, in the acid-rain literature, the concept of critical loads has been defined as a threshold below which depositions of acidic pollutants, either singly or in combination, do no physical damage to receiving ecosystems (Posch et al, 1995).

Uncertainty whether ecosystems are being driven close to their critical values therefore has important welfare implications as, once these thresholds are crossed, wholesale disruption to and perhaps even collapse of ecosystems can occur. In other words, ecological change is discontinuous, and there could be dramatic impacts on biological resources and ecological services. This would suggest that, to the extent that individuals are concerned with the uncertainty surrounding ecological disruptions, their welfare would be especially sensitive to threshold effects and to the uncertainty associated with such effects.

Because of the concern with the potentially serious welfare implications of ecological threshold effects, the ecological economics literature has advocated several possible policy approaches for preventing such effects from occurring. These include the precautionary principle, safe minimum standards and threshold instruments.

The Precautionary Principle

The precautionary principle is increasingly being invoked as a public policy guideline for environmental issues. Major international conferences and treaties in which this principle has been put forward include the UN FCCC, the Earth Summit (UNCED), and Article 130v of the EU Maastricht Treaty.

As noted by Myers (1993), the precautionary principle in essence asserts that there is a premium on a cautious and conservative approach to human interventions in the natural environment where our understanding of the likely consequences of the intervention is limited, and there are threats of serious or irreversible damage to natural systems and processes. In such circumstance, the burden of scientific proof should therefore lie on would-be environmental disrupters to demonstrate that their actions will not result in unacceptable ecological damage.

More formally, Perrings (1991) relates the precautionary principle to the notion of reserved rationality, whereby it may be rational for policy-makers to proceed cautiously with an intervention in the natural environment to safeguard against the possibility of unexpectedly severe future costs – including the advent of sudden surprises such as rapid climatic change and natural disasters. The need to proceed cautiously is reinforced by the lack of past experience with the type of environmental damages that may occur. This in turn may prevent decision-makers from gauging accurately either the likelihood of a catastrophic outcome or the scale of the impacts on human welfare.

Consequently, the precautionary principle requires that an allowance or a margin of error be made for those uses of the environment that may result in unexpected and uncertain – though potentially large – future losses. This margin of error can be translated into a safeguard allowance or the sum total of preventive expenditures that may be committed to mitigate any future damages associated with use of environmental resources today.

However, it is conceivable that the future consequences of any environmental damage may be *irrevocable*, in the sense that uses of the environment today may cause profound and irreversible environmental damage which permanently reduces the welfare of future generations. Many commentators on the current patterns of biodiversity loss note that this may be a characteristic feature of the future damages that are associated with species extinction, habitat destruction, and above all, loss of valuable ecological functions and ecosystem resilience (Ehrlich and Ehrlich, 1992; Myers, 1993). If this is the case, then preventive expenditures or safeguard allowances alone may not be sufficient to avoid irreversible environmental costs being imposed on future generations.

Safe Minimum Standards

If the welfare of future generations can only be assured if the level of biodiversity they inherit is no less than that available to present genera-tions, then the precautionary principle begins to approximate more closely to the policy of invoking safe minimum standards. This policy has a long history associated with the concept of avoiding species extinction. For example, more than 40 years ago, Ciriacy-Wantrup (1952) argued that as a result of irreversible extinction of a species, future societies may discover that they have forgone significant benefits. If there were close substitutes for the goods and services of the threat-ened species, and if there was a technological bias favouring those substitute goods, then the costs of preserving a minimum viable popula-tion of the species and its required supporting habitat would be small.

More recently, the safe minimum standard approach has been advocated as a means of controlling the more general problem of biodiversity decline (see Box 10.2). Although it is now recognized that the current global biodiversity crisis cannot be reduced simply to a problem of species extinction, contemporary proponents of the safe minimum standard approach would argue that this principle should be extended to provide the necessary safeguards for ensuring that future generations inherit at least the same level of biodiversity as available to current generations. For example, Perrings et al (1992) suggest that safe minimum standards are likely to be an essential part of a global biodiversity conservation strategy, given the considerable uncertainty associated with the future environmental impacts of current economic activities, the non-market and public goods nature of environmental assets and the irreversibility of species extinction and loss of ecological functions. In particular, if the existence of ecological thresholds means that unknown irreversible environmental effects may be catastrophic, then the rate of environmental exploitation should not just be slowed down but ultimately restricted.

Bishop (1993) takes this argument a step further by maintaining that, in the absence of an efficient and sustainable economy protecting the interests of future generations, the adoption of a safe minimum standards strategy is the best policy for ensuring this objective. Albeit somewhat crude, safe minimum standards seek to increase the welfare of future generations by conserving biological resources and diversity that may prove useful and valuable and that would otherwise have been lost. Given our ignorance of the future, the strategy would increase the options available to future generations, thus increasing the likelihood that the economy is on a sustainable path. Safe minimum standards by themselves will not guarantee that the economy will ever reach such a sustainable path. However, they will ensure that future generations are better compensated by receiving a larger resource endowment than in the absence of such standards. Just how much larger that endowment will be depends on the willingness of the current generation to tolerate the costs of biodiversity conservation through more stringent enforcement of safe minimum standard rules.

However, as in the case of the precautionary principle, the conditions under which safe minimum standards for biodiversity conservation should be applied are difficult to determine. To some extent they already underline the physical limits involved in more conventional environmental policies such as tradeable permits for pollution and legislation ensuring preservation of species and habitats, as for example the current US Endangered Species Act. Taken as a whole, however, existing environmental policies clearly do not guarantee that future generations will

Box 10.2 *The Safe Minimum Standard and Biodiversity Conservation*

The concept of a safe minimum standard as a policy for conservation has a long history in resource economics that can be traced to Ciriacy-Wantrup (1952) and has generally been thought of in the context of species extinction. Adopting the standard as a policy objective would essentially mean strict avoidance of extinction in day-to-day resource management decisions. Exceptions would occur only when it is determined explicitly that the costs of avoiding extinction are intolerably large or that other social objectives must take precedence.

As outlined by Bishop (1993) the basic arguments in favour of a safe minimum strategy for biodiversity conservation are as follows:

- The strategy rule is generally considered a pragmatic step towards the attainment of an efficient and sustainable economy built on appropriate inter-generational natural resource endowments and an optimal path of capital accumulation over time;
- However, because such an economy does not exist today, and because of ignorance of the future and market (as well as policy) failures, there is great risk in the present practice of trading off biodiversity through market transactions – in the sense that giving up two species for ten hospital beds would constitute a net gain for society. The result is excessive levels of biodiversity loss;
- The criterion of intolerable costs nonetheless implies that there are limits on how much society should pay for biodiversity conservation. However, the burden of proof lies on those seeking a relaxation of the safe minimum strategy to determine costs that are intolerable from those that are merely substantial;
- A safe minimum standard strategy is therefore a practical safeguard for biodiversity conservation until economies have moved onto a development path that is both efficient and sustainable, including the elimination of pervasive market and policy failures that are biased against biodiversity conservation. Once such an ideal is attained, then biodiversity conservation can be assured through market mechanisms and public policy, and the strategy rule need no longer apply.

However, the safe minimum standard strategy carries its own risks:

- The current generation's ignorance over the future value of biodiversity and what constitutes intolerable costs also limits the effectiveness of the strategy in conserving the optimal level of biodiversity. Some biodiversity that may be of great value to future generations may be lost. Alternatively, some biodiversity that has little value may be saved;
- A safe minimum standard strategy is likely to yield outcomes that trade-off biodiversity conservation and overall economic efficiency. Under the safe minimum standard strategy rule, economic development opportunities that would have yielded positive net benefits to both present and future generations but would also have contributed to biodiversity loss may be abandoned;
- The costs associated with safe minimum standards may not be borne equally across all members of society, or all countries. Thus for the sake of intra-generational fairness, and indeed even to induce some countries to

cooperate in a global strategy, it may be necessary to incorporate mechanisms for compensating income groups and countries that are disproportionately affected;

- It may be difficult to manage the transition from the second-best economy governed by safe minimum standards for biodiversity conservation to the ideal economy whereby appropriate market mechanisms and public policies ensure efficient and sustainable management of biodiversity. A critical issue is the timing of the transition, including the speed of adjustment and the degree to which the strategy should be relaxed over time;
- It is possible that the elimination of many market and policy failures concerning resource use and environmental degradation may by themselves be sufficient for conserving biodiversity. The need for safe minimum standards can therefore be overly exaggerated in many cases;
- Safe minimum standard rules for the avoidance of species extinction are less problematic than extending such rules to preserve critical ecosystems and ecological functions. In particular, the margin of error in terms of assessing their future value or the associated costs of their conservation is much greater. Consequently, determining the optimal level of conservation and the appropriate trade-off with economic efficiency objectives is that much more difficult.

Source: Barbier et al, 1994b

inherit a level of biodiversity that is no less than that available to present generations.

Threshold Instruments

In Chapter 8 we discussed the role of market-based and regulatory instruments in environmental policy. However, the existence of threshold values for the various parameters of the ecological systems on which economic activity depends further complicates the design of appropriate policies and the choice of appropriate instruments. In particular, policy makers have to address the additional problem that the costs of exceeding thresholds are fundamentally uncertain (Perrings and Pearce, 1994). The possibility of a major environmental catastrophe or system collapse cannot be ruled out. As a consequence, any policy which compromises the resilience of ecosystems will have uncontrolled effects, and even small policy changes can have dramatic but unforeseen impacts. Under such conditions, the protection of ecosystem sustainability, or resilience, may need to become an explicit and overriding policy objective. To fulfil this objective, limits may have to be imposed on economic activity so as to preclude the possibility of thresholds being crossed, where there is reason to believe that the social costs of system collapse or environmental catastrophe are major. Thus, special threshold instruments may need to be invoked.

As indicated in Box 10.3, if the social costs of exceeding ecological thresholds are greater than the private net gains from doing so, then imposing safe minimum standards and penalties for limiting economic activity is the optimal policy. In fact, protection of the thresholds could be met through strict enforcement of the safe minimum standard (for example, physical restriction or regulation of economic activity) or, as shown in Box 10.3, through the imposition of discontinuous environmental levies and fines at the level of the threshold.

However, what is more significant is not whether a regulatory or market-based instrument is used but that we are once again back to considering non-economic criteria in determining environmental policy. The economic instruments required to protect ecological thresholds are no longer motivated by conventional economic objectives, such as equating marginal net private benefits with marginal external costs. Instead, the motivation is governed by an essentially ethical judgement about the socially acceptable margin of safety in the exploitation of the natural environment, and above all, the acceptable level of biodiversity necessary to maintain ecosystem functioning and resilience (Perrings and Pearce, 1994). In other words, we are firmly in the strong sustainability view of the environment and economic development (see Chapter 2).

Safeguards for the Future: When do They Apply?

The precautionary principle, safe minimum standards and threshold-instrument approaches to biodiversity conservation present a fundamental challenge to developing more innovative policies for respecting ecosystem limits and thresholds. This is one important area for future research in ecological economics. However, there remain some fundamental questions concerning our present capability and willingness to employ these policies more widely.

First, application of such approaches to environmental problems requires decision makers today to be ethically more concerned about inter-generational equity than they appear to be at present. Current attitudes to inter-generational equity as revealed through policy decisions would suggest that modern societies emphasize the enhancement of welfare today with little consideration of the implications for future generations. The underlying assumption is generally that future generations will enjoy the same or even higher levels of welfare than we do currently. Consequently, the potential threat that environmental degradation poses to the economic opportunities available to future generations receives little weight in economic decisions made today.

In contrast, invoking policies based on the precautionary principle, safe minimum standards and threshold instruments to control ecological

Box 10.3 *Environmental Policies and Ecological Threshold Effects*

Policies for controlling environmental damage are usually governed by a standard economic rule for internalizing any environmental externalities. For example, the optimal level of economic activity would be at the point where the marginal net private benefit (profit) of those who degrade the environment is just equal to the marginal external cost of environmental degradation on the rest of society. Depending on their relative cost-effectiveness and other considerations either environmental regulations or market-based instruments could be used to attain the desired level. However, this environmental policy rule clearly depends on either private costs and revenues or environmental damage functions being well known and clearly defined. In particular, the latter must be well behaved (that is continuous and convex, or rising smoothly with the level of environmental degradation).

The presence of *ecological thresholds* would suggest that environmental damage functions are not well behaved but are most likely discontinuous, or jump at the point of the threshold. If the *threshold costs* – the social costs of exceeding the threshold – are greater than the maximum private net benefit of exceeding the threshold, then the standard environmental policy rule, described above, no longer holds and cannot be used to determine choice of instruments. Instead, the optimal policy would be to devise a *penalty function* to prevent private actors from degrading the environment beyond the threshold. This is illustrated for the cases where thresholds are known and not known with certainty.

In the first diagram below, the external costs of biological resource use are discontinuous at some level of economic activity, q^*_s. At that threshold point, the costs jump to some much higher level, and then continue to increase with the level of economic activity. However, the external costs beyond this ecological threshold are uncertain – they consist of adverse but unknown effects on the flow of ecological services to which that resource contributes, including the overall resilience of an ecosystem. The social costs of exceeding the threshold clearly outweigh the net private gains; consequently, it is not optimal to allow economic activity beyond this point, that is to the maximum level of private profit, Π_p, at point q^*_p. The optimal policy is to combine user charges for the expected social costs of biological resource use below the threshold level of activity, $0a$, and a penalty above the threshold level of activity, bc. If this penalty is enforced, it will be sufficient to protect society against the costs of exceeding the threshold, and the greater the difference between the penalty and private profit, the greater the margin of safety.

However, it is very rare that ecological thresholds are known with certainty. For example, the rationale for *safe minimum standards* is based on the lack of knowledge of the threshold level for many species and ecosystems (see Box 10.2). Consequently, the standard which triggers the penalty should be set at a level so as to reduce the risk of overshooting the threshold. As shown in the second diagram, the standard is imposed at a much lower level

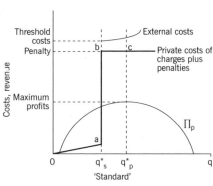

Source: Perrings and Pearce, 1994

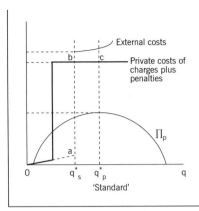

of activity than that which actually breaches the ecological threshold – at a level where ecological damages are known but rising. That is, the penalty function $Oabc$ lies to the left of the discontinuity at q^*_s. Thus the penalty function is associated with a safe minimum standard policy that ensures the preservation of a minimum stock of the biological resource that is consistent with maintaining ecological services and ecosystem resilience.

Source: Perrings and Pearce, 1994

disruption and biodiversity loss would represent a profound shift in attitudes by the present generation in favour of inter-generational equity. Employing safe minimum standards would essentially mean placing limits on economic activities to ensure that they do not impose irreversible environmental costs on future generations. Only slightly weaker, the precautionary principle can be interpreted as saying that if it is known that an action may cause profound and irreversible environmental damage which permanently reduces the welfare of future generations, but the probability of such damage is not known, then it is inequitable to act if the probability is known (Perrings, 1991). Threshold instruments can introduce some element of market incentive, but the main objective of such instruments is to provide a punitive deterrent on economic activity that threatens ecological thresholds. Implementing any of these policies would signal a significant shift in current attitudes to inter-generational equity, possibly to the point where we are actively intervening in favour *of* the welfare of future generations. It is not clear that we are prepared – if ever – to countenance such a change in our ethics.

More importantly, there are important intra-generational aspects to such policies that need addressing. The world's resource endowment, and particularly its biodiversity and remaining natural ecosystems, is not distributed equally. On a global level, the costs of implementing policies based on safe minimum standards, the precautionary principle or threshold instruments are likely to appear more tolerable to one country compared to another. Thus those countries that are more directly dependent on resource exploitation and conversion to achieve a higher level of economic development may not accept any global conservation strategies that disproportionately affect them unless they are adequately compensated by other countries. As discussed in Chapter 7, we are in the process of creating global markets and institutions that are facilitating flows in international compensation for preserving global environmental benefits. However, compensating a country for its efforts in providing environmental assets of international significance is one thing; dictating a country's overall policy approach, and ultimately its ethical attitudes, to the environment is a different matter.

Finally, as we have stressed throughout this chapter, the imposition of any safeguard policy to protect the environment and mitigate against ecological threshold effects can impose significant opportunity costs on a society. The use of such policies must itself proceed with caution (see Box 10.2). For example, it is significant that the Second Sulphur Protocol does not have as its practical aim the achievement of critical loads but a 60 per cent reduction in the exceedence of actual depositions over critical loads (Pearce, 1999). In time, better analysis and information will tell us whether or not such an approach is overly cautious in its concern for the opportunity costs of a zero threshold level target for acid deposition in Europe. Once again, this calls for more policy-relevant interdisciplinary research into this and similar ecological threshold problems so that we can decide on what safeguards for the future need to be implemented, at the minimum costs to the welfare of present generations.

Conclusion

We believe that ecological economics has an important contribution to make to our understanding of the welfare implications of ecological systems and processes. However, we do not consider ecological economics to be a new or transdisciplinary science as such. We consider ecological economics as being essentially a form of interdisciplinary analysis, which is particularly suitable to many complex environmental problems that require the collaboration of ecologists, economists and scientists from other disciplines. As we have emphasized throughout this chapter, such collaboration yields many benefits for economics. There is a considerable amount that economists and other social scientists can learn from ecologists, hydrologists, soil scientists and other scientists about the biophysical and natural workings of the environment that can improve the economic analysis of environmental problems.

11

Conclusions

We have revisited the arguments we first set out in *Blueprint* 1 some ten years ago. We find that the arguments presented there continue to hold today. We have to look to the misworkings of the economy to find the real causes of environmental degradation, and we have to attach price tags to environmental assets if we are to change the way we treat the environment. Everything we do has an environmental impact, and economic decisions pervade all that we do. Ultimately, the prospects for natural environments some 100 years hence are not good. They cannot be, because there is little or nothing to stop at least 50 per cent more people inhabiting an earth where the impact of human activity on the environment is pervasive and profound. We can do the best we can, and that means addressing all those issues that are the subject of policy decisions by households, corporations and governments. That means getting rid of perverse subsidies, establishing property rights to the environment, creating markets, taxing polluters (and that is all of us), and changing our accounting systems.

What has changed in ten years?

First, the language of environmental economics is now a common language, even down to 'internalizing externalities', 'demonstration and capture', and 'creating markets'. We doubt if we would have believed ten years ago that such a rapid change could have come about. We have both spent weeks, if not months, of our lives just trying to explain the basic ideas to an often intrigued but sceptical population of politicians, journalists and scientists. We claim little credit for the change. We are simply relieved it has happened.

Second, the opponents of environmental economics are fewer. Environmentalists and politicians generally have seen at least some of the virtue in the economic approach. Sceptics remain and they are vocal, and that is good. Their vehemence in opposing the economic message is occasionally irritating, and that is good too. Perhaps the most telling comment, however, is that the critics still find it hard to come up with a better or more convincing story about causation and solutions. They speak of moral stances as saving the world and we would like them to be right in their faith in such solutions. But we think that so much of the moralizing is either whistling in the wind or counterproductive. One can take a moral view and also look to pragmatism for effecting those views. Above all, whatever route is taken has to be democratic and we share the wider concern that some modern environmentalism has lost its roots in what people, as opposed to elites, want.

Third, selling the message of environmental economics was one thing. Putting those messages into practice has been another, and we accept that it has all been more difficult than we might have anticipated. The problem is that, even when people are convinced, changing institutions, cultures and policies is extremely difficult in a world where those things have been built up over long periods of time – centuries in the case of the UK, for example. Nonetheless, as we have outlined, many of the changes we advocated have taken place or are taking place: environmental taxes are up and running, though perhaps not in quite the form we might have advocated; tradeable permit systems exist; polluters are paying; and the rich are paying the poor to change their behaviour towards the environment. Perhaps more important than anything is the change in corporate culture. We do not believe that corporations have gone green simply because it is the right thing to do, but, equally, we do not believe we can explain all the corporate initiatives on the environment on the basis of compliance, anticipation of regulation or cost cutting. There is a new commitment to the environment and we believe environmental economics has played its part in securing that change.

Fourth, it is part of human nature to search for new paradigms. Science would not progress but for this curiosity of human beings. But there is a risk that as fast as we discover solutions we reject them because they are no longer new. Huge energies are devoted to rethinking the problem rather than solving it. We do think we know how to solve environmental problems as far as anyone can against the backdrop of vast population change yet to come. The real challenge is perhaps the one most people find the least exciting. We know what to do. We need to get on and do it.

References

Anderson, K (1992) 'The standard welfare economics of policies affecting trade and the environment', in Anderson, K and Blackhurst, R (eds) *The Greening of World Trade Issues*, Harvester Wheatsheaf, London

Ansuategi, A, Barbier, EB and Perrings, C (1998) 'The Environmental Kuznets Curve', in van den Bergh, JCJM and Hofkes, MW (eds) *Theory and Implementation of Economic Models for Sustainable Development*, pp139–164, Kluwer Academic Publishers, Dordrecht

Antle, JM and Heidebrink, G (1995) 'Environment and development: theory and international evidence', *Economic Development and Cultural Change*, vol 43, no 3, pp603–625

Arora, S and Gangopadhyay, S (1995) 'Toward a theoretical model of voluntary overcompliance', *Journal of Economic Behaviour and Organization*, vol 28, no 3, pp289–309

Arora, S and Cason, T (1995a) 'An experiment in voluntary environmental regulation: the participation in EPA's 33/50 program', *Journal of Environmental Economics and Management*, vol 28, pp271–86

Arora, S and Cason, T (1995b) *Why Do Firms Overcomply with Environmental Regulations? Understanding Participation in EPA's 33/50 Program*, Discussion Paper 95-38, Resources for the Future, Washington DC

Arrow, K, Solow, R, Portney, P, Leamer, E, Radner, R, Schuman, H (1993) *Report to the National Oceanic and Atmospheric Administration*, Panel on Contingent Valuation, *Federal Register*, vol 58, no 10

Arrow, K, Bolin, B, Costanza, R, Dasgupta, P, Folke, C, Holling, CS, Jansson, B-O, Levin, S, Mäler, K-G, Perrings, CA and Pimentel, D (1995), 'Economic growth, carrying capacity, and the environment, *Science*, vol 268, pp520–521

Atkinson, G, Dubourg, R, Hamilton, K, Munasinghe, M, Pearce, DW and Young, C (1997) *Measuring Sustainable Development: Macroeconomics and the Environment*, Edward Elgar, Cheltenham

Baharuddin, Hj G (1995) 'Timber Certification: An Overview' *Unasylva*, vol 46, no 183, pp18–24

Baharuddin, Hj G and Simula, M (1994) *Certification Schemes for All Timber and Timber Products*, Report for the International Tropical Timber Organization, Yokohama

Baharuddin, Hj G and Simula, M (1996) *Study of the Development in the Formulation and Implementation of Certification Schemes for all Internationally Traded and Timber Products*, Draft Report to the International Tropical Timber Organization, Yokohama

Balland, J-M and Platteau, J-P (1996) *Halting Degradation of Natural Resources. Is There a Role for Rural Communities?* Clarendon Press, Oxford

Barbier, EB (1989) *Economics, Natural Resource Scarcity and Development: Conventional and Alternative Views*, Earthscan, London

Barbier, EB (1992) 'Economics for the Wilds', in Swanson, TS and Barbier, EB (eds) *Economics for the Wilds: Wildlife, Wildlands, Diversity and Development*, Earthscan, London

Barbier, EB (1994a) 'Valuing Environmental Functions: Tropical Wetlands', *Land Economics*, vol 10, no 2, pp155–173

Barbier, EB (1994b) 'Natural Capital and the Economics of Environment and Development', in Jansson, AM, Hammer, M, Folke, C and Costanza, R (eds), *Investing in Natural Capital: The Ecological Economics Approach to Sustainability*, Island Press, Washington DC

Barbier, EB (1997) 'The economic determinants of land degradation in developing countries', *Philosophical Transactions of the Royal Society*, Series B, vol 352, pp891–899

Barbier, EB (1997) 'Introduction', *Environment and Development Economics*, Special Issue on Environmental Kuznets Curves, vol 2, no 4

Barbier, EB (1999a) 'Endogenous Growth and Natural Resource Scarcity', *Environmental and Resource Economics*, vol 14, no 1, pp51–74

Barbier, EB (1999b) 'Rural poverty and natural resource degradation', in López, R and Valdés, A (eds) *Rural Poverty in Latin America*, World Bank, Washington DC

Barbier, EB (1999c) 'The value of water and watersheds: reconciling ecological and economic externalities', in 1998 *Managing Human-Dominated Ecosystems Symposium*, The Missouri Botanical Gardens Press, St Louis

Barbier, EB, Bishop, JT, Aylward, BA and Burgess, JC (1992), 'Economic Policy and Sustainable Natural Resource Management', in Holmberg JC (ed), *Policies for a Small Planet*, Earthscan, London

Barbier, EB and Burgess, JC (1992) *Malawi - Land Degradation in Agriculture*, Environment Department, Divisional Working Paper no 1992–7, The World Bank, Washington DC

Barbier, EB and Burgess, JC (1996) 'Economic analysis of deforestation in Mexico', *Environment and Development Economics*, vol 1, pp203–239

Barbier, EB and Burgess, JC (1997) 'The economics of tropical forest land use options', *Land Economics*, vol 73, no 2, pp174–195

Barbier, EB, Burgess, JC, Bishop, JT and Aylward, BA (1994a) *The Economics of the Tropical Timber Trade*, Earthscan, London

Barbier, EB, Burgess, JC and Folke, C (1994b) *Paradise Lost? The Ecological Economics of Biodiversity*, Earthscan, London

Barbier, EB, Burgess, JC, Swanson, TM and Pearce, DW (1990) *Elephants, Economics and Ivory*, Earthscan, London

Barbier, EB and Homer-Dixon, T (1999) 'Resource Scarcity and Innovation: Can Poor Countries Attain Endogenous Growth?' AMBIO, vol 26, no 1, pp144–147

Barbier, EB and Lopez, R (1999) 'Debt, poverty and resource management in a rural smallholder economy', Paper for the Royal Economic Society Conference, The University of Nottingham, 29 March–1 April

Barbier, EB and Markandya, A (1990) 'The conditions for achieving environmental sustainable development', *European Economic Review*, vol 34, pp659–669

Barbier, EB, Markandya A, and Pearce, DW, (1990) 'Environmental Sustainability and Cost Benefit Analysis', *Environment and Planning* A, vol 22, pp1259–66

Barbier, EB and Strand, I (1998) 'Valuing mangrove-fishery linkages: a case study of Campeche, Mexico', *Environmental and Resource Economics* vol 12, pp151–166

Barrett, S (1991), 'Environmental regulation for competitive advantage', *Business Strategy Review*, Spring, pp1–15

Barrett, S (1994) 'The Biodiversity Supergame', *Environmental and Resource Economics*, vol 4, pp111–122

Barro, RJ and, Xavier, S-I-M (1995) *Economic Growth*, McGraw-Hill, New York

Bateman,I, Willis, K, Garrod, G, Doktor, P, Langford, I and Turner, RK (1992) *Recreation and Environmental Preservation Value of the Norfolk Broads: A Contingent Valuation Study*, Report to the National Rivers Authority (now the Environment Agency), London

Bateman, I, Willis, K and Garrod, G, (1994) 'Consistency between contingent valuation estimates: a comparison of two studies of UK National Parks', *Regional Studies*, vol 28, no 5, pp457–474

Bateman, I and Langford, I (1997) 'Non-users' willingness to pay for a National Park: an application and critique of the contingent valuation method', *Regional Studies*, vol 31, no 6, pp571-582

Baumol, W and Oates, W (1988) *The Theory of Environmental Policy*, 2nd edition, Cambridge University Press, Cambridge

Bebbington, J (1993) 'The EC Fifth Action Plan: Towards Sustainability', *Social and Environmental Accounting*, vol 13, no 1, Spring, pp9–11

Beckerman, W (1992) 'Economic growth and the environment: whose growth? whose environment?', *World Development*, vol 20, pp481–496

Beeby, A (1993) *Applied Ecology*, Chapman and Hall, London

Bell, FW (1989) *Application of Wetland Valuation Theory to Florida Fisheries*, Report no 95, Florida Sea Grant Program, Florida State University, Tallahassee

Bell, FW (1997) 'The economic value of saltwater marsh supporting marine recreational fishing in the Southeastern United States', *Ecological Economics*, vol 21, no3, pp243–254

Bilsbarrow, R and Geores, M (1994) 'Population, land use and the environment in developing countries: what can we learn from cross-national data?' in Brown, K and Pearce, DW (eds), *The Causes of Tropical Deforestation*, UCL Press, London, pp106–133

Bishop, RC (1993) 'Economic efficiency, sustainability, and biodiversity', AMBIO vol 22, no2–3, pp69–73

Boserup, E (1965) *The Conditions of Agricultural Growth*, Allen and Unwin, London

Bourke, IJ (1995) International Trade in Forest Products and the Environment', *Unasylva* vol 46, no 183, pp11–17

Bovenberg, A and Smulders, S (1995) 'Environmental Quality and Pollution–Augmenting Technological Change in a Two-Sector Endogenous Growth Model', *Journal of Public Economics*, vol 57, pp369–391

Boyce, J (1987) *Agrarian Impasse in Bengal: Institutional Constraints to Technological Change*, Oxford University Press, Oxford

Brennan, A (1992) 'Moral pluralism and the environment', *Environmental Values*, vol 1, pp15-53

Brookshire, D, Eubanks, L and Randall, A (1983) 'Estimating Option Prices and Existence Values for Wildlife Resources', *Land Economics*, vol 59, no 1, pp1–15

BSO/Origin (1990) *Annual Report 1990*, Utrecht

Cabeza-Gutés, M (1996) 'The concept of weak sustainability', *Ecological Economics*, vol 17, pp147–156

Cabinet Office (1996) *Regulation in the Balance: a Guide to Regulatory Appraisal Incorporating Risk Assessment*, Cabinet Office, London

Cairncross, F (1991) *Costing the Earth*, Pinter, London

Cairncross, F (1995) *Green, Inc.*, Earthscan, London

Carson, R (1994) 'Valuing the Preservation of Australia's Kakadu Conservation Zone', *Oxford Economic Papers*, vol 46, supplementary issue, pp727–749

Carson, R, Flores, N, Martin, K and Wright, J (1996) 'Contingent valuation and revealed preference methodologies: comparing the estimates for quasi public goods', *Land Economics*, vol 72, pp80–99

Carson, R, Flores, N and Meade, N (1995) *Contingent Valuation: Controversies and Evidence*, Department of Economics, University of California, San Diego

Carson R, Mitchell, R, Hanemann, M, Kopp, R, Presser, S and Ruud, P (1995) 'Contingent valuation and lost passive use: damages from the *Exxon Valdez'*, Discussion Paper 95-02, Department of Economics, University of California at San Diego

Carson, RT, Jeon, Y and McCubbin, DR (1997) 'The relationship between air pollution emissions and income: US data', *Environment and Development Economics* vol 2, no 4

Ciriacy-Wantrup, SV (1952) *Resource Conservation: Economics and Policies*, University of California Press, Berkeley

Clark, CW (1976) *Mathematical Bioeconomics: The Optimal Management of Renewable Resources*, John Wiley, New York

Clawson, M and Knetsch, J (1966) *Economics of Outdoor Recreation*, Johns Hopkins University Press, Baltimore

Cleaver, K and Schreiber, G (1993) *The Population, Agriculture and Environment Nexus in Sub-Saharan Africa*, Africa Regional Technical Dept, Agriculture and Rural Development Series, no 9, World Bank, Washington DC

Coburn, T, Beesley, M, Reynolds, D (1960) *The London–Birmingham Motorway, Traffic and Economics*, Road Research Laboratory Technical Paper 46, Her Majesty's Stationery Office, London

Cole, MA, Rayner, AJ and Bates, JM (1997) 'The environmental Kuznets curve: an empirical analysis', Special Issue on Environmental Kuznets Curves, *Environment and Development Economics*, vol 2, no 4

Commission on the Third London Airport, (1971) (The 'Roskill Commission'), *Report* and *Papers and Proceedings*, 9 volumes, Her Majesty's Stationery Office, London

Conway, GR (1983) 'Applying Ecological Concepts to the Study of the Intensification of the Use of Indonesia's Agro-Ecosystems', in KEPAS, *The Sustainability of Agricultural Intensification in Indonesia: A Report of Two Workshops of the Research Group on Agro-Ecosystems*. Kelompak Penelitan Agro-Ekosistem, Agency for Agricultural Research and Development, Jakarta, Indonesia

Conway, GR (1987) 'The properties of agroecosystems', *Agricultural Systems*, vol 24, pp95–117

Conway, GR and Barbier, EB (1990) *After the Green Revolution: Sustainable Agriculture for Development*, Earthscan, London

Cornes, R and Sandler, T (1986) *The Theory of Externalities, Public Goods and Club Goods*, Cambridge University Press, Cambridge

Costanza, R (1989) 'What is ecological economics?' *Ecological Economics*, vol 1, pp1–7

Costanza, R, Daly, HE and Bartholomew, JA (1991) 'Goals, agenda, and policy recommendations for ecological economics' in Costanza, R (ed) *Ecological Economics: The Science and Management of Sustainability*, Columbia University Press, New York

Costanza, R, Kemp, WM and Boynton, WR (1993) 'Predictability, Scale, and Biodiversity in Coastal and Estuarine Ecosystems: Implications for Management', AMBIO, vol 22, pp88–96

Coursey, D, Hovis, H and Schulze, W (1987) 'The disparity between willingness to accept and willingness to pay measures of value', *Quarterly Journal of Economics*, vol 102, no 3, pp679–690

Cropper, M and Griffiths, C (1994) 'The interaction of population growth and environmental quality', *American Economic Review*, vol 84, no 2, pp250–254

Current, D, Lutz, E, and Scherr, S (ed) (1995) *Costs, Benefits and Farmer Adaption of Agroforestry: Project Experience in Central America and the Caribbean*, World Bank Environment Paper no 14, World Bank, Washington DC

Dasgupta, AK and Pearce, DW, (1972), *Cost-Benefit Analysis: Theory and Practice*, Macmillan, Basingstoke

Dasgupta, PS and Heal, GE (1979) *The Economics of Exhaustible Resources*, Cambridge University Press, Cambridge

Deacon, RT (1994) 'Deforestation and the Rule of Law in a Cross-Section of Countries', *Land Economics*, vol 70, pp414–430

de Bruyn, SM (1997) 'Explaining the environmental Kuznets curve: structural change and international agreements in reducing sulphur emissions', *Environment and Development Economics*, vol 2, no 4

de Groot, RS (1992) *Functions of Nature*, Wolters-Noordhoff, Amsterdam

Department of the Environment (1991) *Policy Appraisal and the Environment*, Her Majesty's Stationery Office, London

Department of the Environment (1995) *A Guide to Risk Assessment and Risk Management for Environmental Protection*, London,

Department of the Environment (1996) *Indicators of Sustainable Development for the United Kingdom*, Her Majesty's Stationery Office, London

Department of the Environment (1997a) *The Wider Costs and Benefits of Environmental Policy: a Discussion Paper*, London

Department of the Environment (1997b) *The United Kingdom National Air Quality Strategy*, Her Majesty's Stationery Office, London

Department of the Environment, Transport and the Regions (1997) *Experience with 'Policy Appraisal and the Environment' Initiative*, Her Majesty's Stationery Office, London

Department of the Environment, Transport and the Regions (1998) *Policy Appraisal and the Environment: Draft Policy Guidance*, London

Department of Trade and Industry (1996) *Checking the Cost to Business: a Guide to Compliance Cost Assessment*, London

EC (1994) *Panorama of EU Industry*, EC, Luxembourg

EFTEC (1998) *Technical Guidance on Environmental Appraisal*, Department of the Environment, Transport and the Regions, London

Ehrlich, PR and Ehrlich, AE (1981) *Extinction: The Causes and Consequences of the Disappearance of Species*, Random House, New York

Ehrlich, PR and Ehrlich, AE (1992) 'The Value of Biodiversity' AMBIO, vol 21, no 3, pp219–226

Ehrlich, PR and Holdren, J (1971) 'Impacts of population growth', *Science*, vol 171, pp1212–1217

Ehrlich, PR and Wilson, EO (1991) 'Biodiversity studies: science and policy', *Science*, vol 253, pp758–762

Elliot, G (1994) 'The Trade Implications of Recycled Content in Newsprint: The Canadian Experience', in OECD, *Life-Cycle Management and Trade*, OECD, Paris

Ellis, GM and Fisher, AC (1987) 'Valuing the environment as input', *Journal of Environmental Management*, vol 25, pp149–156

ENDS (Environmental Data Services) (1980), 'EEC Commission refuses to cost environmental legislation', Report 47, pp7–18

ENDS (1998) 'Water abstraction decision deals savage blow to cost-benefit analysis', Report 278, pp16–18

English, J, Tiffen, M and Mortimore, M. (1994) *Land Resource Management in Machakos District, Kenya 1930-1990*, World Bank Environment Paper no 5, World Bank, Washington DC

Environmental Investigation Agency (1996) *Corporate Power, Corruption and the Destruction of the World's Forests: The Case for a New Global Forest Agreement*, EIA, London

FAO (Food and Agriculture Organization) (1984) *Land, Food and People*, United Nations, Rome

FAO (1991) *Second Interim Report on the State of Tropical Forests by Forest Resources Assessment 1990 Project*, presented at the 10th World Forestry Congress, September, United Nations, Paris

FAO (1993) *Forest Resources Assessment 1990: Tropical Countries*, United Nations, Rome

Farber, S and Costanza, R (1987) 'The economic value of wetlands systems', *Journal of Environmental Management*, vol 24, pp41–51

Flora, DF and McGinnis, WJ (1991) *Effects of Spotted-Owl Reservations, The State Log Embargo, Forest Replanning and Recession on Timber Flows and Prices in the Pacific Northwest and Abroad*, unpublished review, Trade Research, Pacific Northwest Research Station, USDA Forest Service, Seattle

Folke, C (1991) 'Socioeconomic Dependence of the Life-Supporting Environment' in Folke, C and Kåberger, T (eds) *Linking the Natural Environment and the Economy: Essays from the Eco-Eco Group*, Kluwer Academic Press, Dordrecht

Folke, C and Kautsky, N (1992) 'Aquaculture with its environment: prospects for sustainability', *Ocean and Coastal Management*, vol 17, pp5–24

Foster, CD and Beesley, M, (1963) 'Estimating the social benefits of constructing an underground railway in London', *Journal of the Royal Statistical Society*, Series A, 126, Part 1

Foster, V and Mourato, S (1997) 'Are consumers rational ? Evidence from a contingent ranking experiment', Paper presented to 8th Annual Conference of the European Association of Environmental and Resource Economists, Tilburg

Foster, V, Mourato, S, Ozdemiroglu, E, Pearce, DW, Hett, T and Dobson, S (in preparation), *What Price Virtue? The Social value of the Charitable Sector*

Foundation for Water Research (1997) *Assessing the Benefits of Surface Water Quality Improvements*, FR/CL0005, Foundation for Water Research, Marlow

Fredman, P (1994) 'The existence of existence value', Department of Forest Economics, Swedish University of Agricultural Sciences, Umeå, Sweden, *mimeo*

Freeman, AM (1991) 'Valuing environmental resources under alternative management regimes', *Ecological Economics*, vol 3, pp247–256

Freeman, AM (1993) *The Measurement of Environmental and Resource Values: Theory and Methods*, Resources for the Future, Washington DC

Freeman, AM (1982) *Air and Water Pollution Control: A Benefit-Cost Assessment*, Wiley, New York

Freeman, AM (1990) 'Water pollution policy', in Portney, P (ed) *Public Policies for Environmental Protection*, pp97–150, Resources for the Future, Washington DC

Fukuyama, F (1995) *Trust*, Penguin, Harmondsworth

Garrod, G and Willis, K, (1996) 'Estimating the benefits of environmental enhancement: a case study of the River Darent', *Journal of Environmental Planning and Management*, vol 39, pp189–203

Garrod, G and Willis,K (1999) *Economic Valuation of the Environment*, Edward Elgar, Cheltenham

Global Environment Facility (1998) *Operational Report on GEF Programs*, GEF, Washington DC

Goldin, I and Winters, LA (eds) (1995) *The Economics of Sustainable Development*, Cambridge University Press, Cambridge

Golleti, F (1994) *The Changing Public Role in A Rice Economy Approaching Self-Sufficiency: The Case of Bangladesh*, IFPRI Research Report 98, International Food Policy Research Institute, Washington DC

Gray, R (1993) 'Current practice in environmental reporting', *Social and Environmental Accounting*, vol 13, no 1, pp6–8

Greenley, D, Walsh, R and Young, R (1981) 'Option value: empirical evidence from a case study of recreation and water quality', *Quarterly Journal of Economics*, 96, pp657–673

Grossman, GM and Kreuger, AB (1993) 'Environmental impacts of a North American Free Trade Agreement', in Garber, P (ed) *The US-Mexico Free Trade Agreement*, MIT Press, Cambridge, MA

Grossman, GM and Kreuger, AB (1995) 'Economic growth and the environment', *Quarterly Journal of Economics*, vol 110, no 2, pp353–377

Grove-White, R, (1997) 'The environmental "valuation" controversy: observation on its recent history and significance', in Foster, J (ed), *Valuing Nature: Economics, Ethics and the Environment*, pp21–31, Routledge, London

Hahn, R, (1996) 'Regulatory reform: what do the government's numbers tell us?' in Hahn, R (ed), *Risks, Costs and Lives Saved: Getting Better results from Regulation*, pp208–254, Oxford University Press

Hamilton, K, Atkinson, G and Pearce, DW (1998) 'Savings rules and sustainability: selected extensions', CSERGE, University College, London

Hamilton, K and Atkinson, G (1996) 'Air pollution and green accounts', *Energy Policy*, vol 24, 7, pp675–684

Hanemann, M (1991) 'Willingness to pay and willingness to accept: how much can they differ?', *American Economic Review*, vol 81, no 3, pp635–647

Hanemann, M (1994) 'Valuing the environment through contingent valuation', *Journal of Economic Perspectives*, vol 8, no 4, pp19–43

Hanley, N, Spash, C and Walker, L (1995) 'Problems in valuing the benefits of biodiversity protection, *Environmental and Resource Economics*, vol 5, pp249–272

Hanley, N and Milne, J (1996) *Ethical Beliefs and Behaviour in Contingent Valuation*, Discussion Papers in Ecological Economics, Department of Economics, University of Stirling, 96/1

Hardin, G (1991) 'Paramount positions in ecological economics' in Costanza, R (ed), *Ecological Economics: The Science and Management of Sustainability*, Columbia University Press, New York

Heath, J and Binswanger, H (1996) 'Natural resource degradation effects of poverty and population growth are largely policy-induced: the case of Colombia', *Environment and Development Economics*, vol 1, pp65–83

Hettige, H, Lucas, REB and Wheeler, D (1992) 'The toxic intensity of industrial production: global patterns, trends and trade policy', *American Economic Review*, vol 82, no 2, pp478–481

Highways Agency (1997a) *Economic Assessment of Road Schemes: COBA Manual*, vol 13 of *Design Manual for Roads and Bridges*, Her Majesty's Stationery Office, London

Highways Agency (1997b) *Environmental Assessment*, vol 11 of *Design Manual for Roads and Bridges*, Her Majesty's Stationery Office, London

Holdren, J and Ehrlich, PR (1974) 'Human population and the global environment', *American Science* vol 62, pp282–292

Holling, CS (1973) 'Resilience and Stability of Ecological Systems', *Annual Review of Ecology and Systematics*, vol 4, no 124

Holling, CS (1992) 'Cross-scale morphology, geometry and dynamics of ecosystems', *Ecological Monographs*, vol 62, pp447–502

Holling, CS, Schindler, DW, Walker, BW and Roughgarden, J (1995) 'Biodiversity in the functioning of ecosystems: an ecological primer and synthesis' in Perrings, C, Mäler, K-G, Folke, C, Holling, CS and Jansson, B-O (eds) *Biodiversity Loss: Ecological and Economic Issues*, Cambridge University Press, Cambridge

Holling, CS (1986) 'Resilience of ecosystem: local surprise and global change' in Clark, WC, and Munn, RE (eds) *Sustainable Development of the Biosphere*, pp292–317, Cambridge University Press, Cambridge

Holtz-Eakin, D and Selden, TM (1995) 'Stoking the fires? CO_2 emissions and economic growth', *Journal of Public Economics*, vol 57, pp85–101

Homer-Dixon, TF (1995) 'The Ingenuity Gap: Can Poor Countries Adapt to Resource Scarcity?', *Population and Development Review*, vol 21, pp1–26

Homer-Dixon, TF (1994) 'Environmental Scarcities and Violent Conflict: Evidence from Cases', *International Security*, vol 19, pp5–40

Homer-Dixon, TF, Boutwell, JH and Rathjens, GW (1993) 'Environmental Change and Violent Conflict', *Scientific American*, February, pp38–45

House of Lords, Select Committee on the European Communities (1994–95), 1st Report, *Bathing Water*, HL Paper 6-I; and 7th Report, *Bathing Water Quality Revisited*, HL Paper 6-I, Her Majesty's Stationery Office, London

Howarth, RB and Norgaard, RB (1995) 'Intergenerational Choices under Global Environmental Change', in Bromley, D (ed) *The Handbook of Environmental Economics*, pp111–38, Basil Blackwell, Oxford

Huber, RM, Ruitenbeek, J and Serôa da Motta, R (1998) *Market-Based Instruments for Environmental Policymaking in Latin America and the Caribbean: Lessons from Eleven Countries*, Discussion Paper no 381, World Bank, Washington DC

Hurlbert, SH (1971) 'The non-concept of species diversity: a critique and alternative parameters', *Ecology* vol 52, pp577–586

International Finance Corporation (1992) *Investing in Environment: Business Opportunities in Developing Countries*, IFC, Washington DC

International Institute for Sustainable Development (1994) *Making Budgets Green: Leading Practices in Taxation and Subsidy Reform*, IISD, Winnipeg, Canada

IUCN/UNEP/WWF (1991) *Caring for the Earth: A Strategy for Sustainable Living*, IUCN, Gland

IUCN/UNEP/WWF (1980) *World Conservation Strategy: Living Resource Conservation for Sustainable Development*, IUCN, Gland

Jaffe, A, Peterson S, Portney, P and Stavins, R (1994) *Environmental Regulation and International Competitiveness: What Does the Evidence Tell Us?*, Discussion paper 94-08, Resources for the Future, Washington DC

Kahn, JR and Kemp, WM (1985) 'Economic losses associated with the degradation of an ecosystem: the case of submerged aquatic vegetation in Chesapeake Bay', *Journal of Environmental Economics and Management*, vol 12, pp246–263

Kahneman, D and Knetsch, J (1992) 'Valuing public goods: the purchase of moral satisfaction, *Journal of Environmental Economics and Management*, vol 23, pp248–257

Kaimowitz, D (1995) 'Livestock and deforestation in Central America in the 1980s and 1990s: a policy perspective', in EPTD *Discussion Paper*, no 9, Environment and Production Technology Division, International Food Policy Research Institute, Washington DC

Kareiva, P (1996) 'Diversity and sustainability on the prairie', *Nature*, vol 379, pp673–674

Karou, Y (1993) 'Differentiating use and non-use values for coastal pond water quality improvements', *Environmental and Resource Economics*, 3, pp487–494

Kates, RW (1990) 'Hunger, poverty and the environment'; paper prepared at the Distinguished Speaker Series, Center for Advanced Study of International Development, Michigan State University, Lansing

Kay, JJ (1991) 'A nonequilibrium thermodynamic framework for discussing ecosystem integrity' *Environmental Management* vol 15, pp483–495

Kelley, A (1988) 'Economic consequences of population change in the third world', *Journal of Economic Literature*, vol 26, no 4, pp685–728

Kiekens, J-P (1995) 'Timber Certification: A Critique', *Unasylva* vol 46, no 183, pp27–28

Knetsch, J and Sinden, J (1984) 'Willingness to pay and compensation demanded: experimental evidence of an unexpected disparity in measures of value', *Quarterly Journal of Economics*, vol 99, no 3, pp507–521

Komen, MHC, Gerking, S and Folmer, H (1997) 'Income and environmental R&D: empirical evidence from OECD countries', Special Issue on Environmental Kuznets Curves, *Environment and Development Economics*, vol 2, no 4

Kopp, R and Smith, VK, (1989) 'Benefit estimation goes to court: the case of natural resource damages', *Journal of Policy Analysis and Management*, vol 8, no 4, pp593–612

Kunte, A, Hamilton, K, Dixon, J and Clemens, M (1998) *Estimating National Wealth: Methodology and Results*, Environment Department Paper 57, World Bank, Washington DC

Kuznets, S (1955) 'Economic growth and income inequality', *American Economic Review*, vol 49, pp1–28

Lal, R (1995) *Sustainable Management of Soil Resources in the Humid Tropics*, United Nations University Press, Tokyo

Leibenstein, H (1966) 'Allocative efficiency vs X efficiency', *American Economic Review*, 56, June, pp392–415

Lele, U and Stone, S (1989) *Population Pressure, The Environment and Agricultural Intensification: Variations on the Boserup Hypothesis*, MADIA Discussion Papers no 4, World Bank, Washington DC

Leonard, HJ, with Yudelman, M, Stryker, JD, Browder, JO, de Boer, AJ, Campbell, T and Jolly, A (1989) *Environment and the Poor: Development Strategies for A Common Agenda*, Transaction Books, New Brunswick

Lewis, A and Mackenzie, C (1998) 'Support for investor activism among UK ethical investors', *Journal of Business Ethics*, vol XX, pp1–8

Lipton, M (1988) *The Poor and the Poorest: Some Interim Findings*, World Bank Discussion Paper no 25, World Bank, Washington DC

Loomis, J, Lockwood, M and DeLacy, T (1993) 'Some empirical evidence on embedding effects in contingent valuation of forest protection', *Journal of Environmental Economics and Management*, 24, pp45–55

López, R (1997) 'Environmental Externalities in Traditional Agriculture and the Impact of Trade Liberalization: The Case of Ghana', *Journal of Development Economics*, vol 53, pp17–39

Lovejoy, TE (1980) 'A projection of species extinction' in Barney, GO (ed) *The Global 2000 Report to the President. Entering the Twenty-First Century, vol 2*, Council on Environmental Quality, US Government Printing Office, Washington DC

Lucas, RE (1988) 'On the Mechanics of Economic Development', *Journal of Forestry Economics*, vol 22, pp3–42

Lugo, AE, Parrotta, JA and Brown, S (1993) 'Loss in species caused by tropical deforestation and their recovery through management', AMBIO, vol 22, no 2–3, pp106–109

Lynne, GD, Conroy, P and Prochaska, FJ (1981) 'Economic value of marsh areas for marine production processes', *Journal of Environmental Economics and Management*, vol 8, pp175–186

Maddison, D (ed) (1996) *Blueprint 5: The True Cost of Road Transport*, Earthscan, London

Madariaga, B and McConnell, K (1987) 'Exploring existence value', *Water Resources Research*, vol 23, no 5, pp936–942

Magurran, AE (1988) *Ecological Diversity and its Measurement*, Chapman and Hall, London

Mahar, D and Schneider, RR (1994) 'Incentives for tropical deforestation: some examples from Latin America', in Brown, K and Pearce, DW, *The causes of tropical deforestation*, pp159–170, University College London Press, London

Mäler, K-G (1991) 'The production function approach' in Vincent, JR, Crawford, EW and Hoehn, JP (eds) *Valuing Environmental Benefits in Developing Countries*, Special Report 29, Michigan State University, East Lansing

Mäler, K-G (1995) 'Economic Growth and the Environment', in Perrings, CA, Mäler, K-G, Folke, C, Holling, CS and Jansson, BO (ed) *Biodiversity Loss: Economic and Ecological Issues*, pp213–224, Cambridge University Press, Cambridge

Mankiw, NG, Romer, D and Weil, DN (1992) 'A Contribution to the Empirics of Economic Growth', *Quarterly Journal of Economics*, vol 107, pp407–437

Markandya, A and Shibli, A (1995) 'Industrial Pollution Control Policies in Asia', *Environmental Discussion Paper*, no 3, Harvard Institute for International Development, Cambridge, Mass

Martínez-Alier, J (1995) 'The environment as a luxury good, or "too poor to be green"?', *Ecological Economics*, vol 13, pp1–10

Masera, O, Ordóñez, M and Dinzo, R (1992) *Carbon Emissions and Sequestration in the Forests: Case Studies from Seven Developing Countries: Volume 4 Mexico*, Climate Change Division, Environmental Protection Agency, Washington DC

Matsuyama, K (1992) 'Agricultural Productivity, Comparative Advantage, and Economic Growth', *Journal of Economic Theory*, vol 58, pp317–334

May, RM (1974) *Stability and Complexity in Model Ecosystems*, 2nd ed, Princeton University Press, Princeton, New Jersey

May, RM (ed) (1981) *Theoretical Ecology*, Blackwell, Oxford

McConnell, KE (1997) 'Income and the demand for environmental quality', Special Issue on Environmental Kuznets Curves, *Environment and Development Economics*, vol 2, no 4

McConnell, KE and Strand, IE (1989) 'Benefits from commercial fisheries when demand and supply depend on water quality', *Journal of Environmental Economics and Management*, vol 17, pp284–292

McNeely, JA (1993) 'Economic Incentives for Conserving Biodiversity: Lessons for Africa', AMBIO vol 22, no 2–3, pp144–150

McNeely, JA, Miller, KR, Reid, WR, Mittermeier, RA and Werner, TB (1990) *Conserving the World's Biological Diversity*, IUCN, Gland

Milgrom, P and Roberts, J (1992) *Economics, Organization and Management*, Prentice-Hall International, New Jersey

Moomaw, WR and Unruh, GC (1997) 'Are environmental Kuznets curves misleading us? The case of CO_2 emissions', *Environment and Development Economics*, vol 2, no 4

Morgenstern, R, (1997) *Economic Analyses at EPA: Assessing Regulatory Impact*, Resources for the Future, Washington DC

Musu, I and Lines, M (1995) 'Endogenous Growth and Environmental Preservation', in Boero, G and Silberston, A (eds) *Environmental Economics: Proceedings of European Economic Associations at Oxford*, 1993, St Martins Press, London

Myers, N (1993) 'Biodiversity and the precautionary principle', AMBIO vol 22, no 2–3, pp74–79

Myers, N (1979) *The Sinking Ark: A New Look at the Problem of Disappearing Species*, Pergamon Press, Oxford

Navrud, S and Pruckner, G, (1997) 'Environmental valuation – to use or not to use?', *Environmental and Resource Economics*, vol 10, pp1–26

National Economic Research Associates (1998) *Economic and Social Value of Leakage Reduction*, for the Foundation for Water Industry Research, London

Oates, W, Palmer, K and Portney, P (1994) *Environmental Regulation and International Competitiveness: Thinking About the Porter Hypothesis*, Discussion Paper 94-02, Resources for the Future, Washington DC

Odum, EP (1969) *Ecology and Our Endangered Life-Support Systems*, Sinauer Associates, Sunderland, Massachusetts

Odum, EP (1975) *Ecology*, Holt-Saunders, New York

Odum, EP (1985) 'Trends to be expected in stressed ecosystems', *BioScience*, vol 35, pp419–422

OECD (Organisation for Economic Co-operation and Development) (1991) *Environmental Policy: How to Apply Economic Instruments*, OECD, Paris

OECD (1996) *The Global Environmental Goods and Services Industry*, OECD, Paris

Oldeman, LR, van Engelen, VWP and Pulles, JHM (1990) 'The extent of human-induced soil degradation', Annex 5 in Oldeman, LR, Hakkeling, RTA and Sombroek, WG, *World Map of the Status of Human-induced Soil Erosion: An Explanatory Note*, 2nd ed, International Soil Reference and Information Centre,Wageningen

Opschoor, JB and Vos, HB (1989) *Economic Instruments for Environmental Protection*, OECD, Paris

Pack, H (1994) 'Endogenous Growth Theory: Intellectual Appeal and Empirical Shortcomings', *Journal of Economic Perspectives*, vol 8, pp55–72

Panayotou, T (1995) 'Environmental degradation at different stages of economic development', in Ahmed, I and Doeleman, JA (eds) *Beyond Rio: The Environmental Crisis and Sustainable Livelihoods in the Third World*, Macmillan Press, London

Panayotou, T (1997) 'Demystifying the environmental Kuznets curve: turning a black box into a policy tool', *Environment and Development Economics*, vol 2, no 4

Pearce, DW (1970) 'The Roskill Commission and the location of London's third airport', *Three Banks Review*, September

Pearce, DW (1986) Cost-Benefit Analysis, Macmillan, Basingstoke
Pearce, DW (ed) (1991) Blueprint 2: Greening the World Economy, Earthscan, London
Pearce, DW (ed) (1993) Blueprint 3: Measuring Sustainable Development, Earthscan, London
Pearce, DW (1995) Blueprint 4: Capturing Global Environmental Value, Earthscan, London
Pearce, DW (1998) 'Environmental appraisal and environmental policy in the European Union', Environmental and Resource Economics, vol11, no 3-4, pp489–501
Pearce, DW (1998b) 'Cost-benefit analysis and environmental policy', Oxford Review of Economic Policy, vol 14, no 4, pp84–100
Pearce, DW (1999) 'Economic valuation and ecological economics', in Pearce, DW, Economics and Environment: Essays on Ecological Economics and Sustainable Development, pp40–54,Edward Elgar, Cheltenham
Pearce, DW and Atkinson, G (1993) 'Capital theory and the measurement of sustainable development: an indicator of weak sustainability', Ecological Economics, vol 8, pp103–8
Pearce, DW and Atkinson, G (1995) 'Measuring Sustainable Development', in Bromley, D (ed) The Handbook of Environmental Economics, pp166–181, Basil Blackwell, Oxford
Pearce, DW, Barbier, EB and Markandya, A (1990) Sustainable Development: Environmental Economics in the Third World, Edward Elgar, London
Pearce, DW, Markandya, A, Barbier, E, (1989) Blueprint for a Green Economy, Earthscan, London
Pearce, DW, Moran, D and Krug, W (1999) The Global Value of Biodiversity: A Report to UNEP, CSERGE, London
Penning de Vries, FWT, Rabbinage, R and Groot, JJR (1997) 'Potential and attainable food production and food security in different regions', Philosophical Transactions of the Royal Society, Series B, vol 352, pp917–928
Perez-Garcia, JM (1991) An Assessment of the Impacts of Recent Environmental and Trade Restrictions on Timber Harvests and Exports, Working Paper no 33, Center for International Trade in Forest Products, University of Washington, Seattle
Perrings, C (1991) 'Reserved rationality and the precautionary principle: techno-logical change, time and uncertainty in environmental decision making' in Costanza, R (ed), Ecological Economics: The Science and Management of Sustainability, Columbia University Press, New York
Perrings, C, Folke, C and Mäler, K-G (1992) 'The ecology and economics of biodiversity loss: the research agenda', AMBIO, vol 21, no 3, pp201–211
Perrings, C and Pearce, DW (1994) 'Threshold effects and incentives for the conservation of biodiversity', Environmental and Resource Economics, vol 4, no 1, pp13–28
Perrings, C, Barbier, EB, Brown, G, Dalmazzone, S, Folke, C, Gadgil, M, Hanley, N, Holling, CS, Lesser, WH, Mäler, K-G, Mason, P, Panayotou, T, Turner, RK, and Wells, M (1995) 'The economic value of biodiversity'; Chapter 12 in UNEP, Global Biodiversity Assessment, Cambridge University Press
Perrings, C, Folke, C, Mäler, K-G, Holling, CS and Jansson, B-O (1995) 'The ecology and economics of biodiversity loss' in Perrings, C, Folke, C, Mäler, K-G, Holling, CS and Jansson, B-O (eds) Biodiversity Loss: Ecological and Economic Issues, Cambridge University Press, Cambridge
Peuker, A (1992) Public policies and deforestation: a case study of Costa Rica, Latin America and the Caribbean Technical Department, Regional Studies Program, report no 14, World Bank, Washington DC

Pezzey, J (1989) *Economic Analysis of Sustainable Growth and Sustainable Development*, Environment Department Working Paper, No 15, World Bank, Washington DC

Pimm, SL (1984) 'The complexity and stability of ecosystems', *Nature*, vol 307, pp321–326

Pimm, SL (1991) *The Balance of Nature?* The University of Chicago Press, Chicago

Pinstrup-Andersen, P, Pandya-Lorch, R and Rosegrant, MW (1997) *The World Food Situation: Recent Developments, Emerging Issues, and Long-Term Prospects*; Food Policy Report, The International Food Policy Research Institute, Washington DC

Polasky, S, Solow, A and Broadus, J (1993) 'Searching for Uncertain Benefits and the Conservation of Biological Diversity', *Environmental and Resource Economics* vol 3, pp171–181

Porter, M (1990) *The Competitive Advantage of Nations*, Free Press, New York

Porter, M (1991) 'America's green strategy', *Scientific American*, April, p168

Portney, P (1990) 'Air pollution policy', in Portney, P (ed) *Public Policies for Environmental Protection*, pp27–96, Resources for the Future,Washington DC

Posch, M, de Smet, P, Hettelingh, J-P and Downing, RJ (1995) *Calculation and Mapping of Critical Thresholds in Europe*, National Institute of Public Health and the Environment, Bilthoven, The Netherlands

Putnam, RD (1993) *Making Democracy Work: Civic Traditions in Modern Italy*, Princeton University Press, Princeton

Raven, PH (1988) 'On diminishing tropical forests', in Wilson, EO (ed) *Biodiversity*, National Academy Press, Washington DC

Rebelo, S (1991) 'Long-Run Policy Analysis and Long-Run Growth', *Journal of Political Economy*, vol 99, no 3, pp500–521

Reid, WV and Miller, KR (1989) *Keeping Options Alive: The Scientific Basis for Conserving Biodiversity*, World Resources Institute, Washington DC

Reid, WV, McNeely, JA, Tunstall, DB, Bryant, DA and Winograd, M (1993) *Biodiversity Indicators for Policy-Makers*, World Resources Institute, Washington DC

Reid, WV (1992) 'How many species will there be?' in Whitmore, TC and Sayer, JA (eds) *Tropical Deforestation and Species Extinction*, Chapman and Hall, London

Rees, WJ (1992) 'Ecological footprints and appropriated carrying capacity: what urban economics leaves out', *Environment and Urbanization*, vol 4, no 2, pp121–130

Rees, WE and Wackernagel, M (1994) 'Ecological footprints and appropriated carrying capacity: measuring the natural capital requirements of the human economy' in Jansson, A, Hammer, M, Folke, C and Costanza, R (eds) *Investing in Natural Capital: The Ecological Economics Approach to Sustainability*, Island Press, Washington DC

Richards, JF (1990) 'Land transformation' in Turner, BL, Clark, WC and Kates, WC (eds) *The Earth as Transformed by Human Action: Global and Regional Changes in the Biosphere over the Past 300 Years*, Cambridge University Press, Cambridge

Romer, P (1990) 'Endogenous Technological Change', *Journal of Political Economy*, vol 98, S71–102

Romer, P (1993) 'Two Strategies for Economic Development: Using Ideas and Producing Ideas', in *Proceedings of the World Bank Annual Conference on Development Economics* 1992, pp63–69, World Bank, Washington DC

Romer, P (1994) 'The Origins of Endogenous Growth', *Journal of Economic Perspectives*,vol 8, pp3–22

Royal Commission on Environmental Pollution (1994) *Eighteenth Report: Transport and the Environment*, Cm 2674, Her Majesty's Stationery Office, London

Royal Commission on Environmental Pollution (1996) *Nineteenth Report: Sustainable Use of Soil*, Cm 3165, Her Majesty's Stationery Office, London

Rusell, C and Powell, P (1996) *Choosing Environmental Policy Tools*, Inter-American Development Bank, Environment Division, Washington DC

Sachs, JD and Warner, AM (1995) *Natural Resource Abundance and Economic Growth*, Development Discussion Paper No 517a, Harvard Institute for International Development, Cambridge, MA

Sagoff, M (1988) 'Some problems with environmental economics', *Environmental Ethics*, vol 10, pp55–74

Salop, S and Scheffman, D (1983) 'Raising rivals' costs', *American Economic Review, Papers and Proceedings*, vol 73, pp267–271

Sandler, T (1993) 'Tropical Deforestation: Markets and Market Failures', *Land Economics*, vol 69, no 3, pp225–233

Schneider, RR (1994) *Government and the economy on the Amazon Frontier*, Latin America and the Caribbean Technical Department, Regional Studies Program, report no 34, World Bank, Washington DC

Selden, TM and Song, D (1994) 'Environmental quality and development: is there a Kuznets curve for air pollution emissions?' *Journal of Environmental Economics and Management* vol 27, pp147–162

Shafik, N (1994) 'Economic development and environmental quality: an econometric analysis', *Oxford Economic Papers*, vol 46, pp757–773

Simberloff, D (1986) 'Are we on the verge of a mass extinction in tropical rain forests?' in Elliott, DK (ed) *Dynamics of Extinction*, John Wiley, New York

Simon, J (1981) *The Ultimate Resource*, Martin Robertson, Oxford

Sivakumar, MVK and Valentin, C (1997) 'Agroecological Zones and the Assessment of Crop Production Potential', *Philosophical Transactions of the Royal Society, Series B*, vol 352, pp907–916

Solbrig, OT (1993) 'Plant traits and adaptive strategies: their role in ecosystem function' in Schulze, E-D and Mooney, HA (eds) *Biodiversity and Ecosystem Function*, pp97–116, Springer-Verlag, Heidelberg

Solózamo, R, Repetto, R and Cruz, W (1991) *Accounts Overdue: Natural Resource Depreciation in Costa Rica*, World Resources Institute, Washington DC

Southgate, D, Sierra, R and Brown, L (1991) 'The causes of tropical deforestation in Ecuador: a statistical analysis', *World Development* vol 19, pp1145–1151

Standing Advisory Committee on Trunk Road Assessment (1991) *Assessing the Environmental Impact of Road Schemes*, Department of Transport, London

Stern, D, Common, MS and Barbier, EB (1996) 'Economic growth and environmental degradation: the environmental Kuznets curve and sustainable development', *World Development*, vol 24, no 7, pp1151–1160

Stevens, T, Echeverria, J, Glass, R, Hager, T and More, T (1991) 'Measuring the existence value of wildlife: what do CVM estimates really show?', *Land Economics*, vol 67, no 4, pp390–400

Stiglitz, JE (1974) 'Growth with Exhaustible Natural Resources: Efficient and Optimal Growth Paths', *Review of Economic Studies*, Symposium on the Economics of Exhaustible Resources, pp123–138

Summers, R and Heston, A (1991) 'The Penn world table (mark 5): an expanded set of international comparisons, 1950-1988', *Quarterly Journal of Economics*, vol 106, no 2, pp327–368

Sunderlin, WD and Rodrígez, JA (1996) *Cattle, broadleaf forests and the agricultural modernization law of Honduras*, occasional paper no 7, Centre for International Forestry Research, Jakarta

Sutherland, R and Walsh, R (1985) 'Effect of distance on the preservation value of water quality', Land Economics, 61, pp281–291

Swanson, TM (1995) 'The International Regulation of Biodiversity Decline: Optimal Policy and Evolutionary Product', in Perrings, C, Mäler, K-G, Folke, C, Holling, CS and Jansson, B-O (eds) *Biodiversity Loss: Economic and Ecological Issues*, Cambridge University Press, Cambridge

Tietenberg, T (1990) 'Economic Instruments for Environmental Policy', *Oxford Review of Economic Policy*, vol 6, no 1, pp17–33

Tilman, D and Downing, JA (1994) 'Biodiversity and stability in grasslands', *Nature*, vol 367, pp363–365

Tilman, D, Wedlin, D and Knops, J (1996) 'Productivity and sustainability influenced by biodiversity in grassland ecosystems', *Nature*, pp718–720

Toman, MA, Pezzey, J and Krautkramer, J (1995) 'Neoclassical Economic Growth Theory and Sustainability', in Bromley, D (ed) *The Handbook of Environmental Economics*, pp139–165, Basil Blackwell, Oxford

Turner, RK (1993) 'Sustainability Principles and Practice', in Turner, RK (ed) *Sustainable Environmental Management: Principles and Practice*, Belhaven Press, London

UK Department of the Environment (1996) *The Producer Responsibility Obligations (Packaging Waste) Regulations: a Consultation Paper*, London

UK Government (1990) *This Common Inheritance: Britain's Environmental Strategy*, Cm 1200, Her Majesty's Stationery Office, London

UK Treasury (1997) *Appraisal and Evaluation in Central Government: the 'Green Book'*, Her Majesty's Stationery Office, London

UN (1997) *World Population Prospects*, United Nations, New York; Cambridge University Press, Cambridge

UNCED (1992) *Integration of Environment and Development in Decision Making*, report to the preparatory committee for UNCED, New York

UNEP (1993) *Guidelines for Country Studies on Biological Diversity*, UNEP, Nairobi

UNEP (1992) *Biodiversity Country Studies: Synthesis Report*, UNEP, Nairobi

UNEP (1995) *Global Biodiversity Assessment*, Cambridge University Press, Cambridge

United Nations Population Fund (1994) *The State of the World Population 1994*, UNFPA, New York

Varangis, PN, Crossley, R and Primo Braga, CA (1995) 'Is There a Commercial Case for Tropical Timber Certification?', *Policy Research Working Paper* 1479, World Bank, Washington DC

Victor, P, Hanna, HE and Kubursi, A (1994) *How strong is weak sustainability?* Paper presented at the International Symposium on Models of Sustainable Development, Paris

Vincent, JR (1997) 'Testing for environmental Kuznets curves within a developing country', Special Issue on Environmental Kuznets Curves, *Environment and Development Economics*, vol 2, no 4

Von Weizsäcker, E, Lovins, A and Lovins, LH (1997) *Factor Four: Doubling Wealth, Halving Resource Use*, Earthscan, London

Wallich, P (1994) 'The Analytical Economist: The Wages of Haiti's Dictatorship', *Scientific American*, vol 271, p36

Walsh, R, Loomis, J and Gillman, R (1984) 'Valuing option, existence and bequest values for wilderness', *Land Economics*, 60, pp14–29

Weaver, PM, Gabel, HL, Bloemhof-Ruwaard, JM and Wassenhove, LN (1995) 'Optimising Environmental Product Life Cycles: A Case Study of the European Pulp and Paper Sector', CMER *Working Papers* 95/29/EPS/TM, Centre for the Management of Environmental Resources, INSEAD, Fontainebleau, France

Weissinger, AK (1990) 'Technologies for germ plasm preservation *ex situ'*, in Orians, GH, Brown GM, Kunin, WE and Swierzbinski, JE (eds) *The Preservation and Valuation of Biological Resources*, University of Washington Press, Seattle

Weitzman, ML (1995) 'Diversity functions', in Perrings, C, Folke, C, Mäler, K-G, Holling, CS and Jansson, B-O (eds) *Biodiversity Loss: Ecological and Economic Issues*, Cambridge University Press, Cambridge

Weitzman, ML (1992) 'On diversity', *Quarterly Journal of Economics*, vol 107, pp363–405

Weitzman, M and Löfgren, K-G (1998, 'On the welfare significance of green accounting as taught by parable', *Journal of Environmental Economics and Management*, vol 32, pp139–153

Williams, M (1990) 'Forests', in Turner, BL, Clark, WC and Kates, WC (eds) *The Earth as Transformed by Human Action: Global and Regional Changes in the Biosphere over the Past 300 Years*, Cambridge University Press, Cambridge

Willis, K (1990) 'Valuing non-market wildlife commodities: an evaluation and comparison of benefits and costs', *Applied Economics*, vol 22, no 1, pp12–30

Willis, K, Garrod, G, Benson, J and Carter, M (1996), 'Benefits and costs of the wildlife enhancement scheme: a case study of the Pevensey Levels', *Journal of Environmental Planning and Management*, vol 39, no 3, pp387–401

Willis, K and Garrod, G (1995) 'The benefits of alleviating low flows in rivers', *Water Resources Development*, vol 11, pp243–260

Wilson, EO (1992) *The Diversity of Life*, The Penguin Press, London

WCMC (1987) *Our Common Future*, Oxford University Press, Oxford

WCMC (1992) 'Wetlands', in WCMC (ed) *Global Biodiversity: Status of the Earth's Living Resources*, ch 22, pp293–306

WCMC (1992) *Global Biodiversity: Status of the Earth's Living Resources*, Chapman and Hall, London

World Bank (1992) 'World Development Report 1992', Oxford University Press, New York

World Bank (1997a) *Expanding the Measure of Wealth: Indicators of Environmentally Sustainable Development*, World Bank, Washington DC

World Bank (1997b) *Five Years After Rio: Innovations in Environmental Policy*, World Bank, Washington DC

WWF (1989) *The Importance of Biological Diversity*, WWF, Gland

Index